New Paradigms in Higher Education: The Role of Universities

New Paradigms in Higher Education: The Role of Universities

Jeffery Lawrence

LANRYE
INTERNATIONAL
www.clanryeinternational.com

Clanrye International,
750 Third Avenue, 9th Floor,
New York, NY 10017, USA

ISBN: 978-1-64726-625-7

Cataloging-in-Publication Data

New paradigms in higher education : the role of universities / Jeffery Lawrence.
    p. cm.
Includes bibliographical references and index.
ISBN 978-1-64726-625-7
1. Education, Higher. 2. Education. I. Lawrence, Jeffery.
LB2325 .N49 2023
378--dc23

For information on all Clanrye International publications
visit our website at www.clanryeinternational.com

Contents

Preface

Every book is initially just a concept; it takes months of research and hard work to give it the final shape in which the readers receive it. In its early stages, this book also went through rigorous reviewing. The notable contributions made by experts from across the globe were first molded into patterned chapters and then arranged in a sensibly sequential manner to bring out the best results.

Higher education refers to tertiary education that leads to the award of an academic degree. It is an optional final phase of formal learning that occurs after completing secondary education. Higher education institutions (HEIs) play an important role in fostering a lifelong learning culture. It includes not only colleges and universities but also professional schools that offer training in fields such as theology, business, art, law, medicine and music. Universities play a key role in higher education as the pioneers of many initiatives related to cultural, social, political and economic development that can support the growth of a country. They provide direction for practical learning acquisition and also collaborate with the academic community to achieve their objectives. This book provides significant information on the role of universities in providing higher education. Its extensive content provides the readers with a thorough understanding of the subject.

It has been my immense pleasure to be a part of this project and to contribute my years of learning in such a meaningful form. I would like to take this opportunity to thank all the people who have been associated with the completion of this book at any step.

Jeffery Lawrence

Part I

Understanding Responsibility

Publicly Funded Universities and Responsibility

Lars Geschwind, Jouni Kekäle, Rómulo Pinheiro, and Mads P. Sørensen

Responsible Organisations

Responsibility has become a catchword in all organisations, and it has become commonplace for business organisations to stress their responsible position and behaviour. The key areas of their attention tend to

L. Geschwind (✉)
KTH Royal Institute of Technology, Stockholm, Sweden
e-mail: larsges@kth.se

J. Kekäle
University of Eastern Finland, Joensuu, Finland
e-mail: Jouni.kekale@uef.fi

R. Pinheiro
Department of Political Science and Management, University of Agder, Kristiansand, Norway
e-mail: romulo.m.pinheiro@uia.no

M. P. Sørensen
Aarhus University, Aarhus, Denmark
e-mail: mps@ps.au.dk

include responsibility for the environment, social responsibility, financial responsibility, as well as quality and sustainability issues. The aim is to shape a sustainable future for business and operations and to show that investments in the area serve good purposes not only in terms of profit for stakeholders (as in business organisations) but also in a broader social and ecological sense.[1]

The term 'responsible' has different meanings and connotations depending on the individuals or organisations involved, their immediate geographical, cultural and political contexts, as well as historical periods. According to Webster's (1994) dictionary, the term includes connotations of both (a) being accountable for external powers or stakeholders for one's decision and actions and (b) containing the capacity for one's own (moral) decisions, rational thought and action. In other words, if forced, a person could not be held responsible for the outcomes. There is also a connotation of the responsible actor being reliable or dependable. Synonyms for responsible include accountable, amenable, answerable and liable, whereas antonyms include irresponsible, non-accountable and unaccountable.[2] Higher education institutions (HEIs) presently make up a large proportion of national gross domestic products (GDPs) and their activities affect many people, including staff, students (and parents), employers and other stakeholders. This impact is particularly so in systems like those in the Nordic countries with high participation rates and significant investments in research. These investments come with expectations. HEIs are expected to contribute to the development and resilience of societies. They are supposed to provide students with high-quality, relevant education, useful in both short term and over time. They are also producers of knowledge, supposedly with an impact on the cultural, social, political, technological and economic development of our societies. Societal demands are thus high, and rightly so, which is shown in an increasingly active debate on higher education (HE) and research.

This volume deals with the notion of responsibility and its relation to HEIs, in particular publicly run and funded universities. Our examples are mainly from the Nordic countries, which are often considered as responsible societies in many ways, for instance, with respect to accountable governments and transparent institutions (Hilson 2008). However, our aim is also to provide insights and lessons for the sector as a whole. Given the broad use of the term responsibility, it is no wonder that higher education institutions also feel the need to show that they are operating in a responsible manner. We can identify several reasons for this desire to portray sound operations. First, there appears to be a broad awakening to environmental issues, such as climate change, and other global challenges (Johnsen et al. 2015). Universities are key players in providing new knowledge; hence, it is easy to conclude that they can play a role in overcoming such challenges (Greu et al. 2017). Kaldeway (2018) noted that 'grand challenges' have become a dominant theme in scientific discussions and funding schemes in the twenty-first century. Universities are perhaps the organisation best positioned to answer issues in need of systematic and long-term thinking and enquiry on any matter. On the other hand, due to their strong social embeddedness (Ramirez 2009), universities tend to take over responsibilities for various kinds of social problems,[3] perhaps even when they lack the means and measures for promoting such goals. Second, all fashionable concepts and movements tend to spread and produce normative pressure for other fields and operators, thus contributing to the broadening of the use of the concept, both insofar adoption as well as adaptation (Beerkens 2010). Third, we can identify a long-term, external increase of accountability and numerous responsibilities on universities (Hazelkorn et al. 2018), also in the Nordic countries (Hansen et al. 2019; Pinheiro et al. 2019). The expectations on 'responsibility' by universities from multiple stakeholders appear to have persisted (Bok 1982; Neave 2002), but the manifestations and expectations for solutions in reaching 'responsibility' in higher education seem to have changed. In different eras, there have been different assumptions as regards how higher education provides society with public goods (Kekäle et al. 2017); with more recent developments (from Europe) emphasising the instrumental role of universities in directly tackling social issues such as economic development and climate change (Maassen and Olsen 2007). The ongoing discussion on university responsibility, amongst policy and academic circles alike, goes well along with these external pressures.

The Responsible University: A Concept, Its Relatives and Its Opposites

The university is not a monolithic single institution, but rather best described as an array of multiple, complex and loosely coupled structures (Pinheiro and Young 2017). The term 'multiversity' (Kerr 2001) has been used as a way of characterising the various, sometimes conflicting, functions and roles that modern university systems address (see also Castells 2001). A number of concepts pertaining to the social role of HEIs can be found in the literature. Like firms, HEIs have started to act in novel, entrepreneurial ways aimed at gradually reducing their dependence on state funding, which amongst other aspects includes adopting market-like mechanisms (Etzkowitz 2001). Entrepreneurial universities take risks in combining old identities with new structural features such as strengthening their decision-making structures and bridging their core functions with the outside world (Clark 1998). This contrasts with the notion of the 'civic university' where social engagement is intrinsically linked to teaching and research as well as conceived as an institution-wide activity providing academics with a sense of purpose (Goddard et al. 2016). Similarly, Benneworth (2013) and Watson et al. (2011) refer to the 'engaged university' as one where academics and managers take a prominent role in addressing critical issues facing its surrounding communities within the context of social justice and moral responsibility. These range from poverty and social exclusion (inequality) to help in tackling environmental hazards.

More often than not, the aforementioned social challenges best resolve in the form of multiple interdisciplinary collaborations and close collaboration with various stakeholder groups, along the lines of the 'Mode 2' university (Harloe and Perry 2004). The concept of the 'triple helix' has been popular amongst policymakers and university managers alike as a way of conceiving of mutually beneficial interactions between HEIs and public and private actors (Etzkowitz and Leydesdorff 2000). In Europe, the so-called knowledge triangle has emphasised the importance of the social impact derived from HEIs' activities, by strategically articulating the core functions of teaching and research with innovation and engagement as emergent tasks for all HEIs (Maassen and Stensaker

2011). Finally, North American authors have stressed the important 'moral' role played by universities (Berube and Berube 2010), through teaching and youth socialisation, in the context of broader social justice and widespread societal transformations, ranging from gender equality to human rights to racial tolerance to social mobility, and so on. More recently, the rise of fake news in tandem with post-truth, anti-elite and anti-expert knowledge regimes (Nichols 2017; Peters et al. 2018) are challenging traditional conceptions of what counts as legitimate knowledge, putting additional pressures on universities to proactively respond in accordance to their enlightenment and democratically inspired ideals.

Trust towards public institutions and elected officials are good indicators against which to assess the broader social and political climate in which universities, despite their global outlook and orientations, are closely embedded and expected to answer. Recent studies from the US show that in 2018, a mere 48% of adults expressed confidence in higher education, down from 57% in 2015 (Inside Higher Education 2018). In the Nordics, annual polls surveying HEIs and their activities still show a high level of confidence towards university employees. Similarly, recent public polls in Norway and Sweden reveal relatively high levels of trust towards research and higher education researchers, but there is some evidence that this faith is also changing (Science Nordic 2018; VA-barometern 2018/2019), and thus it should not be taken for granted. Responsibility is also related to the opposite, that is, to be *irresponsible* in the meaning of not behaving with honesty, integrity and decency. Throughout the twentieth century, North American research-intensive universities were the subjects of widespread criticism for their proximity to the industrial, military establishment and (indirect) contribution towards the various war efforts (Geiger 2009). Such developments shed further light on the classic cultural rift within academia, between the natural sciences and the social sciences and the humanities (Snow and Collini 2012), with the latter being more critical towards society in general, including external funders such as industry. Earlier inquiries suggest that 'applied' fields are more prone to collaborate with external stakeholders when compared to more basic ones, who tend to be more inner-oriented (Becher and Trowler 2001); yet empirical support for this claim, over the years and across countries, is contested (cf. Pinheiro et al. 2017).

However, the concept of responsibility also needs some problematisation. In some cases, the opposite—being irresponsible—effectively creates an antidote. There are numerous examples to be found in the media, including several eye-catching cases that have surfaced in the Nordic countries, which challenge the traditional image of trustful Nordic welfare societies with a low level of corruption and deliberate misbehaviour. Probably the most well-known was the Macchiarini affair at Karolinska Institutet in Sweden. Paolo Macchiarini was the Italian former star surgeon who made international headlines when he implanted artificial windpipes into patients but later encountered serious scientific misconduct charges involving fatal consequences (Abbott 2016). Other cases of made up experiments and tests have been revealed as well, with for instance the research at Uppsala University on how fish were affected by plastics, initially published in Nature and internationally recognised before the fraud was proven (Nature 2017).

Conceptions of what is responsible and what is not also change with time and place. In disciplinary fields like philosophy, the distinction may be especially difficult to make. That is why great tolerance has traditionally characterised idealised conceptions of academia. The recent emphasis on short-term accountability and efficiency has set new external expectations, but the dynamics of human invention may not have changed accordingly. Being non-conformist and non-responsive concerning current social expectations might bring long-term benefits and fruitful approaches, but significant innovations and breakthroughs have seldom been accepted overnight (e.g. gravity, electricity). Instead, these innovations encounter considerable scepticism at the onset. There are critical research traditions aimed at social equity, in which uses of power and privileged positions face questioning in attempts to foster more just and equal societies. The concentration of resources may cut down the intellectual and social areas which give meaning and prerequisites for living to many groups of people. Being irresponsible also can signal a sense of genuine autonomy from outside interests and strategic agendas (co-optation) and not being entirely politically correct and adaptive to all of these policies. For example, saying no to third stream/external funding (with perks attached), not adapting as easily as all the others, not being afraid to speak truth to power, and so on.

Responsibility as a New Thing?

The role of universities in society, both locally and globally, has been discussed since medieval times. In fact, universities have never been entirely autonomous or isolated from external demands. At the outset, they were deeply rooted in the Christian Church, not only with interlinkages regarding organisation and staff but also based on the kind of education provided. The main aim for a long period of time was to educate the clergy (de Ridder-Symoens 2003). During the late middle ages and the early modern era, universities contributed to the emerging state bureaucracy, educating civil servants to a growing group of clerks, scripters and other administrators. With the establishment of an administrative and judicial state bureaucracy supporting the King there was an increasing demand for educated civil servants. Consequently, law increasingly became a relevant subject area, while universities populated the newly established royal courts in European countries. In the seventeenth and eighteenth centuries also the medical sciences took further steps, albeit modern medicine had to wait until the early nineteenth century to emerge. Even more, the natural sciences prospered, in particular during the eighteenth century when the foundation formed for subsequent breakthroughs. Still, Divinity or Theology remained the noblest, highest ranked discipline, and the curriculum was dominated by works by the classic thinkers, with Latin as the lingua franca of the scholarly world (Huff 2017).

Not until the early nineteenth century did research become one of the main tasks for university professors, landmarked by the foundation of the University of Berlin in 1810 by Wilhelm von Humboldt (Östling 2018). This crucial transition from one university type to another was related to growing and shifting demands from the Prussian state and what became perceived as a university sector in decline. However, the introduction of research and research-based education was only one of the characteristics. Another was the idea of scholarly freedom and autonomy, even detachment from contemporary societal issues. The nineteenth century was an increasingly problematic time for traditional universities to catch up with new demands from industrialisation and emerging capitalism.

Universities faced criticism for not being up to the task of educating the highly needed professional groups populating offices both in the public and the private sectors. At some universities, external pressure for responsibility led to new faculties, sections and disciplines partially as a response to demands from employers (Wittrock 1993).

At a sector level, the responses from the old, established universities were not considered sufficient. Beginning in the late eighteenth century and continuing throughout the nineteenth century, several new higher education institutions came into existence, including those in the Nordic countries. One specific example included the technical universities focusing on educating engineers for a growing industrialised society. These institutions include KTH Royal Institute of Technology and Chalmers University of Technology in Sweden, Tampere Technical University in Finland, Denmark's Technical University and Norwegian University of Science and Technology, NTNU in Norway. Other both public and private universities opened as well, partly as a response to the existing universities' perceived ability to be responsible. In the aftermath of the Second World War, higher education and research entered a new phase, with a key role in the development of modern welfare societies in the Nordic countries, orchestrated by a designated research and technology policy. During the 1960s, a new expansion wave took place, partly as a result of a much broader democratic movement (Pinheiro and Antonowicz 2015), which opened up universities to a wider public (rising demand) and led to the foundation of a number of new HEIs. Some of these institutions represented a stronger vocational and local character. As a result, most of the Nordic systems entered the mass higher education phase in the 1970s (Trow 2000), supporting the widely shared belief (emanating from human capital theory, cf. Romer 1986) that public investments in education would be beneficial for society as a whole, alongside the idea of higher education as a policy instrument for the development and realisation of the ambitious goals set out by the welfare state (Ahola et al. 2014). Many of the new institutions developed different, distinct profiles than those of the existing universities, as a response to changing demands from society. This period was also the time when binary sectors composed of universities and other types of HEIs were introduced in some countries and considered in most, for various reasons (cf. Kyvik 1981, in the case of Norway). The expansion of the system with a growing student and faculty body, and new institutions embracing, for instance, 'interdisciplinarity' changed the geography of higher education and research (Kyvik 1983). The establishment of universities and university colleges across domestic regions also meant that they became increasingly embedded in regional development, for example, as engines of economic growth (Pinheiro et al. 2018).

The last decades, starting with another wave of expansion in the 1990s, have also meant the introduction of new governance ideas in the sector (Neave and van Vught 1991). Still, higher education and research are heavily relying on the public purse for funding and for regulation. However, the former central steering method has been replaced by more formal autonomy and 'steering from a distance' in relation to goals (see e.g. Degn and Sørensen 2015). This changing social contract between higher education (HE) and society, brokered by the state, also meant the opening up of the university to a wide variety of strategic interests and demands from multiple stakeholders (Neave 2002). A related aspect of this changing social contract is the growing neo-liberal idea of a global market for universities where they collaborate and compete. This competition is measured by, and manifested in, for instance, publications, competitive grants and world rankings (Geschwind and Pinheiro 2017).

Global Policy Initiatives

HE has been recognised as an important sector for addressing global issues such as sustainable development (Gough and Scott 2008). At universities, responsibility can also be linked directly to the sustainability goals of the United Nations (UN). In 2015, the member states of the UN adopted the 2030 Agenda for Sustainable Development and its 17 Sustainable Development Goals (SDGs).[4] This sustainability agenda deals with areas such as poverty, inequality, climate change, environmental degradation, prosperity, peace and justice. All the (17) goals are rather ambitious. For example, goal number 1 is to 'End poverty in all its forms everywhere'. This goal is specified to 'eradicate extreme poverty for all people everywhere, currently measured as people living on less than $1.25 a day' by 2030 and, at the same time, 'reduce at least by half the proportion of men, women and children of all ages living in poverty' according to national standards for poverty.[5]

These 17 goals could be a framework for universities working with issues of responsibility. Universities have already been called upon to take part in the fulfilment of the SDGs. 'The Sustainable Development Solutions Network (SDSN)—Australia/Pacific' has, for example, published a guide to help universities and other higher education institutions to get started implementing and working with the SDGs. In the guide, it is made clear that universities have a key role to play in the fulfilment of the goals, 'for the SDGs to be truly successful at a global scale, universities need to become champions of sustainable development and play a leading role in the implementation of the SDGs' (SDSN Australia/Pacific 2017). Simultaneously, as functioning organisations, universities face a series of immediate challenges associated with the need to secure external funding, raise quality standards and compete on a global scale, which results in a new set of tensions and dilemmas regarding what functions and whose stakeholders to prioritise (Enders and de Boer 2009; Benneworth and Jongbloed 2010; for a discussion on the Nordics see Pinheiro et al. 2014).

Nordic higher education has been affected by the so-called Europeanisation of the HE space (Maassen and Musselin 2009). The 2000 EU-driven Lisbon Agenda has had a profound effect on the instrumentalisation of the sector in securing policy goals—economic growth and innovation—with HE seen as a critical pillar for enhancing the competitiveness of the region as a whole (Sørensen et al. 2016). As part of this process, and following the suggestions from the EU commission (Aghion et al. 2008), Nordic governments have embarked in a bold agenda aimed at modernising their domestic HE landscapes, including a strengthened focus on university-industry relations and the commercialisation of knowledge (Pinheiro 2015), in addition to mergers or amalgamations (Pinheiro et al. 2016). The establishment of a common European area for HE (Bologna) has enabled the diffusion of standardised practices across national systems, enhancing the convergence of structures, practices and procedures (Witte 2008).

Contemporary societies have several pressing issues to address. A broad yet concrete example is provided by the so-called global challenges (e.g. UN 2019) which are at the forefront of a contemporary 'responsible' approach. They are challenging to solve ('wicked problems'), but at least they are stable enough to be studied extensively through academic enquiry. However, seeing, for example, climate change only as an academic problem is insufficient; such problems are also political and practical, embedded deeply in our civilisation and our industrial way of life. In this respect, scientific solutions provide the basis for wider social, political and cultural changes that are required to address such complex problems. This basis for change, in turn, requires action, coordination and collaboration across knowledge domains, sectors and types of organisations, making the emerging concept of 'knowledge co-creation' a rather appealing one amongst policy and managerial circles (Trencher et al. 2013).

Simultaneously, contemporary HE and research systems, not least in the Nordics, are still based on academic freedom as a core value (cf. Vabø and Aamodt 2008), that is, on the assumption and practices according to which individual scholars assumedly know best what is worth teaching and researching. This approach feeds a culture of trust amongst like-minded academic peers, providing the sustained motivation needed for achieving good results. Calls for increasing instrumentalisation, fiercer competitive pressures and closer ties with external interests, such as those of corporations, governments and funders, create new tensions and dilemmas associated with the need to continue to nurture professional virtues like communism, universalism, independent thinking, organised scepticism and disinterestedness aligned with the traditional ethos of science (Merton 1973).

Responsibility is also an issue closely related to the so-called crisis in science (see, e.g. Saltelli and Funtowicz 2017). This crisis is a double crisis, with both exogenous and endogenous manifestations. On the one hand, it is a *trust-crisis*. The public seems to lose faith in science due to scandals and questionable scientific results stemming from, among others, scientific scandals and growing political and economic interference in the science system. On the other hand, the crisis is also an endemic crisis within the science system itself. Here, detrimental research practices and replication problems are at the forefront, in addition to unreflected 'gap filling' as a way of motivating research (Alvesson et al. 2017). Studies have shown that many scientific results cannot be reproduced by other scientists (Ioannidis 2005, 2014). This leads to a waste of valuable time and funding resources—and can potentially harm universities and the public's trust in science. The causes behind the reproducibility crisis are many. Scientific misconduct in the form of Fabrication, Falsification and Plagiarism (FFP) is potentially very harmful but relatively rare (Fanelli 2009). Therefore, increasing focus has been directed to more widespread detrimental practices; so-called Questionable Research Practices (QRPs) such as p-hacking, selective citing, lack of transparency of methods, and so on (Steneck 2006; Bouter et al. 2016). We still know very little about the root causes of these practices, but publication and funding pressures, as well as the absence of internal quality control, amongst others, seem to be some of the causes. In Europe and elsewhere new projects are emerging designed to better understand and deal with FFP and QRPs. In these projects, emphasis is often put on Research Integrity (see, e.g. EU funded projects such as SOPs4RI: 'Standard Operating Procedures for Research Integrity', VIRT²UE: 'Virtue Based Ethics and Integrity of Research', or EnTIRE: 'The Embassy of Good Science'). 'The European Code of Conduct for Research Integrity' (Allea 2017) is a central policy document in this regard. Further, at the national level, some European countries have made their own codes of conduct to strengthen research integrity (see, e.g. the Danish Code of Conduct: Ministry of Higher Education and Science 2014).

Another interesting example of an emerging discussion on responsibility is the concept of Responsible Research and Innovation (RRI). The latter has become a key term within the European Commission and has, since 2011, been part of the EU's seventh research framework programme and the more recent Horizon 2020 (Owen et al. 2012). RRI builds on the two previous framework programmes' idea of socio-technical integration and has, according to Owen et al. (2012, 757), three key dimensions: First, it puts emphasis on 'science for society', that is, it focuses on the 'right impacts' or that science delivers what society needs. Second, there is an emphasis on joining science with society: Science should evolve with the surrounding society. Here, increased institutionalised responsiveness becomes vital. Third, the concept's bridging of responsibility with innovation and research aims at stimulating actors within the field to reflect more critically on their roles and responsibilities as knowledge producers, co-creators and policy advisors.

Putting Responsibility Into Practice

We have noted an overall external pressure for increasing accountability or responsibility for universities. Such pressures are buffered and penetrated through academic 'filters', and the outcomes may legitimately, and in practice, vary over time and from place to place. To display this variance of outcomes, we turn to the seminal works of Becher and Kogan (1980) and Clark (1983). Becher and Kogan (1980, 10–20) divide the levels and structure of any higher education system as follows in this section. What is crucial is that each of these levels contributes to outcomes of responsibility in the system, in the manner described:

1. *Central level* (national and local authorities involved in planning and allocation of resources for HE). National governments, for example, may have their political priorities and tasks, which they may or may not back up with funding for their fulfilment. Such duties, such as life-long learning, inevitably bound resources and tend to rule out alternative possibilities for the use of these scarce resources.
2. *Individual institution* as defined in the law (with instruments of governance and decision-making bodies). Many countries have undergone changes in university legislation in which institutional autonomy and accountability (responsibility) have been strengthened simultaneously. The institutions ought to profile themselves and create distinct strategies with identified aims, as pertaining to 'procedural autonomy' (Schmidtlein and Berdahl 2005). Institutional funding often connects to the successful fulfilment of these aims. The latter tend to filter the work being done, so that specific issues receive more support and attention than others. What is more, accountability results focusing on ex-post evaluations provide an incentive for gaming, where what gets measured is what gets done (Figlio and Getzler 2006). Prioritising is needed, as Clark (1998, 131) notes: 'universities are caught in the cross-fire of expectations', as knowledge increases exponentially and external stakeholders voice their demands. No institution can do it all any longer but must identify core strengths and set strategic priorities. This activity, in turn, affects the ways in which the institution will be able to act responsibly.

3. *Basic Unit* (departments, school of study that has academic responsibility). These units need to establish study programmes based on existing research and expertise. Given the deeply rooted and slow to build
nature of such programmes, basic units cannot easily change their orientation without slowly developing new expertise through research or
recruitments.
4. *Individuals* (teaching and research staff, administrators and ancillary
workers). Academic contributions are strongly dependent on the commitment and motivation of individual scholars (Höhle and Teichler
2013). Since it may take 15–20 years to become an expert in a field,
individuals and their research profiles tend to steer how responsibility
is taking place. This aspect is highlighted by the considerable academic
freedom expressed typically in legislation. For example, in Finland,
this fundamental legislative freedom has not changed, although external steering mechanisms and pressures for accountability have
increased over time (Kekäle et al. 2017).

Clark (1983, 28) noted that academic activities are divided and
grouped in two basic ways: by discipline and enterprise. Enterprise refers
to different institutional levels. Disciplines guide research questions; they
tend to maintain cultures and values, which gather similar-minded scholars together (Becher 1981). Close interaction and cooperation tend to
strengthen these values (Kekäle 2001). Since Gibbons et al.'s (1994) seminal work, shedding light on new modes of knowledge production, much
has been written on the value and challenges of multidisciplinarity, interdisciplinarity and transdisciplinarity in both teaching and scientific
inquiries (Lattuca 2001; Franks et al. 2007). Still, a purely technical university tends to be better equipped for dealing with specific research questions when compared to, for example, an Arts college or a comprehensive
university. Undoubtedly, disciplinary traditions and orientations do affect
the perspectives, inquiries and values pursued (Becher and Trowler 2001),
which again filter the discussion on a given subject. Given the presence of
such filters or structural barriers, we contend that rather broad and universalistic aims and outcomes regarding responsibility, as outlined in
policy documents and the general media (cf. Aghion et al. 2008), are
challenging to realise. Instead, empirically, we are likely to assist the

emergence of local answers and models to particular (localised) manifestations and interpretations of responsibility in the light of specific contextual circumstances; time, place, people, problems, and so on. The aim is to highlight these in the empirical case studies composing the bulk of this volume.

Clark (1998) noted nearly 20 years ago that there was a widening asymmetry between environmental demands and the institutional capacity to respond; today, this asymmetry has become even more pronounced. Academic excellence, social responsibility, global relevance and more responsiveness to emerging demands with fewer resources are expected. This demand, in turn, has led to mission overload with HEIs struggling to find a new balance between primary tasks (teaching and research) and secondary priorities emanating from the outside from a multiplicity of stakeholder groups (Enders and de Boer 2009). This situation is part of the changing social contract (within the last two decades) between HE and society, brokered by the state, with the latter being just one of many parties routinely posing new demands on HEIs (Maassen 2014). This phenomenon needs an assessment against the broader set of (new public management) government-led reforms targeting the public sector at large since the 1980s (Christensen and Lægreid 2011). These reforms have, inter alia, emphasised the role of market mechanisms, such as competition and performance management, and resulted in the rise of efficiency and accountability regimes; also in the realm of HE (Hazelkorn et al. 2018), and including the Nordic countries as well (Pinheiro et al. 2019).

Contemporary debates surrounding HEIs' third mission (of social engagement) have emphasised the role played by HEIs in the transfer of knowledge to society and firms, as engines for economic development and global competitiveness (Harding et al. 2007), and/or bastions for revitalising the socio-cultural profile of cities, regions and states (Laredo 2007). Studies have investigated the interplay between the third mission and the traditional core functions of teaching and research, with overwhelming evidence suggesting higher levels of structural decoupling (Benneworth 2012; Pinheiro et al. 2018). The third mission has gained new momentum in the last decade, as HEIs look for ways to distinguish themselves in a highly competitive market place, including the quest for new revenue streams and patrons (Pinheiro et al. 2015). Significant tensions remain, not least when it comes to finding an adequate balance between local engagement/relevance and global excellence, even though the two are not mutually exclusive (cf. Pinheiro 2016).

Higher Education in the Nordic Countries: Some Key Features

Nordic higher education has been the target of major governmental reforms in the last two decades. On the whole, these reforms have focused on strengthening the autonomy of institutions whilst at the same time enacting structural changes in the internal fabric of HEIs to foster efficiency, accountability and excellence. Managerialist-related features have been at the top of the agenda, with a strengthened focus given to changes in the governance structures of HEIs as well as the introduction of performance-based mechanisms within teaching and research (Vabø and Aamodt 2008). Teaching quality and research (world class) excellence have also featured centrally, as part of a gradual but steady move towards an enterprise-like market-based model centred on rankings and global competition (Geschwind and Pinheiro 2017).

When result-oriented management appeared in the late 1980s and early 1990s in the Nordic countries, university budgets began to include performance-based funding. Furthermore, funders have requirements for research outcomes, which effectively steers projects towards these goals, what some have termed the rise of 'strategic science regimes' (Rip 2004). Since the national legal frameworks regulating Nordic HE have been renewed to foster efficiency and accountability, quality assurance mechanisms have been introduced, structural development and mergers have been carried out, leadership practices have become less collegial and more leader-centred (Degn and Sørensen 2015; Pinheiro et al. 2019). There have been cascading reforms aiming at increasing relevance, accountability and efficiency within the given timeframe, leading (perhaps) to mission overload. Financial steering and competition may increase research efficiency but the benefits appear to be only temporary due to complex regulations by multiple funders, short-term agreements, the accumulation of research funding by academic elite groups, the so-called Matthew effects (Kwiek 2018), and potential clashes with educational values and cultures (Auranen 2014).

Governments across the Nordic region have enacted a variety of reforms aimed at making HEIs more accountable for their own actions and more responsive to external demands and expectations. From an initial look at Norway, the 2003/2004 Quality Reform led to the establishment of a series of governance and leadership changes within HEIs, for example, performance-based management and external actors playing a key role at the board level. Likewise, the Bologna process and the creation of a national agency for quality assurance led to increased oversight, most notably for non-university institutions such as university colleges. A system of contracts came to the fore, changing the relationship between HEIs and the Ministry from one based on trust towards a more transactional arrangement based on agreed-upon strategic goals and tangible outcomes. Societal engagement ('formidling') officially became a task for all HEIs, including the research-intensive ('flagship') universities such as Oslo, Bergen and the Norwegian University of Science and Technology (NTNU). In 2015, and for the first time, the Norwegian government adopted a long-term (2015–2024) plan for research and HE, outlining the need to concentrate resources in areas of national strategic importance (seas, climate, health care, etc.) and as a means of securing world class research excellence on a global scale (Kunnskapsdepartementet 2015). Amongst other aspects, the report stresses the responsibility of the public sector, HEIs included, in helping tackling both local and global problems, which entails 'a responsibility for bringing their best experts forward' (Ibid., p. 44).

In Finland, the most profound of the recent changes in HE policy is the new Universities Act (558/2009) of 2009. Although the act was a fundamental move, it can be seen to be well in line with the overall long-term development in HE and the university-society relationship: increasing institutional autonomy, albeit within the framework of greater accountability (responsibility). Aarrevaara et al. (2009) reported that the essence of the reform is that the overall responsibility for improving the conditions of the division of labour will be transferred to the universities as they will become independent legal entities. According to the Ministry of Education, the aim was to increase top international expertise, establish stronger and more effective higher education units, and improve the competitiveness of the university system with better professional management.

It is, according to the university law, the responsibility of universities in Denmark to 'conduct research and offer research-based education at the highest international level within its academic fields' (University Act 2011). Further, the University Act states that universities also have an obligation to collaborate with the surrounding society, to contribute to the development of international collaboration, to contribute to promoting growth, prosperity and the development of society. The university is also by law obligated to exchange knowledge and competences with society and encourage its employees to take part in the public debate (University Act 2011).

Also, in the Swedish higher education legislation, there are references to responsibility. The steps taken towards increased formal autonomy for higher education institutions by reforms in 1993 and 2011 have accentuated the need for responsible action. It reflects in the Higher Education Act that HEIs should collaborate with the surrounding society and inform these societies of their activities as well as work for research results to come to use. Furthermore, actions should be undertaken with the highest possible efficiency, effectiveness and quality as well as trustworthiness and ethics. HEIs are also expected to contribute to a sustainable development and gender equality, provide international perspectives, and promote widening participation (Högskolelag 1992/1434).

In short, Nordic HEIs are faced with increasing pressures to be both responsive and responsible, and this volume is a first attempt to take stock of ongoing developments across the Nordic countries, including shedding light on key trends and tensions, trade-offs and dilemmas as well as illuminating possible ways ahead in the Nordic countries and beyond. Some of the contributions in this volume problematise the geographical dimension of higher education in its relation to responsibility: how can a university contribute to society in various contexts? Both the regional and global dimensions surface for discussion in empirical chapters. Other contributions are more focused on *how* the core activities, research and education, are undertaken, for instance, in the form of so-called co-creation of knowledge, interdisciplinarity or massive open online courses (MOOC) and publication strategies related to languages, in particular the role of English as the scientific lingua franca. Last but not least, the internal, organisational procedures and practices are under discussion, as in recruitment processes and various 'irresponsible repertoires', that is, how university management can find themselves in responsibility dilemmas, potentially breaching the public value. Altogether the volume provides an array of examples of, and critical discussions of, the 'responsible university', it challenges, opportunities, in particular in the Nordic countries, but also beyond.

Notes

1. See, for example, http://www.responsiblebusiness.com/.
2. https://www.merriam-webster.com/dictionary/responsible#other-words.
3. https://www.eairweb.org/forum.
4. https://www.un.org/sustainabledevelopment/.
5. https://www.un.org/sustainabledevelopment/poverty/.

References

Aarrevaara, T., Dobson, I., & Elander, C. (2009). Brave New World: Higher Education Reform in Finland. *Higher Education Management and Policy, 21*(2), 89–106.

Abbott, A. (2016). Medical Nobel Prize Committee Deals with Surgical Scandal. *Nature News, 537*(7620), 289.

Aghion, P., Dewatripont, M., Hoxby, C., Mas-Colelle, M., & Sapir, A. (2008). *Higher Aspirations: An Agenda for Reforming European Universities.* Brussels: Bruegel.

Ahola, S., Hedmo, T., Thomsen, J. P., & Vabø, A. (2014). *Organisational Features of Higher Education. Denmark, Finland, Norway and Sweden.* NIFU Working Paper 2014:14. Oslo: NIFU.

Allea. (2017). The European Code of Conduct for Research Integrity. Retrieved from https://ec.europa.eu/research/participants/data/ref/h2020/other/hi/h2020-ethics_code-of-conduct_en.pdf.

Alvesson, M., Gabriel, Y., & Paulsen, R. (2017). *Return to Meaning: A Social Science with Something to Say*. New York: OUP Oxford.

Auranen, O. (2014). *University research performance: Influence of funding competition, policy steering and micro-level factors*. PhD Thesis, University of Tampere. Tampere: Tampere University Press.

Becher, T. (1981). Towards a Definition of Disciplinary Cultures. *Studies in Higher Education, 6*(2), 109–122.

Becher, T., & Kogan, M. (1980). *Process and Structure in Higher Education*. London: Heinemann.

Becher, T., & Trowler, P. (2001). *Academic Tribes and Territories: Intellectual Enquiry and the Culture of Disciplines*. Buckingham: Society for Research into Higher Education & Open University Press.

Beerkens, E. (2010). Global Models for the National Research University: Adoption and Adaptation in Indonesia and Malaysia. *Globalisation, Societies and Education, 8*(3), 369–381.

Benneworth, P. (2012). The Relationship of Regional Engagement to Universities' Core Purposes: Reflections from Engagement Efforts with Socially Excluded Communities. In R. Pinheiro, P. Benneworth, & G. A. Jones (Eds.), *Universities and Regional Development: A Critical Assessment of Tensions and Contradictions*. Milton Park and New York: Routledge.

Benneworth, P. (2013). *University Engagement with Socially Excluded Communities*. Dordrecht: Springer.

Benneworth, P., & Jongbloed, B. (2010). Who Matters to Universities? A Stakeholder Perspective on Humanities, Arts and Social Sciences Valorisation. *Higher Education, 59*(5), 567–588. https://doi.org/10.1007/s10734-009-9265-2.

Berube, M. R., & Berube, C. T. (2010). *The Moral University*. New York and Toronto: Rowman & Littlefield Publishers.

Bok, D. C. (1982). *Beyond the Ivory Tower: Social Responsibilities of the Modern University*. Cambridge, MA: Harvard University Press.

Bouter, L. M., Tijdink, J., Axelsen, N., Martinson, B. C., & Riet, G. t. (2016). Ranking Major and Minor Research Misbehaviors: Results from a Survey Among Participants of Four World Conferences on Research Integrity. *Research Integrity and Peer Review, 1*, 17.

Castells, M. (2001). Universities as Dynamic Systems of Contradictory Functions. In J. Muller, N. Cloete, & S. Badat (Eds.), *Challenges of Globalisation. South African Debates with Manuel Castells* (pp. 206–233). Cape Town: Maskew Miller Longman.

Christensen, T., & Lægreid, P. (2011). *The Ashgate Research Companion to New Public Management*. Surrey: Ashgate.

Clark, B. R. (1983). *The Higher Education System. Academic Institutions on Cross-National Perspective*. Berkeley: University of California Press.

Clark, B. R. (1998). *Creating Entrepreneurial Universities: Organizational Pathways of Transformation*. New York: Pergamon.

De Ridder-Symoens, H. (2003). *A History of the University in Europe: Volume 1, Universities in the Middle Ages* (Vol. 1). Cambridge: Cambridge University Press.

Degn, L., & Sørensen, M. P. (2015). From Collegial Governance to Conduct of Conduct: Danish Universities Set Free in the Service of the State. *Higher Education, 69*(6), 931–946.

Enders, J., & de Boer, H. (2009). The Mission Impossible of the European University: Institutional Confusion and Institutional Diversity. In A. Amaral, G. Neave, C. Musselin, & P. Maassen (Eds.), *European Integration and the Governance of Higher Education and Research* (Vol. 26, pp. 159–178). Dordrecht: Springer.

Etzkowitz, H. (2001). The Second Academic Revolution and the Rise of Entrepreneurial Science. *Technology and Society Magazine, 20*(2), 18–29.

Etzkowitz, H., & Leydesdorff, L. (2000). The Dynamics of Innovation: From National Systems and "Mode 2" to a Triple Helix of University–Industry–Government Relations. *Research Policy, 29*(2), 109–123.

Fanelli, D. (2009). How Many Scientists Fabricate and Falsify Research? A Systematic Review and Meta-Analysis of Survey Data. *PLoS ONE, 4*(5), e5738.

Figlio, D. N., & Getzler, L. S. (2006). Accountability, Ability and Disability: Gaming the System? In T. Gronberg & D. Jansen (Eds.), *Improving School Accountability* (pp. 35–49). Bingley: Emerald Group Publishing Limited.

Franks, D., Dalea, P., Hindmarsha, R., Fellows, C., Buckridgea, M., & Cybinskia, P. (2007). Interdisciplinary Foundations: Reflecting on Interdisciplinarity and Three Decades of Teaching and Research at Griffith University, Australia. *Studies in Higher Education, 32*(2), 167–185.

Geiger, R. L. (2009). *Research & Relevant Knowledge: American Research Universities Since World War II*. New Jersey: Transaction Publishers.

Geschwind, L., & Pinheiro, R. M. (2017). Raising the Summit or Flattening the Agora? The Elitist Turn in Science Policy in Northern Europe. *Journal of Baltic Studies, 48*(4), 513–528. https://doi.org/10.1080/01629778.2017.1305178.

Gibbons, M., Limoges, C., Noworthy, H., Schwartzman, S., Scott, P., & Trow, M. (1994). *The New Production of Knowledge. The Dynamics of Science and Research in Contemporary Societies*. London: Sage.

Goddard, J., Hazelkorn, E., & Vallance, P. (2016). *The Civic University: The Policy and Leadership Challenges*. Cheltenham: Edward Elgar Publishing.

Gough, S., & Scott, W. (2008). *Higher Education and Sustainable Development: Paradox and Possibility*. New York: Taylor & Francis.

Grau, F.X., Goddard, J., Hazelkorn, E., & Tandon, R. (2017). Recommendations for Academia, Academic Leaders and Higher Education and Research Policymakers. In Grau, et al. (Eds.), *Towards a Socially Responsible Higher Education Institution: Balancing the Global with the Local*. GUNI – Global University Network for Innovation. Higher Education in the World. Towards a Socially Responsible University: Balancing the Global with the Local. Retrieved from http://www.guninetwork.org/report/higher-education-world-6.

Hansen, H. F., Geschwind, L., Kivistö, J., Pekkola, E., Pinheiro, R., & Pulkkinen, K. (2019). Balancing Accountability and Trust: University Reforms in the Nordic Countries. *Higher Education* (online first). https://doi.org/10.1007/s10734-019-0358-2.

Harding, A., Scott, A., Laske, A., & Burtscher, C. (Eds.). (2007). *Bright Satanic Mills: Universities, Regional Development and the Knowledge Economy*. Aldershot: Ashgate.

Harloe, M., & Perry, B. (2004). Universities, Localities and Regional Development: The Emergence of the 'Mode 2'University? *International Journal of Urban and Regional Research, 28*(1), 212–223.

Hazelkorn, E., Coates, H., & McCormick, A. C. (2018). *Research Handbook on Quality, Performance and Accountability in Higher Education*. Cheltenham and Northampton: Edward Elgar Publishing.

Hilson, M. (2008). *The Nordic Model: Scandinavia Since 1945*. London: Reaktion Books.

Högskolelag. (1992/1434). Retrieved from https://www.riksdagen.se/sv/dokument-lagar/dokument/svensk-forfattningssamling/hogskolelag-19921434_sfs-1992-1434.

Höhle & Teichler. (2013). Determinants of Academic Job Satisfaction in Germany. In P. Bentley, H. Coates, I. R. Dobson, L. Goedegebuere, & V. L. Meek (Eds.), *Job Satisfaction Around the Academic World* (pp. 125–133). Dordrecht: Springer. https://doi.org/10.1007/978-94-007-5434-8_7.

Huff, T. E. (2017). *The Rise of Early Modern Science: Islam, China, and the West*. Cambridge: Cambridge University Press.

Inside Higher Education. (2018). Retrieved from https://www.insidehighered.com/news/2018/10/09/gallup-survey-finds-falling-confidence-higher-education.

Ioannidis, J. P. (2005). Why Most Published Research Findings Are False. *PLoS Med, 2*(8), e124.

Ioannidis, J. P. (2014). How to Make More Published Research True. *PLoS Med, 11*(10), e1001747.

Johnsen, H., Torjesen, S., & Ennals, R. (2015). *Higher Education in a Sustainable Society*. London: Springer International Publishing.

Kaldeway, D. (2018). The Grand Challenges Discourse: Transforming Identity Work in Science and Science Policy. *Minerva, 56*(2), pp. 161–182. Retrieved from https://link.springer.com/article/10.1007/s11024-017-9332-2.

Kekäle, J. (2001). *Academic Leadership*. New York: Nova Science Publishers.

Kekäle, J, Diogo, S., & Varis, J. (2017). *Changes in the University-Society Relationship and Its Outcomes in Major Higher Education Reforms in Finland*. A Paper Presented at the Good University Aarhus Workshop. Unpublished Manuscript.

Kerr, C. (2001). *The Uses of the University*. Cambridge, MA: Harvard University Press.

Kunnskapsdepartementet. (2015). Long-term Plan for Research and Higher Education. Retrieved from Oslo. Retrieved from https://www.regjeringen. no/contentassets/e10e5d5e2198426788ae4f1ecbbbbc20/en-gb/pdfs/ stm201420150007000engpdfs.pdf.

Kwiek, M. (2018). High Research Productivity in Vertically Undifferentiated Higher Education Systems: Who Are the Top Performers? *Scientometrics, 115*(1), 415–462.

Kyvik, S. (1981). *The Norwegian Regional Colleges: A Study of the Establishment and Implementation of a Reform in Higher Education*. Oslo: Norwegian Institute for Studies in Research and Higher Education.

Kyvik, S. (1983). Decentralisation of Higher Education and Research in Norway. *Comparative Education, 19*(1), 21–29.

Laredo, P. (2007). Revisiting the Third Mission of Universities: Toward a Renewed Categorization of University Activities? *Higher Education Policy, 20*(4), 441–456.

Lattuca, L. R. (2001). *Creating Interdisciplinarity: Interdisciplinary Research and Teaching Among College and University Faculty*. Nashville: Vanderbilt University Press.

Maassen, P. (2014). A New Social Contract for Higher Education? In G. Goastellec & F. Picard (Eds.), *Higher Education in Societies* (pp. 33–50). Rotterdam: SensePublishers.

Maassen, P., & Musselin, C. (2009). European Integration and the Europeanisation of Higher Education. In *European Integration and the Governance of Higher Education and Research* (pp. 3–14). Dordrecht: Springer.

~n, P., & Olsen, J. P. (2007). *University Dynamics and European Integration.* ordrecht: Springer.

.assen, P., & Stensaker, B. (2011). The Knowledge Triangle, European Higher Education Policy Logics and Policy Implications. *Higher Education, 61*(6), 757–769.

Merton, R. K. (1973). *The Sociology of Science: Theoretical and Empirical Investigations.* Chicago: University of Chicago Press.

Ministry of Higher Education and Science. (2014). Danish Code of Conduct for Research Integrity. *Copenhagen.* Retrieved from https://ufm.dk/en/publications/2014/the-danish-code-of-conduct-for-research-integrity.

Nature. (2017). *Investigation Finds Swedish Scientists Committed Scientific Misconduct.* Probe centered on controversial paper that claimed microplastic pollution harms fish. Retrieved from https://www.nature.com/articles/d41586-017-08321-2.

Neave, G. (2002). The Stakeholder Perspective Historically Explored. In J. Enders & O. Fulton (Eds.), *Higher Education in a Globalising World: International Trends and Mutual Observations: A Festschrift in Honour of Ulrich Teichler* (pp. 17–37). Berlin: Springer.

Neave, G., & van Vught, F. (1991). *Prometheus Bound: The Changing Relationship Between Government and Higher Education in Western Europe.* Oxford: Pergamon.

Nichols, T. (2017). *The Death of Expertise: The Campaign Against Established Knowledge and Why It Matters.* New York: Oxford University Press.

Östling, J. (2018). *Humboldt and the Modern German University: An Intellectual History.* Lund: Lund University Press.

Owen, R., Macnaghten, P., & Stilgoe, J. (2012). Responsible Research and Innovation: From Science in Society to Science for Society, with Society. *Science and Public Policy, 39*(2012), 751–760.

Peters, M. A., Rider, S., Hyvönen, M., & Besley, T. (2018). *Post-Truth, Fake News: Viral Modernity & Higher Education.* Singapore: Springer.

Pinheiro, R. (2015). Citius, Altius, Fortius: Mobilising the University for the 'Europe of Knowledge'. In B. Culum, F. Robeiro, & Y. Politis (Eds.), *New Voices in Higher Education Research and Scholarship* (pp. 1–17). Hershey, PA: IGI-Global.

Pinheiro, R. (2016). Assessing Change in Higher Education from the Perspective of Excellence Versus Relevance. In N. Cloete, L. Goedegebuure, Å. Gornitzka, J. Jungblut, & B. Stensaker (Eds.), *Pathways Through Higher Education Research: A Festschrift in Honour of Peter Maassen* (pp. 37–40). Oslo: University of Oslo.

Pinheiro, R., & Antonowicz, D. (2015). Opening the Gates or Coping with the Flow? Governing Access to Higher Education in Northern and Central Europe. *Higher Education, 70*(3), 299–313.

Pinheiro, R., Geschwind, L., & Aarrevaara, T. (2014). Nested Tensions and Interwoven Dilemmas in Higher Education: The View from the Nordic Countries. *Cambridge Journal of Regions, Economy and Society, 7*(2), 233–250. https://doi.org/10.1093/cjres/rsu002.

Pinheiro, R., Geschwind, L., & Aarrevaara, T. (Eds.). (2016). *Mergers in Higher Education: The Experiences from Northern Europe, Higher Education Dynamics.* Dordrecht: Springer.

Pinheiro, R., Geschwind, L., Hansen, H., & Pulkkinen, K. (Eds.). (2019). *Reforms, Organizational Change and Performance in Higher Education: A Comparative Account from the Nordic Countries.* Cham: Palgrave.

Pinheiro, R., Langa, P., & Pausits, A. (2015). One and Two Equals Three? The Third Mission of Higher Education Institutions. *European Journal of Higher Education, 5*(3), 233–249.

Pinheiro, R., Normann, R., & Johnsen, H. C. G. (2017). External Engagement and the Academic Heartland: The Case of a Regionally-embedded University. *Science and Public Policy, 43*(6), 787–797.

Pinheiro, R., & Young, M. (2017). The University as an Adaptive Resilient Organization: A Complex Systems Perspective. In J. Huisman & M. Tight (Eds.), *Theory and Method in Higher Education Research* (pp. 119–136). Bingley: Emerald.

Pinheiro, R., Young, M., & Sima, K. (2018). *Higher Education and Regional Development: Tales from Northern and Central Europe.* Cham: Palgrave.

Ramirez, F. O. (2009). World Society and the Socially Embedded University. 사회과학논집, *40*(2), 1–30.

Rip, A. (2004). Strategic Research, Post-modern Universities and Research Training. *Higher Education Policy, 17*(2), 153–166.

Romer, P. (1986). Increasing Returns and Long-Run Growth. *Journal of political economy, 94*(5), 1002–1037.

Saltelli, A., & Funtowicz, S. (2017). What is science's crisis really about? *Futures, 91*, 5–11.

Schmidtlein, F., & Berdahl, R. (2005). Autonomy and Accountability: Who Controls Academe? In P. Altbach, R. Berdahl, & P. Gumport (Eds.), *American Higher Education in the Twenty-First Century: Social, Political, and Economic Challenges* (pp. 71–90). Baltimore: John Hopkins University Pres.

Science Nordic. (2018). Retrieved from http://sciencenordic.com/swedish-women-less-trusting-researchers.

SDSN Australia/Pacific. (2017). *Getting Started with the SDGs in Universities: A Guide for Universities, Higher Education Institutions, and the Academic Sector*. Australia, New Zealand and Pacific Edition. Sustainable Development Solutions Network – Australia/Pacific, Melbourne. Retrieved from http://ap-unsdsn.org/wp-content/uploads/University-SDG-Guide_web.pdf.

Snow, C. P., & Collini, S. (2012). *The Two Cultures*. London: Cambridge University Press.

Sørensen, M. P., Young, M., & Bloch, C. (2016). Excellence in the Knowledge-Based Economy: From Scientific to Research Excellence. *European Journal of Higher Education, 6*(3), 217–236. https://doi.org/10.1080/21568235.2015.1015106.

Steneck, N. H. (2006). Fostering Integrity in Research: Definitions, Current Knowledge, and Future Directions. *Science and Engineering Ethics, 12*, 53–74.

Trencher, G., Yarime, M., McCormick, K. B., Doll, C. N., & Kraines, S. B. (2013). Beyond the Third Mission: Exploring the Emerging University Function of Cocreation for Sustainability. *Science and Public Policy, 41*(2), 151–179.

Trow, M. (2000). From Mass Higher Education to Universal Access: The American Advantage. *Minerva, 37*(4), 303–328.

UN. (2019). https://sustainabledevelopment.un.org/?menu=1300.

University Act. (2011). Retrieved from https://ufm.dk/en/legislation/prevailing-laws-and-regulations/education/files/the-danish-university-act.pdf.

VA-barometern. (2018/2019). VA-rapport 2018:6. Stockholm: Vetenskap och Allmänhet. Retrieved from https://v-a.se/downloads/varapport2018_6.pdf.

Vabø, A., & Aamodt, P. O. (2008). Nordic Higher Education in Transition. In T. Tapper & D. Palfreyman (Eds.), *Structuring Mass Higher Education. The Role of Elite Institutions*. London: Routdlege.

Watson, D., Hollister, R., Stroud, S. E., & Babcock, E. (2011). *The Engaged University: International Perspectives on Civic Engagement* (1st ed.). London: Routledge.

Webster's. (1994). *Encyclopedic Unabridged Dictionary of the English Language*. New York: Gramercy Books.

Witte, J. (2008). Aspired Convergence, Cherished Diversity: Dealing with the Contradictions of Bologna. *Tertiary Education and Management, 14*(2), 81–93. https://doi.org/10.1080/135838808020518.

Wittrock, B. (1993). The Modern University: The Three Transformations. In S. Rothblatt & B. Wittrock (Eds.), *The European and American University Since 1800. Historical and Sociological Essays*. Cambridge: Cambridge University Press.

Part II

The Emergence of Responsible Universities and the Way Forward

2

Responsible University: A Government Perspective

Mikko Kohvakka, Arto Nevala, and Hanna Nori

Introduction

In recent decades, responsibility has become a buzzword, but also a dilemma, in higher education (HE). Shared by all and faced by each alone, responsibility is a universal concept; yet there is no consensus on how to define it. Today, there is disagreement about the responsibility of universities. Many say universities have become more responsible, while others argue against this claim. Has this always been the case? And is it even possible to find one 'true' definition of responsibility? To find this out, we need to look back at history.

In this chapter we take a government perspective and discuss what a responsible university has meant in Finnish HE policy and how perceptions of it have changed from the late 1950s to the so-called great

M. Kohvakka (✉) • A. Nevala
University of Eastern Finland, Joensuu, Finland
e-mail: mikkko@uef.fi; arto.nevala@uef.fi

H. Nori
University of Turku, Turku, Finland
e-mail: hanna.nori@utu.fi

university reform of the 2010s. To answer this question, we adopt a socio-spatial approach. First, we describe how the idea of the spatial (regional) responsibility of universities changed as Finland moved from the so-called Nordic-Keynesian welfare state era to a more international 'Schumpeterian' competition state period. Secondly, within the above-mentioned spatial and temporal framework, we examine socio-economic equality in Finnish HE, the promotion of which has been a key objective of Finnish social and education policy since the 1950s. We measure socio-economic equality in terms of the participation of different socio-economic groups in university studies, and we analyse which student background related factors are important for access to university studies. We thus examine responsibility in terms of equality of entry to university and the processes of student admission.

Access to university in Finland is limited according to the so-called numerus clausus system. For many disciplines, there have been, and still are, considerably more applicants than places to study. As a result, admission can be highly competitive, and especially in high-prestige institutions and disciplines (so-called elite fields) only a small proportion of applicants are admitted. In this competition for student places, the socio-economic position of parents plays an important role, as several studies have shown. Changes in the socio-economic background of students thus serve to indicate how the 'responsible university' has been defined in the Finnish HE system during the last five decades.

Theoretically, we claim that a key aspect of any modern social and political concept such as a responsible university is its 'temporalized' nature (Koselleck 2002; Kettunen 2012). Thus, researchers dealing with issues of responsibility in HE policy should also ask how the responsible university has been conceptualized and connected with political agendas and political agency in different times and places. From this perspective, emphasizing historical contingency, we claim that a responsible university should be seen—above all—as a tool for governing the tension between experience and expectation, which is an essential part of HE politics and policy (Rose 1999; Kettunen 2012). We recognize that responsible university is a current concept, used analytically by social scientists to make sense of HE policy and generate social cohesion in the twenty-first century. However, we should also seek to explain the historical processes by which different political ideas of universities' responsible behaviour have crystallized in past decades. In this context, then, a responsible university could be defined as a category of practice or every-day experience, developed and deployed by ordinary social actors at different times and in different places (Brubaker and Cooper 2000).

On the one hand, our analysis is based on research carried out by ourselves and other scholars. In addition, our main research material consists of official university policy documents and the most recent statistics on the socio-economic backgrounds of students, and statistics related to the other background factors important for university access. In regard to research methods, we primarily use both qualitative textual analyses, especially policy document analysis, and quantitative methods, such as calculating different key ratios, to scrutinize contemporaries' interpretations of a responsible university.

This chapter proceeds as follows: firstly, the case of Finland and a brief examination of the history of the Finnish HE system will be introduced in the Nordic context. Then, the proceeding sections will analyse the changing meanings of a socio-spatially responsible university from the late 1950s to the beginning of the 2010s by paying attention both to the issues of regional responsibility of universities and socio-economic equality in student admissions. Finally, the concluding section will bring together the most important findings in the Nordic context. This section also looks at the current trend in Finnish HE policy and reflects on whether it is fruitful to discuss responsible universities generally and take them as pre-existing categories or whether it is more appropriate to see them as unique entities representing the strategies, values and viewpoints that are characteristic of a certain time and place.

The Case of Finland—From Welfare State to Competition State

After World War II, political tensions and the struggle between different ideologies, both in domestic policy and in international relations, intensified demand for closer ties between nation states and their citizens. In the Nordic countries, too, most politicians saw the preservation of civil peace as the highest priority and thus adopted a stance that equated responsibility with social and regional equality. Practically, this meant a need to build a welfare state, to strengthen the social responsibility of the state and improve the visibility of social responsibility in every part of society and in every corner of state territory (Giulianotti et al. 2017; Alestalo et al. 2009; Jalava 2012). This process, called spatial Keynesianism, was seen as a responsible way to act not only because the state territory was considered a valuable national resource and factor of production but also because the idea of equal opportunity was seen as the basis of state sovereignty during the Cold War period (Moisio 2012). Hence, the Nordic-Keynesian welfare state pursued de-centralized socio-spatial formations based on regional political ideas emphasizing national integrity and the creation of various regional institutions, like universities, throughout the state.

In the Finnish HE system, the Nordic welfare state and spatial Keynesianism meant an immense increase in student numbers. In the early 2010s the number of university students (170,000) was more than 11 times higher than it had been in the late 1940s (15,000). It could be argued that since the early 1970s the elite form of Finnish HE, emphasizing privilege of birth and shaping the mind and character of the top social classes, was partially replaced by the mass HE system to which a much broader age group had possibility of access. However, certain features of the previous elite system remained embedded within the new mass education period (Trow 1974).

Due to this rapid expansion and massification, new universities were established. Today, 14 universities operate within the Ministry of Education and Culture's administrative branch, in addition to which the National Defence University operates under the defence administration. In addition, during the deep economic downturn of the early 1990s, Finland adopted a so-called dual system with new polytechnics (universities of applied sciences) founded alongside the universities to tighten the bond between the HE system and society.

The new dual system was an apex of the Nordic welfare state and spatial Keynesianism. At the same time, the collapse of the Soviet Union, European integration, and, especially, the steps towards globalization of financial markets, industrial production, technology and communication opened windows to other ways of conceptualizing responsible behaviour and new spaces of social change. For many nations, territorially equalizing welfare state strategies appeared as an obstacle as states were increasingly adopting non-material and spatially differentiating policies and practices. This was also the case in Sweden, Norway, Denmark and Finland, where governments were concerned about national success in an international competitive marketplace. The new discourse of a Schumpeterian competition state arose, championing the ideas of urbanism, internationalization and high technology as new national survival strategies (Heiskala and Hämäläinen 2007; Moisio 2012).

In HE policy, the transformation from a Nordic-Keynesian welfare state towards a more international, Schumpeterian competition state meant that university funding was cut and it was necessary for universities to allocate scarcer public funds to carefully chosen fields that had the prerequisites to prosper amid fierce international competition without constant subsidies from the public sector. The new Schumpeterian HE policy aimed at improving cooperation between universities, reducing overlap and establishing bigger, stronger and more competitive scientific units. This so-called structural development of HE was, however, only partly realized during the 1990s, and the HE network remained almost untouched until the so-called great university reform in 2010 (Nevala and Rinne 2012; Rinne 2012).

The guidelines for the reform were defined in the 2010 University Act, which triggered a major structural and cultural change in the way universities are led. From then on, Finnish universities were either institutions subject to public law, or foundations subject to private law in which the authority for personnel policies, financial administration and strategic decisions was delegated from the state to the universities. Moreover, universities began to fulfil their commitments to society by strategically using their own external, supplementary funds, although the Ministry of Education and Culture, as the main funder, still had a strong steering influence on the universities' activities (Aarrevaara et al. 2009). These developments led to a radical departure from previous decades in how the socio-spatially responsible university was interpreted, as the following two sections will explore.

Spatial Keynesianism and the Inward-Looking Idea of Spatially Responsible Universities

In Finland during the era of spatial Keynesianism, the ruling centre-left governments saw utilization of the resources of the state's peripheral regions as beneficial to the nation as a whole. In practice, the politics of one nation, aiming at a coherent nation state with balanced educational and economic opportunities throughout the state territory, were supported by education, investment and regional policies that became intertwined in the 1960s and 1970s (Moisio and Leppänen 2007). The centre-left governments became aware of the need to create an education system that would moderate regional differences and overcome differences between the social classes. It is no coincidence that the preparation of a new state-wide comprehensive school at the primary level and the enactment of a law on the development of a HE system over the period 1967–1986 were fulfilled at the same time, in the mid-1960s (Kohvakka 2016).

The Act for the Development of Higher Education, 1967–1986, fostered social and regional equality by facilitating access to universities and guaranteeing resources for HE during an era when six multidisciplinary universities, two technology universities and one business school were about to begin operating alongside Finland's eight existing institutions (Välimaa 2005, 2018). Together with Norway, Finland implemented a more deliberate regionalization policy than, for example, Sweden (Dahllöf 1994) and created territorially the most encompassing network of HE institutions in the Nordic countries (Kogan and Bauer 2000; Dhondt and Nevala 2015). However, in Finland, all new HE institutions were research universities, whereas Norway, Sweden and Denmark placed their emphasis on the non-university sector, that is, vocationally oriented colleges (Höltta 1999; Kyvik 2004; Välimaa 2018). Leading politicians and civil servants of the time thought that the responsible behaviour of universities meant processes in which the intellectual capital of the whole state territory would be harnessed by the universities to support the national mission of state planning (Science Policy Council 1973). According to this logic, state administration and regional research and education merged into a seamless whole in which government officials, professors and researchers worked together to strengthen the bond between the state territory and its citizens in every way (Moisio and Leppänen 2007).

The strong belief in the importance of state intervention and planning in producing economic growth and in the social utility of positivist scientific knowledge meant that some branches of science became more important than others. Particularly, social sciences, such as sociology, social policy, economics and regional studies, were crucial in supporting 'the power container' (Giddens 1985): the state's supremacy in politics, as well as in economic, cultural and social policy (Taylor 1996). The social sciences were ready to accept the special task offered to them and the privileged position that accompanied the offer (Allardt 2000). As a result, social sciences in Finland adopted a state-centric view in which other spatial scales, notably the international and the regional/local, became subsumed into the national frame of reference.

The dominance of spatial Keynesianism and the national scale overshadowed the scrutiny of corporate activity and other activities stretching beyond state-centric thinking. Technology universities and business schools experienced particular difficulty adapting to the state's normative regulation system, which restricted autonomous and non-public interaction between industry and universities in the 1970s. These universities took part in several initiatives that were contrary to state monopoly capitalism and favoured the institutional autonomy of universities and the interests of economic life (Michelsen 1994; Pihkala 2000). In addition, they adopted a critical stance towards the government's argument that the primary task of universities was to support regionally harmonious and equal territorial development of the state space (Kohvakka 2015).

Criticism of spatial Keynesianism emerged in the late 1970s at the same time as the dual crises of stagnation and mass unemployment that forced West European governments to raise taxes to cover growing social entitlement costs. All this put the Keynesian welfare state ideology in turmoil. During these crises, the prevailing idea of state-led regulation as a responsible way to act was challenged by a new way of thinking about responsibility that demanded market liberalization and new public management methods (Brenner 2004; Harvey 2005). At first, the Nordic countries responded to the crises moderately by strengthening and widening the welfare state. However, at the beginning of the 1980s, trust in a strong public sector and state-centric practices as the cornerstones of responsible behaviour started to lose ground—first in Denmark (Hansen 1990; Degn and Sørensen 2015) and later also in other Nordic countries. The development of spatial Keynesianism reached its culmination in Finland in the mid-1980s. Since then, the gradual rise of Schumpeterian competition logic, based on a belief in all-embracing competitiveness, individualism and the efficiency of a free and open market, challenged the old, institutionalized principles of collectivism, conservatism and protectionism.

A Competition State and a New Meaning of Spatial Responsibility

The deep economic depression of the early 1990s was the main driver of the gradual shift from the Nordic-Keynesian welfare state to Schumpeterian competition state in Finland. The new narrative brought to the public by market liberal politicians, officials and business leaders redefined a socio-spatially responsible university as an entity emphasizing private benefit over public enrichment. In this redefinition process abstract principles of egalitarian rationality, stability and procedural legitimacy were challenged by discourses valuing economic rationality, efficiency and legitimacy by results (Kohvakka 2015). Ideas of international competition and competitiveness gained prominence in university strategies and became closely connected with a drive to increase both universities' and the state's competitiveness through know-how and improved research activity (Ministry of Education 1991; Ministry of Education 1996; Heiskala and Hämäläinen 2007; Moisio and Leppänen 2007; Kohvakka 2016). The previously dominating strategies of the spatially responsible university, which were mainly inward-looking, emphasizing the national scale and territorialized practices, were challenged by new outward-looking strategies stretching beyond the national and stressing new de/reterritorialization practices.

The new ways of thinking about the universities' socio-spatial responsibility entailed new concepts such as networks, innovations, clusters and city-districts that were all associated with the urban environment (Moisio and Leppänen 2007). In government programmes and national development plans for education and research, universities were no longer assumed to be the principal providers of regional stability within their home region. Instead, due to growing societal pressure, universities began producing new urban and transregional landscapes that transcended the traditional territorial boundaries of regions and created new university-city and university-industry alliances where membership was not based solely on geographical proximity but on the shared aims and abilities to cultivate knowledge, technology and innovations. Representatives of the engineering sciences and business studies who considered that the state authorities had regulated contact with economic life in the 1970s and the early 1980s now took their place in the spotlight as corporate activity and theories of institutional economics were no longer bounded by state-centric thinking (Husso and Raento 2002).

Despite new definitions of socio-spatial responsibility, the historically constructed Keynesian logic of regional development still had its impact on territorial practices in HE. As the universities in the late 1990s and early 2000s were creating urban-centric, transregional research and development hubs by establishing branch units, or 'university centres' (Nokkala and Välimaa 2017), in cities without a university, the new polytechnics that had been established throughout the country started to foster an 'old-school', inward-looking territorial regionalism. As vocational HE institutions, 32 polytechnics focused their practices on education with social relevance to meet the new needs of the knowledge-based economy and the labour market. Polytechnics were, above all, locally or regionally scaled institutions run by a single municipality or a federation of municipalities within a single region (Välimaa 2005). Polytechnics' activities were thus largely predetermined by their geographical location and therefore promoted collaborative activities that fostered the relatively uniform pattern of regional space associated with spatial Keynesianism and its inclusive approaches to regional development (Harrison et al. 2017).

However, this division of labour of outward-looking universities and inward-looking polytechnics was to be short-lived. Already by the end of the 2000s, polytechnics (now called universities of applied sciences) started to close campuses and branch units located in peripheral, rural municipalities. The strategic focus of the polytechnic was no longer on providing and guaranteeing equal study possibilities throughout its own region. Instead, their spatial (re)orientation and understanding of responsible behaviour began to resemble that of universities. By the early 2010s, there was broad consensus among politicians and officials that the mission of polytechnics was to provide HE for professional expert jobs and to carry out applied research and development and innovation activities that promoted industry, business and regional development in an urban, globally oriented environment (Salminen and Ylä-Anttila 2010; Välimaa and Neuvonen-Rauhala 2008).

To succeed in this urbanization process, the state authorities encouraged polytechnics to empower new 'spatial imaginaries' (Harrison et al. 2017), namely, city-regions and transregional alliances. This was done by supporting deeper collaboration both between polytechnics and with universities. Cooperative institutions were rewarded for merging themselves into a bigger, transregional units or consortia, which signalled greater alignment with the Schumpeterian (market-driven) understanding of more targeted and exclusive forms of regional development. The visibility of polytechnics in rural areas decreased in the same proportion as they decreased in number, from 32 in the early 2000s to 25 in the late 2010s. At the same time, multi-campus universities began to run down their branch campuses in small towns in the name of centralization, the concentration of limited resources in larger city-regions that, allegedly, shared aspirations to compete for elite status nationally and globally (Vartiainen 2017).

A form of urban-centric, internationally oriented elitism thus made its return to the spatial practices of HE institutions in Finland during the first decade of the 2000s. Next, we will turn our attention to the changes in the social background of students and the prerequisites for admission and examine whether a similar development towards the return of elitism as the representation of responsible behaviour can be discerned.

Towards Socio-economic Equality?

As previously mentioned, one of the principal goals of Finnish education policy since the 1950s has been to equalize the participation of different socio-economic groups in HE, thereby promoting educational equality and thus 'responsible' progress. During the post-war decades the dominant trend regarding the socio-economic background of university students was equalization. As Fig. 2.1 shows, the differences between socio-economic groups regarding participation in university education have evened out, but have not disappeared by any means.

Proportional participation: Percentage of socio-economic groups in university divided by percentage of these groups in population aged 45–54 years. For example, group I in 1980: 36.5%/14.5% = 2.52.

Figures greater than 1.0 indicate over-representation of the socio-economic group.

Socio-economic groups (based on parent/guardian employment): I: Upper white-collar and entrepreneurs, II: Lower white-collar and small

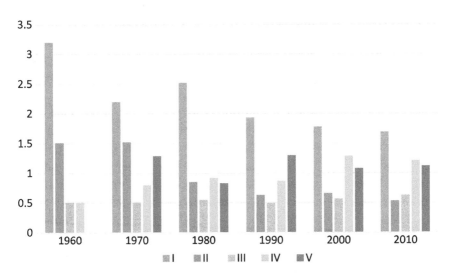

Fig. 2.1 Proportional participation of children from different socio-economic groups in university education in the years 1950–2010. *Sources*: Socio-economic background of new university students from 1925 to 2010; Demographic statistics of Finland, years 1960–2010

entrepreneurs, III: Blue-collar, IV: Agricultural, V: Others (pensioners, unemployed, etc.).

The figure contains uncertainties with respect to classification and comparability, however. For example, pensioners were not classified as pensioners but according to their former employment prior to the year 1975. Furthermore, the socio-economic groups needed to be large to allow longitudinal comparison, which makes them internally heterogeneous. The figure nevertheless indicates the trend in development relatively reliably.

The proportion of children of upper white-collar personnel and entrepreneurs (group I) going to university declined rapidly in the early 1980s and has since steadily diminished. This can be partly explained by the change in the demographic structure in Finland: in the year 2010 there were almost three times as many people in upper white-collar and entrepreneurial jobs (age group 45–54 years) than there were in the 1970s. In other words, since the high-level white-collar group has greatly expanded, the number of their children entering university education has increased more slowly. In comparison, almost the same number of working-class students (group III) enrolled in universities in the 2000s as in the 1980s, and their relative participation rate grew only a little. The same phenomenon can be seen with lower level office workers' children (group II), whose representation in university education has diminished dramatically since the early 1970s.

The children of pensioners and unemployed (group V) increased their share of university enrolment initially, partly due to the change in the classification of statistics, but later their proportion dropped. In the 1980s and early 1990s, the children of pensioners were well represented in university education. In the late 1990s and early 2000s, the number of pensioners stopped growing and, as a result, their children's participation in university education also diminished. The children of unemployed people have had a very slender representation in university education throughout, and that is still the case: the participation ratio of children of unemployed people in 2000 was 0.50 (socio-economic background of new university students, year 2000). The unemployed can thus be regarded as a marginalized sector of the population also with respect to university education. Interestingly, the agricultural population (group

IV) was underrepresented until the 1990s, but later their representation grew, and the figures show clear over-representation in the 2000s. One possible explanation is that although there are now much fewer agricultural entrepreneurs than before, they have bigger farms and more income and therefore better possibilities to send their children to university (Nori 2011).

In terms of the social background of students, in fields with high social status, such as law, medicine, business and technology, there were clearly more people from upper class families than in universities on average. In these so-called elite fields, as many as 47% of new students came from upper level professional, white-collar or entrepreneur families (group I) in the 1990s and 2000s. The difference is best illustrated by comparing these proportions with those of the opposite extreme, pedagogy (including teacher education), in which only some 30% of students came from the highest social group during the same period (Nevala 1999). It is important to note that graduates from these 'elite fields' often work in prestigious professions. Hence, the equalization of HE has taken place primarily in the lower status fields, such as the humanities and social sciences and education. This can be interpreted that the main differences in the socio-economic background were primary between the fields of study and thus the 'elite university' can be found in Finland inside the 'mass university' (Ahola 1995; Nevala 1999; Nori 2011; Kivinen et al. 2012).

To sum up the development to the beginning of the 2000s, we find two major changes: equalization on the one hand and persistent inequality on the other. The changes in Finnish society and educational policy from the 1960s onwards have unquestionably affected the recruitment and background of university students. Educational equality advanced and, at the same time, education functioned as a significant means of social mobility as there was a growing demand for a skilled university-educated workforce in the welfare state. Nevertheless, it should also be borne in mind that there have been, and still are, significant differences between universities and fields of study regarding enrolment in university education (Jalava 2012; Nevala and Nori 2017; Kivinen et al. 2012).

From the 1960s to the early 2000s, Finnish HE policy was mainly national, the state was one of the key players, and it was closely related to the general goals of the Nordic-Keynesian welfare state, such as regional and social equality. The state controlled universities through different norms, that is, legislation, but universities had, however, extensive scientific autonomy. HE during this period can therefore be interpreted as having being responsible to the state, for the increased willingness of citizens to gain education, and for regional development. By contrast, the impact of business life on HE policy was minimal.

Social Equality and the Fragmentation of Universities in the 2000s

Since the beginning of this century, Finland has transformed into a competition state. At the same time, structural changes in HE that started in the 1990s have continued and intensified. From our point of view, there are two essential aspects of change. On the one hand, the impact of so-called market forces on HE policy and HE practices has intensified. On the other hand, the fragmentation of HE is reflected in the fact that the routes to university education are nowadays considerably varied. Thus, the background factors affecting access to HE are now more diversified than in the past. To examine the changes in student admission from the 2000s onwards, we compared university applicants in 2003 (Nori 2011) and 2014 (Nevala and Nori 2017). The new University Act came into force in 2010, and by comparing datasets for 2003 and 2014, we can bring into focus the effects of the university reform on students' choices. We also studied the internal fragmentation of the Finnish university: what differences in student background exist between disciplines? The factors contributing to admission were studied using binary logistic regression analysis (Table 2.1).

Table 2.1 clearly shows that applicant's age, municipality group, basic education, main activity (employment status) and parents' education have an impact independent of other background factors. Firstly, the older the applicant is, the more difficult it is to be accepted. In 2003, the odds ratio (OR) for age was 0.98, which means the probability of access reduces by 2% per each additional year of age. The significance of age has increased during the past 11 years; in 2014 the OR was as high as 0.93

Table 2.1 Factors having an impact on university admission in 2003 and 2014

Variable	2003 Odds ratio	95% confidence interval	p value	2014 Odds ratio	95% confidence interval	p value
Age	0.98	0.97–0.99	0.000	0.93	0.92–0.94	0.001
Municipality group						
Province	1.11	0.95–1.29	0.181	1		
City	1.30	1.15–1.46	0.000	1.20	1.08–1.34	0.001
Conurbation	1			0.96	0.83–1.11	0.591
Matriculation examination						
No	1			1		
Yes	1.35	1.09–1.66	0.004	2.42	1.91–3.08	0.001
Main activity						
Unemployed	1			1		
Employed	1.28	1.14–1.44	0.000	3.00	2.54–3.54	0.001
Student	1.54	1.36–1.73	0.000	7.50	6.35–8.85	0.001
Conscript	1.37	1.18–1.60	0.000	4.90	4.06–5.90	0.000
Mother's level of education						
Upper secondary				1		
Lowest tertiary				1.04	0.97–1.12	0.242
Lower degree tertiary				1.04	0.95–1.13	0.425
Higher degree tertiary				1.33	1.23–1.45	0.001
Doctorate or equivalent				1.56	1.34–1.81	0.001
Father's level of education						
Basic education	1			–		
Upper secondary	1.06	0.97–1.16	0.205	1		
Lowest tertiary	1.16	1.05–1.29	0.004	1.08	1.00–1.16	0.045
Lower degree tertiary	1.19	1.06–1.35	0.004	1.18	1.09–1.27	0.001
Higher degree tertiary	1.36	1.21–1.54	0.000	1.29	1.20–1.38	0.001
Doctorate or equivalent	1.80	1.51–2.15	0.000	1.26	1.12–1.42	0.001

Source: Background information concerning university applicants in 2003 and 2014, Statistics Finland

Note: Odds ratio (OR) is defined as the ratio of the probability of success and the probability of failure. OR can range between 0 and infinity (note: OR is a different number from the participation factor in Fig. 2.1)

(one year reduces odds of acceptance by 7%). Today, a 30-year-old applicant's chance of successful admission is approximately 70% lower than that of a 20-year-old (Nevala and Nori 2017). This is a startling result.

Geographical origin also influences the applicant's odds of admission (in 2003, the reference category was conurbation, in 2014 it was province). The probability of urban applicants being admitted to university is greater than that of others, and there have been no changes in this respect over the past ten years. Urban applicants were over-represented among all applicants. There may be a number of reasons why urban applicants are accepted more often than applicants from rural areas. For example, the most successful upper secondary schools with the 'best' students are located in Finland's biggest cities—especially in the metropolitan area. Also, participation in preparatory courses is easier in cities than in the provinces.

In 2003, the probability of an applicant with a matriculation certificate securing a study place at university was 35% higher than that of applicants without matriculation. By 2014, it had risen to as high as 2.4-fold (or 140% higher). Applicants who have not completed a matriculation examination also often have non-academic parents. This means that they are twice as disadvantaged as others (Haltia et al. 2017).

An applicant's 'main activity' (employment status) also impacts their chances of admission. The situation of the unemployed is naturally the weakest. During the past 11 years there have been significant changes in the odds ratios regarding main activity. In 2003, the probability of admission was highest among full-time students, who had a 1.5-fold (50%) higher chance of compared to unemployed applicants. By 2014, this difference had increased to 7.5-fold (650%). This shows the beleaguered position of the unemployed in admission selection. Being unemployed may also be a result of poorer grades in upper secondary school or vocational school, which is, again, directly related to success in the student admission process.

In the 2003 data there was no variable describing the mother's education level. According to the 2014 data, it seems that mother's education has stronger impact on access opportunities than father's education. Admission odds increase in line with mother's education level. The offspring of a mother who has completed a doctoral education has a 1.6-fold (60%) higher likelihood of being accepted than a descendant of a mother who only has an upper secondary degree. With respect to father's education, the years 2003 and 2014 are not fully comparable. In 2003, the reference category was basic education and, in 2014, secondary education. In both years, the probability of admittance increases as the father's level of education increases. It seems, however, that the significance of father's education level has somewhat diminished over the years.

The effect of family background is manifested mainly through parental education, and, again, the mother's education seems to be more relevant. In Finland, as in the other Nordic countries, social mobility is more common on average than in other Western nations. The social and cultural capital of parents does not, therefore, determine the future status of their offspring, but education does nevertheless continue to play a role as a channel of social rise—albeit to a lesser extent than in previous decades.

Today, new university students are selected from different social groups more equally than ever before. However, there is an increasing variety of access rates and admission levels between different institutions, disciplines and training programmes. For example, students from privileged backgrounds typically choose, and are admitted to, highly selective disciplines such as medicine, dentistry and law, whereas students from lower social backgrounds typically enrol in less selective and vocationally orientated programmes (Nori 2018). Consequently, even in the 2010s, students' socio-economic backgrounds differ between disciplines. Figure 2.2 shows the representation (%) of white-collar and blue-collar parents of university students in different disciplines (mother's and father's socio-economic status as combined averages) in 2014.

The lines for lower white-collar employees and blue-collar workers are in many respects similar. On the right-hand side, the shares of upper white-collar employees are the highest, and on the left they are the lowest. Law, medicine, psychology, economics and engineering have a considerably high proportion of upper white-collar employees. Psychology appears to be a field in which social selectivity has risen considerably over the last 20 years. In the mid-1990s (Kivinen and Rinne 1995) the field was classified as quite popular across the board; nowadays, the sector is more elitist in terms of students' parental social status. The share of blue-collar parents is the highest in military science. Other fields that have been defined as popular include health sciences, pharmacy, social sciences

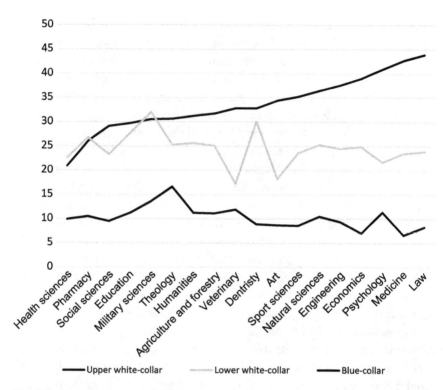

Fig. 2.2 Representation of university students' parents (upper and lower white-collar employees and blue-collar workers) per discipline (%), mothers and fathers combined, in 2014

and educational sciences. These fields have the fewest students with upper white-collar parents. These are also typically women-dominated fields.

There are also regional inequalities in student admission. Universities in metropolitan areas admit more students with a high social background, while relatively more students with a lower social background are admitted to small provincial universities (Kivinen et al. 2012; Nori 2011). Compared to universities of applied sciences, traditional universities recruit students from higher social backgrounds (Potila et al. 2017). Within the traditional university sector, differences between disciplines are also much deeper than in the non-university sector (Saari et al. 2015).

When we consider student selection from the perspective of responsibility, it seems that responsibility has shifted from the state to individuals and, in part, to their families. The importance of the applicant's age, previous education and 'main activity' in accessing university has clearly increased over the last ten years. This means that the choices made by individuals and families are becoming increasingly important.

The state is no longer responsible, either, for implementing regional equality. The main mission of universities in the view of the state is to boost national and international competitiveness. Structural changes and political decisions have led to new developments in university admissions based on principles of competition and availability of choice. This means that universities must acquire the best students with the highest potential, and to this end they actively market their educational offerings. Student admission is one of the key mechanisms through which the 'market value' of universities and other HE institutions is produced. Within the market, students are expected to choose the 'best' institution for them, and institutions are supposed to choose the 'best' students. Under these conditions, students are expected to be individually responsible for their educational choices. Marketization, in that sense, is embedded in competition for status and prestige in the rank hierarchies of HE.

Finland, the Nordic Countries—And Beyond: Conclusions

The strategy of the Nordic-Keynesian welfare state regime emphasized major public investment in the development of infrastructure and equal opportunities across the state territory. This interpretation of responsible action lasted from the late 1950s to the late 1980s. From the 1990s onwards, the emerging Schumpeterian competition state strategy put less stress on territorial and social equalization processes in HE and focused, instead, on growth and success through privatization, specialization and international competitiveness. However, the change in the definition of what a 'responsible university' means was gradual. It could be argued that the narrative of socio-spatial responsibility in HE, which was quite diverse in the 1990s and the early 2000s, became rather uniform in the 2010s.

The period from the 1990s to the beginning of the 2010s was a critical turning point. It triggered pressure for far-reaching changes throughout society. During this critical period many issues, such as the definition of socio-spatial responsibility, became fluid and open to debate. Ultimately, the Schumpeterian logic pushing for more selective and exclusive socio-spatial and socio-economical arrangements prevailed over the Keynesian practices of governing and managing development regionally and across different social groups. The reason why the struggle between the Keynesian and Schumpeterian logics continued for nearly two decades can be found in the historically constructed socio-spatial structures which generated friction, causing Schumpeterian practices to lose energy.

The Nordic-Keynesian welfare state period was also a period of advancing educational equality in Finland. Reform of the basic education system and expansion of secondary education, together with the expansion of the university institution, significantly increased the participation of children of previously marginalized socio-economic groups in university education. Thus, in the 1980s, university students in Finland were more selectively drawn from different socio-economic groups compared to most other countries. At that time, educational equality in HE in Finland was on a par with Sweden (Nevala 1999).

Sweden was, at the time, one of the world's most equal countries in terms of the socio-economic background of university students, based on a broad international comparison. For example, in the UK, France and Germany, over-representation of the highest socio-economic groups among university students was clearly greater than in Finland, Sweden or the other Nordic countries. On the other hand, differences between disciplines regarding the socio-economic background of students were clearly visible in the 1980s both in the Nordic countries and elsewhere. However, the differences were not as big as they were to become in later decades (Erikson and Jonsson 1996; Nevala 1999).

Despite similar trends in HE in the Nordic region, differences can be found between the four major Nordic countries—Finland, Sweden, Norway and Denmark. Expansion does not seem to be a universal remedy for narrowing the participation gap between different social groups.

From 1985 to 2010, Finland and Norway achieved the most substantial reductions in overall HE inequality, the decrease in Denmark was more modest, while Sweden showed no signs of decreasing inequality. There were also large disparities in selectivity between different fields of study during this period, although the majority of fields had moved towards greater equality. The 'elite' fields, such as law and medicine, still favoured socially privileged students, although the social gap has narrowed in Finland and Norway. Socio-economic inequality is thus most visible between fields of study than between universities, although there are also notable differences between universities regarding student background (Thomsen et al. 2017). Comparing the Nordic countries internationally, two essential issues arise. The Nordic HE systems are quite unified in history, structure and function, and stand out in this respect from other countries (Willems and de Beer 2012; Rinne 2012). Another essential feature is that, despite the above considerations, the impact of home background on access to HE is lowest in the Nordic countries. For example, the impact of parental educational background on access to HE is lower in the Nordic countries than anywhere in the world (Marginson 2015).

Since the 'great university reform' in 2010, universities have been made more responsible for competitiveness, efficiency and internationalization and less responsible for socio-spatially equal educational opportunities. In addition, state control over universities is stronger now than it has been for decades. This time, however, state control is not only normative, but also financial, for example, through the employment of cash distribution models. At the same time, the impact of increasing alliance with industry on HE policy has intensified, especially in the 2000s. All of these changes have created a new interpretive framework for Finnish HE policy for perceiving the central aspects of responsible behaviour, which, currently, are closely associated with targeting and exclusion. For example, universities aspiring to academic excellence on the international stage have partly outsourced their regional tasks to nearby polytechnics, while municipalities and regional councils have a say in university affairs only if their expectations, discourses and activities are in line with their respective universities (Moisio et al. 2018).

From the points of view of educational equality, exclusion of people groups, and the concept of responsibility, the ongoing reform of the student admission system is crucial (Ministry of Education and Culture 2016). The reform will increase the significance of general upper secondary school achievement (i.e. matriculation examination), and a quota for students applying for their first study place in HE has been established. The ministry has stated that more than 50% of applicants must be selected on the basis of the matriculation examination, although it is the responsibility of universities to decide on this exact percentage. We expect that the stratification that has subsequently emerged within HE systems will also lead to equivalent changes in student admission patterns. One critical consideration is the impact on 'second chance' applicants, that is, those who have not completed the matriculation examination and whose motivation and desire to continue their studies is born later in life, for example, after vocational studies or working years. It is also likely that low-educated families in rural and semi-urban areas located far from large urban settlements will be among those most affected by the reform. In short, the former interpretation of responsible behaviour in HE policy that emphasized socio-spatial equality will give way increasingly to a new interpretation of responsible university highlighting individualism and competition.

However, as the ongoing reform of student admissions in Finland has not yet fully materialized, the long-term effects on recruitment patterns are yet to be seen. Likewise, it remains to be seen how the elitist Schumpeterian logic will endure in the future as socio-spatial unevenness—or injustice, as the critics put it—rapidly grows between and within regions (Saari et al. 2016). Critical voices and active political resistance against this logic is currently thin on the ground.

Finally, regarding the concept of responsible university, we have used the concept in a way that reveals its flexible, time-dependent and place-dependent nature. We should not think of responsible universities as pre-assigned, static arenas of universalistic, coextensive activity. On the contrary, responsible universities are relational and political constructs. As this chapter has tried to illustrate, politics and policies always tend to favour certain people or social groups, disciplines, places and geographical scales of social action over others, and to reshape the concept of responsible university in line with certain ideological, socio-political and politico-economic values and attitudes. In a truly responsible university, therefore, political struggle and friction must be ever present.

Acknowledgements We would like to thank the editors and other writers of this book, as well as Professor Jussi Välimaa for their instructive comments.

References

Aarrevaara, T., Dobson, I. R., & Elander, C. (2009). Brave New World: Higher Education Reform in Finland. *Higher Education Management and Policy, 21*(2), 2–18.

Ahola, S. (1995). *Eliitin yliopistosta massojen korkeakoulutukseen. Korkeakoulutuksen muuttuva asema yhteiskunnallisen valikoinnin järjestelmänä [From Elite to Mass Higher Education. Changing Structures of Selection in Finnish Higher Education].* Turku: Turun yliopiston koulutussosiologian tutkimuskeskuksen raportti n:o 30.

Alestalo, M., Hort, S. E. O., & Kuhnle, S. (2009). *The Nordic Model: Conditions, Origins, Outcomes, Lessons.* Berlin: Hertie School of Governance.

Allardt, E. (2000). Yhteiskuntatieteet [Social Sciences]. In P. Tommila & A. Tiitta (Eds.), *Suomen tieteen historia 2: Humanistiset ja yhteiskuntatieteet [History of Finnish Science, Part 2: Humanities and Social Sciences]* (pp. 477–535). Porvoo: WSOY.

Brenner, N. (2004). Urban Governance and the Production of New State Spaces in Western Europe, 1960–2000. *Review of International Political Economy, 11*(3), 447–488.

Brubaker, R., & Cooper, F. (2000). Beyond Identity. *Theory and Society, 29*(1), 1–47.

Dahllöf, U. (1994). A Short Introduction to the Nordic Scene. In U. Dahllöf & S. Selander (Eds.), *New Universities and Regional Context* (pp. 207–211). Uppsala: Uppsala University.

Degn, L., & Sørensen, M. P. (2015). From Collegial Governance to Conduct of Conduct: Danish Universities Set Free in the Service of the State. *Higher Education, 69*(6), 931–946.

Demographic Statistics of Finland, years 1960–2010.

Dhondt, P., & Nevala, A. (2015). The Typical Dilemma Between University Expansion and Rationalization: Belgium (and Finland) Since the 1960s. *Kasvatus & Aika, 9*(3), 21–36.

Erikson, R., & Jonsson, J. O. (1996). *Can Education Be Equalized? The Swedish Case in Comparative Perspective.* Boulder, CO: Westview Press.

Giddens, A. (1985). *The Nation State and Violence.* Cambridge: Polity Press.

Giulianotti, R., Itkonen, H., Nevala, A., & Salmikangas, A.-K. (2017). Sport and Civil Society in the Nordic Region. *Sport in Society.* https://doi.org/10.1080/17430437.2017.1390906.

Haltia, N., Jauhiainen, A., & Isopahkala-Bouret, U. (2017). *Ei-ylioppilastaustaiset korkeakouluopiskelijat [Non-upper Secondary School Graduates in Higher Education].* Helsinki: Opetus- ja kulttuuriministeriö.

Hansen, H. (1990). Implementation of Modernization: Paradoxes in the Public Control of Higher Educational Institutions—The Case of Denmark. *Scandinavian Political Studies, 13*(1), 37–56.

Harrison, J., Smith, D. P., & Kinton, C. (2017). Relational Regions in 'in the Making': Institutionalizing New Regional Geographies of Higher Education. *Regional Studies, 51*(7), 1020–1034.

Harvey, D. A. (2005). *Brief History of Neo-Liberalism.* Oxford: Oxford University Press.

Heiskala, R., & Hämäläinen, T. J. (2007). Social Innovation or Hegemonic Change? Rapid Paradigm Change in Finland in the 1980s and 1990s. In T. J. Hämäläinen & R. Heiskala (Eds.), *Social Innovations, Institutional Change and Economic Performance. Making Sense of Structural Adjustment Processes in Industrial Sectors, Regions and Societies* (pp. 80–94). Cheltenham: Edward Elgar.

Hölttä, S. (1999). Regional Cooperation in Postsecondary Education in Europe—The Case of Nordic Countries. *Journal of Institutional Research in Australasia, 8*(2), 31–46.

Husso, K., & Raento, P. (2002). Science Policy and Research in Finland. *Fennia—International Journal of Geography, 180*(1–2), 261–274.

Jalava, M. (2012). *The University in the Making of the Welfare State. The 1970s Degree Reform in Finland.* Frankfurt am Main: Peter Lang.

Kettunen, P. (2012, November 1–4). The Conceptualization of the Social in the Making of a Welfare State—Finland as a Nordic Case. *Science History Association Conference*, Vancouver.

Kivinen, O., & Rinne, R. (1995). *The Social Inheritance of Education. Equality of Educational Opportunity Among Young People in Finland.* Helsinki: Statistics Finland.

Kivinen, O., Hedman, J., & Kaipainen, P. (2012). Koulutusmahdollisuuksien yhdenvertaisuus Suomessa. Eriarvoisuuden uudet ja vanhat muodot [Equality of Schooling Possibilities in Finland. New and Old Modes of Inequality]. *Yhteiskuntapolitiikka, 77*(5), 579–586.

Kogan, M., & Bauer, M. (2000). Higher Education Policies. Historical Overview. In M. Kogan, M. Bauer, I. Bleiklie, & M. Henkel (Eds.), *Transforming Higher Education. A Comparative Study* (pp. 37–54). London: Jessica Kingsley.

Kohvakka, M. (2015). The Scalar Logics of Universities as Part of Statehood Transformation in Finland, 1970–1990. *Fennia—International Journal of Geography, 193*(1), 117–133.

Kohvakka, M. (2016). *Proaktiivisuutta, sopeutumista vai vastarintaa? Lappeenrannan teknillinen korkeakoulu ja Joensuun yliopisto osana valtion ja korkeakoulujärjestelmän tilallista muutosta Suomessa 1960-luvulta 1990-luvun alkuun* [Proactivity, Adaptation or Resistance? The Lappeenranta University of Technology and the University of Joensuu as Part of the Spatial Change of the State and the Higher Education System in Finland from the 1960s to the Early 1990s]. Joensuu: Itä-Suomen yliopisto.

Koselleck, R. (2002). *The Practice of Conceptual History: Timing History, Spacing Concepts*. Stanford: Stanford University Press.

Kyvik, S. (2004). Structural Changes in Higher Education Systems in Western Europe. *Higher Education in Europe, 29*(3), 393–409.

Marginson, S. (2015, June 26). *The Landscape of Higher Education Research 1965–2015 Equality of Opportunity: The First Fifty Years*. SRHE 50'th Anniversary Colloquium. Retrieved February 15, 2019, from https://www.srhe.ac.uk/downloads/SimonMarginsonKeynote.pdf.

Michelsen, K.-E. (1994). *Lappeenrannan teknillinen korkeakoulu 1969–1994 [Lappeenranta University of Technology 1969–1994]*. Lappeenranta: Lappeenrannan teknillinen korkeakoulu.

Ministry of Education. (1991). *Koulutuksen ja korkeakouluissa harjoitettavan tutkimuksen kehittämissuunnitelma vuosille 1991–1996 [Development Plan for Education and Research Conducted in Universities 1991–1996]*. Helsinki: Ministry of Education.

Ministry of Education. (1996). *Koulutus ja tutkimus 2000. Koulutuksen ja korkeakouluissa harjoitettavan tutkimuksen kehittämissuunnitelma vuosille 1995–2000 [Education and Research 2000. Development Plan for Education and Research Conducted in Universities 1991–1996]*. Helsinki: Ministry of Education.

Ministry of Education and Culture. (2016). *Valmiina valintoihin. Ylioppilastutkinnon parempi hyödyntäminen korkeakoulujen opiskelijavalin-noissa [Ready for Admissions. Making Better Use of the Matriculation Examination in Student Admissions]*. Helsinki: Publications of the Ministry of Education and Culture.

Moisio, S. (2012). *Valtio, alue, politiikka. Suomen tilasuhteiden sääntely toisesta maailmansodasta nykypäivään [State, Region, Politics. The Regulation of Spatial Relations in Finland from the Second World War to the Present]*. Tampere: Vastapaino.

Moisio, S., & Leppänen, L. (2007). Towards a Nordic Competition State? Politico-Economic Transformation of Statehood in Finland, 1965–2005. *Fennia—International Journal of Geography, 185*(2), 63–87.

Moisio, S., Kohvakka, M., & Norola, M. (2018) Kaupungin ja yliopiston vuo-rovaikutus Suomessa [City-University Interaction in Finland]. *Hallinnon tutkimus, 37*(1), 22–36.

Nevala, A. (1999). *Korkeakouluksen kasvu, lohkoutuminen ja eriarvoisuus Suomessa [Growth, Fragmentation and Inequality in Higher Education in Finland]*. Helsinki: SKS.

Nevala, A., & Nori, H. (2017). Osallisuuden vanhat ja uudet jakolinjat. Yliopisto-opiskelijoiden sosioekonomisen taustan muutokset ja koulutuksell-inen tasa-arvo [Old and New Dividing Lines of Involvement. Changes in the Socio-economic Background of University Students and Educational Equality]. In A. Toom, M. Rautiainen, & J. Tähtinen (Eds.), *Toiveet ja todel-lisuus—kasvatus osallisuutta ja oppimista rakentamassa [Hopes and Reality—Growth in Building Involvement and Learning]*. Jyväskylä: Suomen kasvatustieteellinen seura.

Nevala, A., & Rinne, R. (2012). Korkeakoulutuksen muodonmuutos [Changing Higher Education]. In P. Kettunen & H. Simola (Eds.), *Tiedon ja osaamisen Suomi. Kasvatus ja koulutus Suomessa 1960-luvulta 2010-luvulle [Knowledge and Expertise in Finland. Education and Training in Finland from the 1960s to 2000s]* (pp. 203–228). Helsinki: SKS.

Nokkala, T., & Välimaa, J. (2017). Finnish Mergers: Change in the Context of Continuity. In H. de Boer, J. File, J. Huisman, M. Seeber, M. Vukasovic, & D. F. Westerheijden (Eds.), *Policy Analysis of Structural Reforms in Higher Education: Processes and Outcomes* (pp. 225–244). Cham: Palgrave Macmillan.

Nori, H. (2011). *Keille yliopiston portit avautuvat—tutkimus suomalaisiin yliopis-toihin ja eri tieteenaloille valikoitumisesta 2000-luvun alussa [For Whom Will the University Gates Open? A Study of the Selection for Admission to Finnish*

Universities and Fields of Study in the Beginning of the 21st Century]. Turku: University of Turku.

Nori, H. (2018). Kiipijöitä ja Uusintajia—Keitä ovat 2010-luvun yliopisto-opiskelijat? [Who are the university students of the 2010s?]. In R. Rinne, N. Haltia, S. Lempinen, & T. Kaunisto (Eds.), *Eriarvoistuva maailma—tasa-arvoistava koulu? [Unequalising World—Equalising School?]* (pp. 205–222). Jyväskylä: Kasvatusalan tutkimuksia.

Pihkala, E. (2000). Taloustieteet [Economics]. In P. Tommila & A. Tiitta (Eds.), *Suomen tieteen historia 2: Humanistiset ja yhteiskuntatieteet [History of Finnish Science, Part 2: Humanities and Social Sciences]* (pp. 536–611). Porvoo: WSOY.

Potila, A.-K., Moisio, J., Ahti-Miettinen, O., Pyy-Martikanen, M., & Virtanen, V. (2017). *Opiskelijatutkimus 2017.* EUROSTUDENT VI -tutkimuksen keskeiset tulokset. Opetus- ja kulttuuriministeriön julkaisuja 2017:37 [Student Survey 2017. Key Results of Finnish Eurostudent VI Survey. Publications of the Ministry of Education and Culture, Finland 2017:37].

Rinne, R. (2012). The Nordic University Model from a Comparative and Historical Perspective. In J. Kauko, R. Rinne, & H. Kynkäänniemi (Eds.), *Restructuring the Truth of Schooling—Essays on Discursive Practices in the Sociology and Politics of Education* (pp. 85–112). Jyväskylä: Finnish Education Research Association.

Rose, N. (1999). *Powers of Freedom. Reframing Political Thought.* Cambridge: Cambridge University Press.

Saari, J., Aarnio, L., & Rytkönen, M. (2015). *Kolme näkökulmaa koulutuksen valikoivuuteen: Nuorten koulutusvalinnat tilastojen ja kertomusten valossa [Three Perspectives on the Selectivity of Schooling: Young People's Study Choices in the Light of Statistics and Narratives].* Helsinki: Opiskelun ja koulutuksen tutkimussäätiö.

Saari, J., Inkinen, A., & Mikkonen, J. (2016). *Korkeakoulutuksen alueellinen tasa-arvo ja segregaatio [Regional Equality and Segregation of Higher Education].* Helsinki: Opiskelun ja koulutuksen tutkimussäätiö.

Salminen, H., & Ylä-Anttila, P. (2010). *Ammattikorkeakoulujen taloudellisen ja hallinnollisen aseman uudistaminen [Renewal of the Economic and Administrative Status of Polytechnics].* Helsinki: Opetus- ja kulttuuriministeriö.

Science Policy Council of Finland. (1973). *Suomen tiedepolitiikan suuntaviivat 1970-luvulla [Guidelines for Finnish Science Policy in the 1970s].* Helsinki: Valtion tiedeneuvosto.

Socio-economic Background of New University Students from 1925–2010. University of Eastern Finland, Department of Geographical and Historical Studies.

Taylor, P. J. (1996). Embedded Statism and the Social Sciences: Opening up to New Spaces. *Environment and Planning A, 28*(11), 1917–1932.

Thomsen, J.-P., Bertilsson, E., Dalberg, T., Hedman, J., & Helland, H. (2017). Higher Education Participation in the Nordic Countries 1985–2010—A Comparative Perspective. *European Sociological Review, 33*(1), 98–111.

Trow, M. (1974). Problems in the Transition from Elite to Mass Higher Education. In *Policies for Higher Education* (pp. 51–104). Paris: OECD.

Välimaa, J. (2005). Social Dynamics of Higher Education Reforms: The Case Finland. In Å. Gornitzka, M. Kogan, & A. Amaral (Eds.), *Reform and Change in Higher Education* (pp. 245–268). Dordrecht: Springer.

Välimaa, J. (2018). *Opinteillä oppineita. Suomalainen korkeakoulutus keskiajalta 2000-luvulle [Finnish Higher Education from the Middle Ages to the 2000s]*. Jyväskylä: University Press of Eastern Finland.

Välimaa, J., & Neuvonen-Rauhala, M.-L. (2008). Polytechnics in Finnish Higher Education. In J. S. Taylor, J. Brites-Ferreira, M. de Lourdes Machado, & R. Santiago (Eds.), *Non-university Higher Education in Europe* (pp. 77–98). Dordrecht: Springer.

Vartiainen, P. (2017). Campus-Based Tensions in the Structural Development of a Newly Merged University: The Case of the University of Eastern Finland. *Tertiary Education and Management, 23*(1), 53–68.

Willems, N., & de Beer, P. (2012). Three Worlds of Educational States? *Journal of European Social Policy, 22*(2), 105–117.

3

Universities, Public Value and Irresponsibility

Paul Benneworth

Introduction

Why do we currently feel the overwhelming need to talk about the responsible university? It is not as if the 'irresponsible University' is a category to which any self-respecting Higher Education Institution (hereafter HEI) could reasonably aspire. The discourse of responsibility has emerged at the European policy level around concerns with the domination of science and technology over society. In the context of the knowledge economy, society is hugely dependent on implementing new technologies, placing substantial power in scientists and engineers' hands to create knowledge that may benefit or penalise society (Owen et al. 2012; De Saille 2015). The responsibility agenda for universities therefore relates to ensuring that universities do not succumb to the temptation to abuse this power, to leverage their privileged position for private institutional benefit (Bozeman 2002).

P. Benneworth (✉)
Western Norway University of Applied Sciences, Bergen, Norway
e-mail: paul.benneworth@hvl.no

This has been driven by a recent transformation in higher education: rising costs in the 1980s led to the introduction of new management techniques within the higher education sector, shifting funding more directly towards the production of (societally valuable) outputs, such as graduate numbers or Ph.D. (Middleton 2000). In parallel with this, university managers were granted substantive autonomy to govern their institutions to better deliver these outputs (Kickert et al. 1997; De Boer et al. 2007). Regulators were created and ministries developed funding formulae to sharpen university responsiveness: performing well within these systems and securing the resources for their survival became an existential question for universities.

And herein lies the challenge: managers facing these existential funding challenges have become increasingly focused upon ensuring their institutional private survival by delivering outputs *regardless* of the effects this has on society (Watermeyer 2019). This intense private self-interest may induce behaviour which—whilst technically legal—breaches societal norms. When businesses breach public values, this may result in consumer boycotts or scandals; for universities, the risk is even higher, of undermining public trust in universities as institutions and their unique societal privileges. The recent emergence of the 'responsible university' discussion may therefore reflect a wider societal reaction to a fear, a fear that universities' irresponsible behaviour may be undermining public trust.

This chapter poses the research question of 'under what conditions might university management find themselves breaching public value', to understand what are the conditions under which the modern university might behave irresponsibly when facing these existential dilemmas. It firstly develops a literature framework to understand why universities are perceived to need to behave responsibly, and proposes a set of 'repertoires of irresponsibility' in which universities' managements may find themselves placed in responsibility dilemmas. It then draws on three empirical vignettes (small stylised case studies developed from secondary material) to explore the dynamics by which universities find themselves enacting these 'repertoires of irresponsibility'. These three vignettes are then analysed to identify processes enabling irresponsibility within contemporary higher education. Four factors are identified driving institutional irresponsibility, and conceptual and administrative improvements to address these drivers are proposed. The chapter concludes that any university wishing to claim it behaves responsibly must as a minimum demonstrate how they have developed suitable institutional frameworks addressing these four factors to ensure that institutional behaviour whilst dealing with existential irresponsibility dilemmas remains socially acceptable.

Towards a Conceptual Framework for the Responsible University

Higher education literature has indicated that the totality of universities' responsibilities to societies constitutes a 'compact' between universities and society (Barnett 2000). Society expects individual researchers to prospectively anticipate society's wishes and interests, and that higher education institutions will behave in the 'public interest' (however defined). Living up to these expectations is necessary for society to grant universities the privilege and freedom to effectively create knowledge (Jackson et al. 2005). This section develops a framework for understanding how societal interests become projected onto universities, proposing that irresponsibility is the result of universities finding themselves in dilemmas where institutional survival seems dependent upon unfairly exploiting their privilege and power.

The University as a Societally Engaged Institution

Universities as institutions have always required social support to justify the resources they require to thrive, and their institutional longevity was based on their capacity to deliver immediate sponsor benefits whilst resisting pressures for immediate usefulness (Benneworth 2014). Universities are as a kind of 'Goldilocks' institution and their coupling to societal interests must be 'just right'. They must not be too oriented towards immediate practical application, but resist at the same time the temptation to be obscure and abstract. A certain degree of remoteness from society allows them to preserve and create abstract knowledge and understanding applicable in many contexts (the universality characteristic of science). But they receive sponsor resources precisely because that knowledge and understanding is relevant and valuable. When universities drift too far from creating useful knowledge, then societal partners complain: when Scottish universities became introspective and separated from technology development in support of industrialisation in the late eighteenth century, their privileges were threatened by (newly created) learned societies (Phillipson 1988). Likewise, when universities became too instrumental and concerned with providing a conveyor belt of trained workers, then society revolted to restore space to ensure that higher education equipped them for society rather than simply creating a pliant workforce (Daalder and Shils 1982).

The reason for the university's institutional longevity is precisely because of their extreme adaptability to changing sponsor needs (Benneworth 2014). As Bender (1988) demonstrates, every societal upheaval in Europe (and latterly North America) led to changes in the nature of universities and indeed the formation of new universities to respond to these needs. Initially, these changes related to the nature of absolute power, the shift from spiritual to temporal, the rise of cities, from empire to the nation-state, with new centres of power requiring highly skilled priests, administrators and rulers to support central powers. From the nineteenth century onwards, the emphasis shifted from administrative-political to economic power, with Germany's Humboldtian and the USA's Land Grant universities creating research and extension missions. Emancipation became an important role in the late nineteenth and twentieth centuries, creating leaders for neglected communities, whether Canada's Nova Scotian Antigonish communities, or Calvinists and Catholics in the Netherlands. More recently, what Delanty (2002) called the 'democratic mass university' expanded university education to create engaged citizens equipped for deliberative processes in increasingly technological societies.

There is a raging contemporary academic debate regarding the consequences of these contemporary changes for universities (Clark 1998; Pinheiro and Stensaker 2013; Barnett 2011). In the context of new public management (hereafter NPM), there has been an attempt to articulate societal benefits in terms of things that can be measured and managed, with the emergence of what Laredo (2007) called a 'third mission' for universities.

This includes specific services for businesses, community and government that exploit university knowledge resources for societal gain, and is addressed in more detail in section "NPM, the Third Mission and the University in the Knowledge Society".

NPM, the Third Mission and the University in the Knowledge Society

A crisis of government legitimacy in the 1970s drove a diagnosis that state institutions had become captured by 'producer interests' where bureaucratic legitimacy was more important than serving citizens. Reform was necessary to ensure that public services served citizens and the so-called new public management sought to place the citizen-user interests at the heart of policy development and implementation by sensitising providers in various ways to citizens' interests (Kickert 1995; Kickert et al. 1997). These approaches operated by aggregating user interests, often through market mechanisms, leading some to term it 'neo-corporatism' (cf Rhodes 2003), seeing governments set targets for universities and funding universities against their performance to those targets.

Ensuring that these market mechanisms would aggregate public interest necessitated widespread reforms to regulatory mechanisms. Market signals are incredibly precise, with customer choices and purchasing behaviours signalling what is and is not valued; creating markets in public services therefore allows very fine-grained signals to be regarding which providers are better or worse. But making public service providers capable of responding to these signals required changing institutions' internal governance, to allow dynamic rather than bureaucratic responses to dynamic conditions and market signals. In what is now sometimes referred to as the 'modernisation' of universities (cf. Commission of the European Communities 2006), universities were reformed to give management more direct power to force their institutions to respond to these signals. Management power was increased, professional decision-making weakened, and legal frameworks were changed to allow university to behave 'strategically' to best meet the demands of their target markets, and making them responsive to these market mechanisms (De Boer et al. 2007; Jongbloed et al. 2007).

HEIs are now expected to pursue a limited number of strategic missions identified by institutional management; a limited number of missions have become popular, such as pursuing internationalisation, places in the rankings, teaching quality or research excellence. A key issue for this modernisation is that it reduced universities' capacities to pay attention to other areas. A problem of 'mission stretch' or 'mission overload' has been identified for universities: they are expected to respond to a range of different external agendas which are not easily reconciled in a single coherent strategy (Enders and De Boer 2009). Under conditions of resource scarcity, universities acting rationally prioritise their spending on those missions and activities which produce the greatest institutional return.

The Urgency of Articulating a New Responsible University Model

New public management has become so widely normalised within higher education that there has been a qualitative shift towards what some have called the 'marketisation' of higher education (Brown and Carasso 2013). Indeed, some have gone so far to contend that the university has become 'toxic', dominated by zombie leadership, chasing academic 'rock stars' and unchallenging of neoliberal ideology (Smyth 2017). Even if one does agree with Smyth's critique of the consequences of the university 'modernisation' project, it is clear that marketisation reduced the attention that universities pay to upholding public service ideals. Although the public's representatives (governments) pushed higher education marketisation, ironically enough, the resultant situation encourages university behaviours with which publics may feel uncomfortable.

Even the most fierce advocates of market-based systems concede that markets can produce economically suboptimal situations, such as monopolies, where a single supplier can set prices artificially high. However, such market failures are easily identifiable because their negative economic consequences represent a failure in terms of the underlying (economic) system logic. More complex to deal with are situations where ostensibly well-functioning markets produce *economically justifiable* outcomes that are at odds with public values. These are much harder to address precisely because the failures are obvious in terms of the underlying system logic. The correct functioning of patent law allowed retroviral HIV drugs manufacturers to block African countries facing AIDS epidemics from importing cheap generic versions to prevent mass fatalities (Bozeman 2002; Bozeman and Sarewitz 2005). It was only the resultant public outcry, particularly from shareholder activists in the global north, that saw this situation overturned when South Africa went unpunished in importing drugs from Thailand.

Our contention here is that irresponsible universities behave in ways that are not market failures but rather represent *public value failures*: in pursing goals of survival in the market they take choices that give outcomes at odds with prevailing public values. Bozeman's diagnosis is that public value failures occur when there are no mechanisms to effectively articulate public value, there is benefit hoarding, short-termism and a domination of competition over public service provision. Table 3.1 transposes Bozeman's (2002) public value failures across to the higher education sector, and highlights university behaviours *potentially* corresponding to such public value failures.

Of course, other more traditional failures may lead to universities behaving irresponsibly, from simple management errors, to political interference, scientific malpractice or corruption. Although this behaviour is irresponsible, it does not represent a public value failure that is a consequence of well-functioning governance—a university where cheating or corruption was discovered represents a governance failure as well as public value failure, and a public outcry is not necessarily necessary to address the issue.

Table 3.1 presents an authorial proposition that these cases genuinely represent public value failures, rather than an empirical establishment of those value failures. In the case of the Dutch performance agreements, for example, universities agreed performance targets with an Independent Commission, and 'creating public value' did not feature in any of the targets. There were no mechanisms to agree and aggregate public interests in these agreements beyond a few politically motivated demands such as reducing administrative employee numbers and increasing student completion rates. But that does not demonstrate that this is a public value

Table 3.1 University irresponsibility repertoires as manifestations of public value failure

Public value failures	Repertoires of university irresponsibility	Concrete examples
No mechanisms to articulate public value	Absence of accountability mechanisms that allow publics to comment on and shape university engagement activities	The Performance Agreements in the Netherlands agreed between Government, a Commission and HEIs (Jongbloed et al. 2018).
'Imperfect monopolies' occur	Emergence of private providers with access to same titles and accreditation despite inferior product/higher profitability	University of Phoenix selling low-value courses to unsuitable students to harvest federal student support loans (Universities and Colleges Union 2011)
Benefit hoarding occurs	Setting of high levels of fees to restrict access to teaching and research already in receipt of substantive public subsidy	Almost all UK universities set £9000 fee justified in terms of 'prestige pricing' to benefit students paying higher fee
Scarcity of providers of public value	A failure to spend resources received from government and fees into teaching activities, to shore up organisational activities	University of Bangor investing in new campus whilst cutting staff numbers
Short-termism and avoidance of long-term investment	De-risking balance sheet (pensions, permanent contracts), downgrading longer term commitments to key stakeholders	The UK Universities Superannuation Scheme Pension strike to defend direct benefit pensions which harm institutional borrowing
Competition prioritised over delivering public services	Excessive emphasis on spending on branding and marketing, shifting resources away from services to selling.	The rise and fall of UK far eastern and Gulf state campuses seeking to build new markets despite dubious human rights records

Source: author's own design following Bozeman's (2002) classification

failure, that something scandalous has happened, comparable with the public outcries surrounding HIV retrovirals. To address this research question, and in line with Watermeyer (2019) this chapter therefore explores three more detailed cases on the basis of the public record. These cases are termed 'vignettes' to be explicit that these are not three worked-through detailed case studies. They nevertheless provide the basis for a reflection in the discussion and conclusions section of the conditions under which universities may find themselves drawn towards enacting repertoires of 'irresponsible behaviour'.

Methodology: Three Stylised 'Vignettes'

This chapter asks the research question 'under what conditions might university management find themselves breaching public value?' To address that question, evidence is sought regarding managerial decision-making in examples of universities and public value failure. Table 3.1 suggests that public value failures may emerge through six behavioural repertoires that emerge in contemporary higher education. Three vignettes are used to structure material to reflect on whether Bozeman's framework may be applicable to higher education in terms of understanding university irresponsibility as a public value failure or whether an alternative framework is necessary. Three cases are analysed where universities have faced a dilemma of maximising private benefits, and in so doing chose a course of action that generated a public outcry indicative of sufficient magnitude to indicate a public value failure (Bozeman's criteria).

The criterion to define 'university public value failure' is that there is in the case a chain of events from university action through public outcry leading to a university leader resigning. As this chapter primarily deals with structural failures rather than actions resulting from rogue leaders, the cases seek to clarify how university governance structures collectively imbue initial action with institutional legitimacy resulting in a situation at odds with public values; there are no examples of the more traditional governance failures referred to above. This approach is clearly exploratory and intensive, there is no representativity and therefore care must be taken in seeking to extrapolate the results more widely.

Each case provides a short and simplified narrative of the key elements of the controversies, the background, the issue, and why the university actors felt justified in taking action that later ended up becoming framed in different ways as a public value failure. The empirical material was gathered in a number of antecedent research projects, and written about in a number of cases elsewhere for a variety of purposes. These stylisations cannot claim to be *comprehensive* or complete but rather *sufficient* to observe the tensions and lines of force driving university behaviours around these dilemmas. These three examples (the universities of Amsterdam, Bath and the London School of Economics) are universities that have elsewhere invested in delivering responsible activities and producing substantive public benefit. This material is not a criticism of individual institutions but attempting to understand the dynamics of dilemmas that may undermine university responsibility. And although they are not drawn from Nordic countries, they are taken from HE systems (the UK and the Netherlands) facing the same increasingly strong financial and research excellence performance pressures which are now starting to spread through the Nordic countries (such as through publication points systems in various Nordic countries that attach funding to publishing in particular outlets).

The Vignettes of Responsibility Dilemmas

This chapter presents three vignettes of irresponsible behaviour, relating to 'urban speculation', 'executive pay' and 'unacceptable research donations'. Each vignette was sufficient to breach public values in terms of an executive resignation, and represent valid examples of this irresponsible behaviour. Universities have long engaged in urban speculation: in the 1960s Chicago where the (private) University of Chicago, created with a strong public mission in the nineteenth century, sought to increase its campus attractiveness by displacing local residents in Woodlawn to allow gentrification (Shils 1988; Webber 2005; Benneworth et al. 2013). In the Netherlands, steadily growing university executive pay was one of the reasons for the Dutch government to introduce the *Wet Normering Topinkomens* ('Law on standardising top salaries') in November 2012 which capped maximum permissible public sector pay to the Prime Minister's salary. In terms of unacceptable research donations, the choice in 2000 of the University of Nottingham to accept £3.4 million funding from a tobacco company to fund a 'centre of business ethics' (Elliot Major 2002) led to a mass departure of a 20-strong cancer research group to Imperial College London (MacLeod 2001). Each example provides a means to understand the pressures that the contemporary university faces to behave irresponsibly: these vignettes therefore offer a view into the future of the pressures under which Nordic universities may find themselves if there are increased pressures towards accountability, competitiveness and market-steering in Nordic higher education systems.

Universities as Urban Speculators

The first vignette explores how one university became enrolled in speculative urban development that breached public values (Benneworth 2016). There has been a recent change in the nature of university urban activities as universities have become increasingly financialised as organisations, needing secure income flows to guarantee loans necessary for investing in improved campuses (Engelen et al. 2014). The case study concerns the University of Amsterdam (referred to here as UvA after its Dutch abbreviation), which in 2014 announced a restructuring of its humanities faculty as a consequence of the lack of profitability of its students (see Benneworth 2015, for more detail). The university had embarked on a campus redevelopment to rationalise its use of space: in the course of that redevelopment process UvA incurred debts which imposed a harsh financial discipline on the university. That discipline began to have consequences for both staff (in terms of rising workloads and temporary contracts) and students. Students felt increasingly that they were treated as a commodity to be 'educated' as quickly and cheaply as possible, rather than as citizens undertaking a learning journey with the right to influence their own education.

A growing negative feeling amongst humanities students led to a group of students occupying a humanities faculty building earmarked for sale to real estate developers in central Amsterdam (the *Bungehuis*). The occupiers demanded more democratic dialogue between management and students and an end to the university's financialisation. That occupation was ended by riot police after ten days, after dialogue between occupying students and university senior management broke down. Two weeks later, a longer occupation began of the *Maagdenhuis*, the university's central administration building, triggered by both a general widespread dissatisfaction with UvA's democratic deficit alongside the specific negative consequences this had had for staff and students across the university. Staff and students symbolically declared the creation of a new university, arranging teach-ins and guest lectures. This occupation attracted a great deal of sympathy and support from external academic communities, and when this second occupation was also ended with a show of force from local police, there was a general wave of public revulsion and political pressure. UvA's president resigned within one week following the forced, brutal ending of the protest, UvA terminated a partnership with the local University of Applied Sciences, and promises were made to staff and students to introduce a new more democratic governance model.

This case can be styled as a failure of universities to devote public resources to the ends for which they were intended, in particular to recruit good staff and provide students with an empowering and enriched learning environment in which they could be educated. Dutch reforms to university governance in 1992 had eliminated university democracy, replacing it with a right to be consulted ('co-determination'). Successive governments had since 1994 appointed business representatives to universities' oversight boards, who were prepared to set fiduciarily responsible budgets regardless of the negative consequences for academic activity. As Engelen et al. (2014) indicate, this had entrenched a financialisation discourse so deeply within Dutch university governance that it was invisible to those who were taking decisions. Indicators of *financial* health— solvency and liquidity—were mistaken for indicators of *institutional* health, and were not challenged when they imposed restrictions on institutional teaching and research activities. University leadership by academics had slowly been replaced by a primacy of the fiduciary responsibility to cover financial covenants to creditors for building projects, and to allow those covenants to determine what was possible within the primary business of teaching and research.

The Crisis of University Executive Pay

A second element of university marketisation came in the rhetorical construction of a 'market' for executive positions within public universities following the American or corporate model. Unlike the Netherlands, the UK has no regulations restraining university executive pay. The role of university Vice Chancellor (Chief Executive) really began transforming with the introduction of student fees and the construction of a competitive UK student market. In 1981, the then Conservative government introduced an 18% sector-wide funding cut and until 2001, UK higher education, primarily concerned with day-to-day survival, had lacked resources to invest in renewal. During that period, universities' highest paid staff were typically medical professors holding dual appointments with teaching hospitals. The 1998 introduction of student fees provided universities with a separate and capitalisable income stream, but that brought with it consumer pressure from students for a good experience and a pleasant study environment, which led to increased investments in university properties. From 2001, the UK Finance Ministry doubled public funding to the sector, trebling Ph.D. stipends and increasing funding for research in both institutional block grants and research councils funds. Universities needed to become expert in financial management and ensure they could demonstrate to their funders (students, banks and the government) that they were managing these resources in a prudent way.

It was around that point that the idea of a university 'executive' (as distinct from a *collegial* primus inter pares) emerged and executive pay started to rise. As student fees were trebled (2005) and trebled again (2010) to £9000, universities framed their management as providing business leadership, mobilising the argument (not always unreasonably) that the international nature of the labour market for such leadership necessitated appropriate remuneration. University governance arrangements saw pay typically determined by a remuneration committee which had neither instinct nor incentive to encourage pay restraint, and in some cases included the very Vice Chancellors whose pay it was setting. Pay surveys suggests that the pay growth, in general, of executives was no faster than the general wage growth for the period (BBC 2017) although there were some exceptions to this rule. The issue of public value failure emerged in 2017 when an annual pay survey of vice chancellors revealed that the highest paid university executive in that year was the long-serving Vice Chancellor of the University of Bath, who was a member of her own pay committee, and whose pay had increased that year from £406,000 to £468,000 (Adams 2017a, b), and in total by £200,000 over five years. In response to these revelations, a member of the UK Upper House began a high profile campaign to remove her from her post, receiving support in this from the then Minister for Higher Education, who announced an inquiry into pay levels in higher education more generally. The Higher Education Council for England also announced an inquiry into governance arrangements at the University of Bath, which found that the remuneration committee was at fault (HEFCE 2017), prompting the executive concerned to take an enhanced retirement package including a sabbatical period.

This case can be styled as an absence of institutional accountability mechanisms to robustly challenge dominant management interests within an institution, and that could allow the public interest to be heard sufficiently early to be meaningful in discussions. The heart of the damning Higher Education Funding Council for England (HEFCE) inquiry report was that there had been a massive failure of governance by the University's 'Court', a non-executive stakeholder body intended to raise issues of general public concern. At the Court meeting of 23 February 2017, a stakeholder had indeed criticised the lack of transparency in the remuneration committee and its decisions. A motion was proposed that the Court should make a representation to the university governance body ('Council') but that was overturned by a vote in which members of the pay body criticised voting against the motion, and in which no declarations of interest had been made. Thus, despite the presence of a stakeholder body that could have alerted the university centrally to the approaching public value failure, the capture of those bodies by university executives and a lack of rigid challenge and oversight led to a situation where public values were transgressed.

Unacceptable Research Donations

The third vignette is the case of universities accepting sponsorship from legal but controversial funding sources. The requirement for universities to cover their own costs in a market environment to sustain long-term financial viability clearly changed the calculus regarding acceptable donations sources. This chapter takes the case of the London School of Economics (hereafter LSE), a constituent college of the federal University of London, established in 1895 by a number of leading social democratic thinkers to support societal development. The public value failure in the LSE case was in accepting a number of donations from the Libyan government that subsequently came to be regarded as providing a veneer of legitimacy for a despotic regime. At its core, in 2009 the LSE accepted a donation from the Gaddafi Foundation of £1.5 m for the establishment of a North Africa programme (an extensive treatment of this case is provided in Woolf 2011).

The donation was to prove one of the last steps in a slowly developing relationship between the LSE and the Libyan regime, a relationship that began with President Gaddafi's son taking a Master's degree then a Ph.D., and in which the son's difficulties with studying had paralleled growing connections between LSE staff and Libya (Woolf 2011). Upon the completion of his Ph.D. (and before the formal conferment) the son had been approached to make a donation to LSE from the Gaddafi Foundation by the director of a research centre (within more general fundraising efforts). At its first subsequent meeting, the Governing Body ('Council') did not fully question the funding's origin, despite it being flagged up for them as questionable by the internal Development Committee. Critically, the Council failed to realise that the Foundation was funded by companies investing in Libya whose permission to invest had been determined by and therefore was dependent upon, and not independent from the regime. An initial delay in acceptance for its scrutiny led to apparent embarrassment, followed by the donation's speedy acceptance in June 2009 (Woolf 2011).

The donation was structured as a series of five donations of £300,000 to establish a North Africa research programme; its acceptance led an emeritus professor to write to the Council complaining about the ethical concerns of accepting the donation. This note highlighted the Foundation's intimate connections to Gaddafi's regime, challenging the apparent consensus that the son represented a reforming influence opening the country up to freedom and towards democracy. This note was discussed at the second Council meeting in October 2009, but the Council were to uphold the decision; in 2010 the Gaddafi father and son gave lectures at the LSE on governance and reform, which were later to be overshadowed by the regime's response to the uprising of 2011. In 2011, a series of revelations in the press revealed the relationship's controversial nature, including that elements of the doctorate were plagiarised, and that there were other commercial contracts between LSE and the Libyan regime that suggested a serious lapse of judgement. This led to the suspension of the North Africa programme, the closure of the affected research centre, the launch of the Woolf inquiry and ultimately the resignation of the Director of LSE (Vasagar and Sweney 2011; Vasagar and Syal 2011; LSE 2011).

This case can be stylised as a failure of accountability mechanisms to represent the public interest within key decision-making arenas. Woolf's inquiry report was clear that all principal actors believed they were acting in LSE's best interests, but despite that, there was a substantive failure of governance. The inquiry indeed singled out the perverse incentive for fundraising from non-traditional sponsors, and the failure to develop institutional controls to ensure that only publicly acceptable sponsorship was accepted. The internal control system had worked, flagging up the potentially problematic nature of the donation, but the Council meeting firstly failed to undertake due diligence and then failed to reflect adequately on the donation when urged to by a knowledgeable emeritus professor. Attempts to broaden the income base and expand into new markets building on emerging opportunities led to what Collini (2011) referred to as being 'willing to take risks about the legitimacy or cleanness of any source'. This willingness to take risks derived from the responsibility dilemma but also became a willingness to accept funding that was (with the benefit of hindsight) obviously intended to facilitate a normalisation of a rogue state (Libya) in both international relations and trade and investment terms.

Towards a First Synthesis of Irresponsibility Enabling Repertoires

The previous section presented three stylised cases of universities high-lighting the role that institutional governance plays in the events chain leading to irresponsibility. These three cases suggest four emerging issues for universities reconciling competition within market frameworks along-side sustaining their public value role:

- The effect of institutional complexity within universities simplifying complex cases in ways that hide their controversial nature from gover-nance structures.
- The effects of different forms of responsibility—fiduciary, ethical, cor-porate—intersecting in ways in which these ethical concerns were downplayed.
- In cases where universities made strategic investments, completing associated projects became an end in itself rather than the primary teaching and research ends they were supposed to deliver.
- No institutional mechanisms within which public interests could be articulated and heard within deliberative processes that very quickly disconnected from external referents.

The first of these relates to the complexity of the university as an insti-tution and the need for very different kinds of activities and communities to relate to each other within a single institution, reducing complex issues to a simple essence. In dealing with very sensitive judgements of respon-sibility, units within the university reduced issues to something suffi-ciently simple to deal with, in terms of what mattered to that unit. But at the same time, those decisions then 'travelled' within the institution, car-rying the baggage of what mattered to that first unit. Other communities within the same institution then had their own understanding framed by that simplistic reading, thereby losing nuance. In the UvA case, it made sense for the UvA *at the board level* to think about the financial sustain-ability of the institution as a question of the profitability-per-student, but as soon as that simplification travelled to a *Faculty*, then it was immediately open to challenge as being counter to public value. Likewise, in the LSE case, the Development Committee's substantive concerns were lost in its translation to the governing body, and the decisions of the academic departments who admitted the Gaddafi *fils* hoping to expose a dictator to liberal thinking were lost when the Ph.D. had been awarded and he became a potential corporate sponsor.

The second of these relates to the existence of different versions of responsibility within a single institution, and the complementarity and incompatibility of these different versions, and their incommensurability with public value. The first was *fiduciary responsibility*, and the require-ment for universities to remain a going concern and to meet their respon-sibilities to their lenders. Universities in both the Netherlands and the UK had undergone decades of neglect in investment in their real estate and attempted to catch up by borrowing to invest, to facilitate better competition. The second was of *individual responsibility* to hit financial targets imposed from above, leading to individuals taking decisions which whilst fitting with the overall institutional aim were at odds with the communities within which they operated, whether the Faculty of Humanities or the LSE Department of Government. Third was a *respon-sibility to attract the best institutional leaders*, whether in the case of the UK by allowing high executive pay, or in the Netherlands by allowing management to compensate for the national pay ceiling by using these board positions to demonstrate fiduciary responsibility and to take well-remunerated non-executive positions (the then-UvA chair was also on the oversight board of Schiphol Airport).

The third element was the emergence of an (implicit) institutional mission or set of goals that was more important than the universities' primary activities (teaching and research) which led to the dominance of logics which were sufficiently far from those of the teaching and research activities to create these public value failures. In the case of UvA, the creation of the new university campus organisation (based on four core locations) became a real estate 'tail' that began visibly and uncomfortably 'wagging the dog' of the faculties. In the LSE case, leveraging influence to win donations strengthening core research programmes and profile became (temporarily) more important than building institutional profile and attractiveness on the basis of those core teaching and research programmes' intrinsic strength. In the case of Bath, strong institutional leadership became an end in its own right, and led to the intermingling of leadership with the checks and balances supposed to provide a public input and accountability, thereby undermining the representation of the public interest.

The final element was the absence of internal mechanisms to provide a strong voice to the public interest and ensure that that public voice achieves an effect in university governance. Notable in each case was that concerns of public value were raised internally long before the effects became visible externally. But it was only when external stakeholders picked up on it and transformed the controversy into a 'public value failure' that the resignation occurred. The issue here appears as the absence of mechanisms allowing internal contrarian voices to achieve an effect, prior to the controversy escalating to the level where it become an issue demanding an institutional sacrifice. UvA had a faculty and university council that had approved the plans for the restructuring and the real estate plans, and even had raised critical voices about those plans, but was not able to compel the university to respond. LSE had a Development Committee that scrutinised and criticised the controversial donation but at the time that passed through to Council, the trenchant criticism was diluted and outweighed by other factors. Bath's Court was effectively captured by managerial interests so stakeholder voices were not heard sufficiently when attempting to flag up the controversial nature of pay decisions. Part of the creation of the modern university as highlighted in section "NPM, the Third Mission and the University in the Knowledge Society" was the creation of a strong steering centre, but irresponsibility seems to be enabled by a lack of appropriate checks and balances that allow outside stakeholders to exert influence in these internal governance mechanisms.

Discussion and Conclusions

This chapter asked the research question 'under what conditions might university management find themselves delivering public value failures' to understand why universities, with their strong public service orientations, might end up breaching public value in their behaviours. These three vignettes allow four systemic factors to be identified regarding university governance arrangements associated with public value failures, namely (i) organisational complexity, (ii) conflicting varieties of responsibility, (iii) tunnel vision around strategic projects and (iv) the absence of a public voice. Bringing these back to the conceptual framework proposed in Table 3.1, these four factors appear to correspond with various elements of Bozeman's framework.

Table 3.2 implies that these four factors appear to provide a means to explain the question of irresponsibility and public value failure in

Table 3.2 Systemic factors driving university public value failures

Public value failures	Repertoires of university irresponsibility	Concrete examples
No mechanisms to articulate public value	Absence of accountability mechanisms that allow publics to comment on and shape university engagement activities	(iv) The absence of a public voice
'Imperfect monopolies' occur	Emergence of private providers with access to same titles and accreditation despite inferior product/higher profitability	Not observed
Benefit hoarding occurs	Setting of high levels of fees to restrict access to teaching and research already in receipt of substantive public subsidy	(ii) Conflicting varieties of responsibility present within the institution
Scarcity of providers of public value	A failure to spend resources received from government and fees into teaching activities, to shore up organisational activities	(i) Organisational complexity
Short-termism and avoidance of long-term investment	De-risking balance sheet (pensions, permanent contracts), downgrading longer term commitments to key stakeholders	(iii) Tunnel vision around strategic projects
Competition prioritised over delivering public services	Excessive emphasis on spending on branding and marketing, shifting resources away from services to selling	(ii) Conflicting varieties of responsibility present within the institution

Source: author's own design based on Table 3.1

universities. These four factors taken together describe a situation where intense competition between HEIs leads to relatively closed decision-making processes neither interested in nor reactive to public voices. The need to involve a range of different actors within a university leads to a simplification of the choices to be made, and in that simplification, intense competition sees corporate and fiduciary considerations dominate more ethical ones. This suggests that these public value failures are a consequence of new public management systems and if not inevitable, hard to address in a systemic way without softening or undermining NPM principles, whether market-steering, competition or autonomy. This suggests a suitable evidentiary standard for analyses of 'Responsible Universities' in that they need make clear precisely how the universities making these 'big claims' for responsibility have managed to shield themselves or circumvent these four factors. From a Nordic perspective, this suggests that as these system-steering pressures intensify in coming years, there is a risk that there will be more of these public value failures, and public policy makers should therefore seek to ensure that universities have the autonomy to resist these pressures and behave responsibly rather than opportunistically.

Secondly, although caution is required given this research's rather exploratory nature, these three cases highlight that the governance arrangements which promote NPM are those in which these public value failures can take place; indeed some of these NPM features appear to raise the chances of public value failure. This implies that building responsible universities is not merely a task for universities and their staff but also an issue for all of those that are in some way regulating university steering systems, including regulation and quality agencies, higher education ministries, and even finance ministries and accountancy standards bodies. This research suggests that a shift towards the responsible university need be accompanied by a shift towards public value management in higher education more generally. In the Nordic context, policy makers should reflect upon and seek to address the inherent tensions and pressures that NPM creates for higher education decision-makers that can lead to collective decisions to behave irresponsibly, and contrary to Nordic public values and the interests of Nordic societies.

Acknowledgements Many thanks to the four editors of the volume for inviting me to participate in the seminar series that led to this chapter, and also to their comments on several earlier versions of the contribution. Many thanks are also due to Lisa Neith, Regio Twente and Universiteit Twente, for her comments on the pre-submission version of the paper. My treatment of Gaddafi *fils* may be influenced by the fact that he granted mercy to a close family friend in 2010. Any errors or omissions remain of course the responsibility of the author.

References

Adams, R. (2017a, July 13). University Vice-Chancellors Are Paid Too Much, Says Lord Adonis. *Guardian Newspaper*. Retrieved October 25, 2018, from https://www.theguardian.com/education/2017/jul/13/university-vice-chancellors-are-paid-too-much-says-lord-adonis.

Adams, R. (2017b, November 19). Calls for Bath University Vice-Chancellor to Resign Over Further Pay Rise. *Guardian Newspaper*. Retrieved October 25, 2018, from https://www.theguardian.com/education/2017/nov/19/calls-for-bath-university-vice-chancellor-to-resign-over-further-pay-rise.

Barnett, R. (2000). Realising a Compact for Higher Education. In K. Moti Gokulsing & C. DaCosta (Eds.), *A Compact for Higher Education*. Aldershot: Ashgate.

Barnett, R. (2011). *Becoming a University*. London: Routledge.

BBC. (2017, September 7). *Reality Check: Has Vice Chancellor Pay Been Spiralling?* Retrieved October 25, 2018, from https://www.bbc.com/news/education-41187447.

Bender, T. (Ed.). (1988). *The University and the City. From Medieval Origins to the Present*. New York/Oxford: Oxford University Press.

Benneworth, P. (2014). Decoding University Ideals by Reading Campuses. In P. Temple (Ed.), *The Physical University*. London: Routledge.

Benneworth, P. S. (2015). The Maagdenhuis Occupation, the Crisis of 'Soft Coupling', and the New University. *Krisis: Journal for Contemporary Philosophy*, *2*, 62–67. http://www.krisis.eu/content/2015-2/Krisis-2015-2-10-Benneworth.pdf.

Benneworth, P. S. (2016). Tensions in University–Community Engagement Creative Economy, Urban Regeneration and Social Justice. In R. Comunian & A. Gilmore (Eds.), *Higher Education & the Creative Economy*. Abingdon: Routledge.

Benneworth, P., Charles, D., Hodgson, C., & Humphrey, L. (2013). The Relationship of Community Engagement with Universities' Core Missions. In P. Benneworth (Ed.), *University Engagement with Socially Excluded Communities* (pp. 85–102). Dordrecht: Springer.

Bozeman, B. (2002). Public-Value Failure: When Efficient Markets May Not Do. *Public Administration Review, 62*(2), 145–161.

Bozeman, B., & Sarewitz, D. (2005). Valuing S&T Activities: Public Values and Public Failure in US Science Policy. *Science and Public Policy, 32*(2), 119–136.

Brown, R., & Carasso, H. (2013). *Everything for Sale: The Marketization of UK Higher Education.* London: Routledge/SHRA.

Commission of the European Communities. (2006). *Delivering on the Modernisation Agenda for Universities: Education, Research and Innovation.* Communication from the Commission to the Council and European Parliament, COM 2006 (208) final.

Clark, B. R. (1998). *Creating the Entrepreneurial University.* Oxford: IAU Press/Pergamon.

Collini, S. (2011, March 4). The University Funding System Is Set up to Invite Supper with the Devil. *The Guardian Newspaper.* Retrieved October 25, 2018, from https://www.theguardian.com/commentisfree/2011/mar/04/university-funding-lse-libya-legitmacy-source.

Daalder, H., & Shils, E. (1982). *Universities, Politicians and Bureaucrats: Europe and the United States.* Cambridge: Cambridge University Press.

De Boer, H. F., Enders, J., & Leisyte, L. (2007). Public Sector Reform in Dutch Higher Education: The Organizational Transformation of the University. *Public Administration, 85*(1), 27–46.

Delanty, G. (2002). The University and Modernity: A History of the Present. In K. Robins & F. Webster (Eds.), *The Virtual University: Knowledge, Markets and Management.* OUP Oxford.

de Saille, S. (2015). Innovating Innovation Policy: The Emergence of 'Responsible Research and Innovation'. *Journal of Responsible Innovation, 2*(2), 152–168.

Elliot Major, L. (2002). Fag End of Funding. *The Guardian Newspaper,* December 12, 2000. Retrieved October 25, 2018, from https://www.theguardian.com/education/2000/dec/12/highereducation.theguardian.

Enders, J., & De Boer, H. (2009). The Mission Impossible of the European University: Institutional Confusion and Institutional Diversity. In *In European Integration and the Governance of Higher Education and Research* (pp. 159–178). Dordrecht: Springer.

Engelen, E., Fernandez, R., & Hendrikse, R. (2014). How Finance Penetrates iIts Other: A Cautionary Tale on the Financialization of a Dutch University. *Antipode, 46*(4), 1072–1091.

HEFCE. (2017). Report of an Inquiry Into a Governance Matter at the University of Bath. Retrieved October 25, 2018, from http://webarchive. nationalarchives.gov.uk/20180319121927/http://www.hefce.ac.uk/reg/ staffpay/bath/.

Jackson, R., Barbagallo, F., & Haste, H. (2005). Strengths of Public Dialogue on Science-Related Issues. *Critical Review of International Social and Political Philosophy, 8*(3), 349–358.

Jongbloed, B., Enders, J., & Salerno, C. (2007). Higher Education and Its Communities: Interconnections, Interdependencies and a Research Agenda. *Higher Education, 56*(3), 303–324.

Jongbloed, B., Kaiser, F., van Vught, F., & Westerheijden, D. F. (2018). Performance Agreements in Higher Education: A New Approach to Higher Education Funding. In *European Higher Education Area: The Impact of Past and Future Policies* (pp. 671–687). Cham: Springer.

Kickert, W. (1995). Steering at a Distance: A New Paradigm of Public Governance in Dutch Higher Education. *Governance, 8*, 135–157.

Kickert, W. J. M., Klijn, E. H., & Koppenjan, J. F. M. (Eds.). (1997). *Managing Complex Networks. Strategies for the Public Sector* (1st ed.). London: SAGE Publications.

Larédo, P. (2007) "Revisiting the Third Mission of Universities: Toward a Renewed Categorization of University Activities?" *Higher Education Policy, 20*, 441–456.

LSE. (2011). LSE Global Governance to Close on 31 July 2011. *LSE Press Release.* Retrieved from http://www.lse.ac.uk/website-archive/newsAndMedia/newsArchives/2011/07/globalgovernance.aspx.

MacLeod, D. (2001, June 12). Cancer Research Team Quits Nottingham. *The Guardian Newspaper.* Retrieved October 25, 2018, from https://www.theguardian.com/education/2001/jun/12/highereducation.medicalscience1.

Middleton, C. (2000). Models of State and Market in the 'Modernisation' of Higher Education. *British Journal of Sociology of Education, 21*(4), 537–554.

Owen, R., Macnaghten, P., & Stilgoe, J. (2012). Responsible Research and Innovation: From Science in Society to Science for Society, with Society. *Science and Public Policy, 39*, 751–760.

Phillipson, N. T. (1988). Commerce and Culture: Edinburgh, Edinburgh University and the Scottish Enlightenment. In T. Bender (Ed.), *The University and the City. From Medieval Origins to the Present*. New York/Oxford: Oxford University Press.

Pinheiro, R., & Stensaker, B. (2013). Designing the Entrepreneurial University: The Interpretation of a Global Idea. *Public Organization Review*, 1–20.

Rhodes, R. A. W. (2003). What Is New About Governance and Why Does It Matter? In J. E. S. Hayward & A. Menon (Eds.), *Governing Europe*. Oxford: Oxford University Press.

Shils, E. (1988). The University, the City and the World: Chicago and the University of Chicago. In T. Bender (Ed.), *The University and the City. From Medieval Origins to the Present* (pp. 210–229). New York/Oxford: Oxford University Press.

Smyth, J. (2017). *The Toxic University: Zombie Leadership, Academic Rock Stars and Neoliberal Ideology*. London: Palgrave Macmillan.

Universities and Colleges Union. (2011, August). *High Cost, High Debt, High Risk: Why Privately Funded Universities Are a Poor Deal for Taxpayers and Students*. UCU Briefing. Retrieved January 21, 2019, from https://www.ucu.org.uk/media/7668/High-cost-high-debt-high-risk-UCU-briefing-on-the-for-profit-education-sector-Aug-11/pdf/HighCostHighDebtHighRisk.pdf.

Vasagar, J., & Sweney, M. (2011, March 1 and 4). LSE Plans Libya Scholarship Fund with Gaddafi Donation. *Guardian Newspaper*. Retrieved October 25, 2018, from https://www.theguardian.com/education/2011/mar/01/lse-libya-scholarship-fund.

Vasagar, J., & Syal, R. (2011, March 4). LSE Head Quits Over Gaddafi Scandal. *Guardian Newspaper*. Retrieved October 25, 2018, from https://www.theguardian.com/education/2011/mar/03/lse-director-resigns-gaddafi-scandal.

Watermeyer, R. (2019). *Competitive Accountability in Academic Life: The Struggle for Social Impact and Public Legitimacy*. Cheltenham: Edward Elgar.

Webber, H. S. (2005). The University of Chicago and Its Neighbours: A Case Study in Community Development. In D. Perry & W. Wiewel (Eds.), *The University as Urban Develop: Case Studies and Analysis*. New York: M. E. Sharpe.

Woolf, D. (2011). *An Inquiry into the LSE's Links to Libya and the Lessons to Be Learned*. Report of the Woolf Inquiry. London: Council of the London School of Economics. Retrieved October 25, 2018, from http://www.lse.ac.uk/News/News-Assets/PDFs/The-Woolf-Inquiry-Report-An-inquiry-into-LSEs-links-with-Libya-and-lessons-to-be-learned-London-School-of-Economics-and-Political-Sciences.pdf.

4

Publication of Research Results: A Question of Language and Translation

Mads P. Sørensen, Mitchell Young, and Pernille Bak Pedersen

Introduction

This chapter focuses on the difficult balance that universities and university researchers in the Nordic countries, and beyond, are expected to achieve today with regard to the publication of research results. On the one hand, universities are expected to perform and compete globally, while on the other hand, they still have responsibilities nationally and locally. Nordic universities are primarily public entities financed by tax payments, but a bigger and bigger part of their activities is directed towards the global knowledge market. Nordic universities compete with universities in the rest of the world for high performing, international students and for the best scientists; they work with international partners in transnational networks and produce highly specialized research for the global science community and they employ an increasing number of

M. P. Sørensen (✉) • P. B. Pedersen
Aarhus University, Aarhus, Denmark
e-mail: mps@ps.au.dk; pernillebp@au.dk

M. Young
Charles University, Prague, Czech Republic

academic staff from non-Nordic countries (Gregersen 2014). As part of this development, Nordic universities also produce a significant and growing number of research publications in English. In the present chapter, we examine this development and discuss which implications it has for universities that want to be responsible both towards local taxpayers and the global science system.

Today, around 86% of all research publications from Danish universities are published in English, and as we will show in this chapter, especially the Humanities and the Social Sciences have seen a dramatic change in research publication language over the last 20 years, from Danish to English. This development is not unique for Denmark but part of a global trend. With the transnationalization of research production and research institutions (Sørensen and Schneider 2017), an increasing focus on metrics and pressure to attain excellence (Sørensen et al. 2016), and the subsequent growing orientation towards the global science system, or what Wagner (2008) calls "the new invisible college", the research language par excellence has become English. This has been the case in the natural sciences and health sciences for many years, but within the last couple of decades, the Humanities and the Social Sciences have seen a similar shift in publication language away from national languages towards English. This development requires our attention and understanding—and we need to reflect on what a responsible language strategy is for present-day universities outside the Anglo-Saxon world.

That one language dominates within academia is historically not a new situation. When the first universities were founded in the twelfth century, the dominating language was Latin. Due to the universities' strong connection to the church, this continued to be the case for many centuries. Latin was thus the dominant language at universities up until the beginning of the nineteenth century when nationally oriented universities were founded—inspired by the Humboldt University in Berlin (founded in 1809/1810). With the modern university's strong connection to the nation state and its role as an institution for the educating of civil servants, for example, national languages gradually took over Latin's commanding role (Bull 2004, 37).

Denmark is an example of this development. When Copenhagen University was founded in 1479, the official language of the university was Latin, and it stayed that way until the eighteenth century, when Danish gradually began to take over as the preferred teaching language (Mortensen and Haberland 2012). As a language of publication, Danish also became increasingly popular during the eighteenth century. Right from its establishment in 1742, the Royal Danish Academy of Science and Letters, for example, published its treatises in Danish. According to Mortensen and Haberland (2012, 181), Danish was, at that time, associated with progress, whereas Latin was the language of tradition. In the nineteenth century, following Humboldt's idea of emphasizing a stronger connection between the state and the university, Danish gradually took over both as the dominant language for teaching and for publication. The last fortress for Latin at Copenhagen University was the doctoral thesis. Up until the middle of the century, most theses were still written in Latin and the public defence of the theses had to be done in Latin (Mortensen and Haberland 2012, 182). The last year a doctoral thesis written in Latin was accepted for public defence at Copenhagen University was in the year 1900.

Similarly, Danish has, today, come under pressure at Higher Education Institutions in Denmark. Wächter and Maiworm (2014, 43) found that 38% of all educational programmes at Danish Higher Education Institutions were taught in English in 2013/2014—and, as mentioned above, around 86% of all research publications from Danish universities in 2017 were published in English. This development is not unique for Denmark but a global trend. Everywhere, English has become the dominant language for research communities, scientific journals and academic conferences (Kaplan 1993; Ammon 2001; Altbach 2013; Montgomery 2013). The topic has even become institutionalized as the academic field of "ERPP" (English for Research Publication Purposes) with its own conference PRISEAL (Publishing and Presenting Research Internationally— Issues for Speakers of English as an Additional Language) and the recently launched Journal of English for Research Publication Purposes.[1] This leading role of English within academia has been understood in different ways (Kuteeva and McGrath 2014). It has been interpreted as a new "Lingua Franca"—a practical tool that makes it possible for researchers from different countries to understand each other—but also as a

"Tyrannosaurus rex", that is, the idea that English intimidates and eats up all the other national languages within the academy (Swales 1997).

What this transformation away from national languages towards English means for researchers' text production has most profoundly been investigated by Lillis and Curry (2010). In a comprehensive ethnographic study, they examined the production of academic texts by 50 researchers from Slovakia, Hungary, Spain and Portugal. They followed the texts from draft to final versions, examined correspondence between the authors and the brokers (journals), and interviewed the authors. Among the main findings in their study were that publishing in English has pervaded evaluation and rewards systems for academics in all the countries studied (see also Gazzola 2012 for further discussion on the relationship between language and academic performance indicators). They describe the difficulties which that creates for academics for whom English is a second language, an aspect of their work that comes to similar conclusions as others who investigated this problem in other regions and disciplines (Flowerdew 1999; Hanauer and Englander 2011; Martín et al. 2014). Finally, they show that English is not a neutral medium but represents a distinct politics with a clear centre-periphery dynamic in which the centre is not merely the English language but the Anglophone academic world that dominates it. Consequently, any research that focuses on localities outside the Anglophone centre must be explicitly justified in order to become publishable.

In Denmark, Madsen in 2008 looked into the personal language strategies of researchers working within the Natural Sciences at Aarhus University (Madsen 2008). A key finding in her study was that it was the receiver group that was decisive for the researcher's choice of language. To her respondents, the increasing use of English primarily had to do with efficiency in communication. Without framing it in this way, Madsen's interviewees thus gave reasons for using English that resonate well with the idea of English as a lingua franca that enables them to communicate better with colleagues at conferences, and which makes it possible for peers outside Denmark to read and review their scientific publications and applications. However, it is also clear that there is more prestige given to English in the academy. Among other things, this has to do with the language of the best journals, which are all in English. The interviewees emphasized that one has to master English well, in order to do well in academia. Madsen analyses this development with inspiration from the French sociologist Pierre Bourdieu and points out that English is a "linguistic capital" in the academic field (Madsen 2008, 78).

A comparative study of the Nordic countries' language policies (Saarinen and Taalas 2017) shows that Denmark is unique among them in not having official language legislation or regulation at any level: national, sectorial (i.e. higher education) or institutional (i.e. as a requirement for institutional policy), though it is noted that most institutions have instituted one of their own volition. However, the issue is very much on the political agenda, as there have been several policy papers and reviews by the Danish Ministry of Culture in the first decade of the 2000s as well as significant media attention to the topic. On the surface both the state and the institutional policy papers support parallel lingualism (Danish and English)—but an analysis of the covert ideologies in the papers shows that this means more Danish and less English in the state policy papers and more English and less Danish in the policy papers of the institutions (Hultgren 2014a). In a separate article, Anna Kristina Hultgren (Hultgren 2014b) examines the relationship between rankings and what she terms 'Englishisation' using Denmark's eight universities as cases. While finding no statistically significant correlation between high rankings and levels of English presence among all the universities, she does find a relationship between low English presence and low rankings. These mixed results, she argues, mean that we cannot see English adaptation solely as a "passive capitulation to the global dominance of the English language" (Hultgren 2014b, 405), but also have to understand it as a strategic and context-dependent choice of the university.

In the following, we will first examine the development in English language research publications in Denmark in general. Thereafter, we focus on the development at Aarhus University, which is a comprehensive and prominent international university. Despite its young age (founded in 1928), it is one of the highest ranked universities in the Nordic countries and within the top 100 on various international ranking lists.[2] The University has grown rapidly over the last two decades and has today around 40,000 students and 8000 members of staff.

As it will become clear in the following, all scientific fields in Denmark in general and at Aarhus University have experienced a radical change in publication language over the last two decades. Yet, it is the Social Sciences and the Humanities that have seen the biggest changes over these years. In order to better understand this development, we supplement the quantitative mapping of the changes in publication languages with interviews with researchers from the two departments within the Social Sciences and the Humanities at Aarhus University that have experienced the most dramatic changes since 2001.[3] The interviews focus on the researchers' experiences of this development and their thoughts on the positive and negative implications of publishing more in English and less in Danish. We also talked to them about their understanding of university researchers' responsibilities towards the global science community and the local and national contexts in which they work.

The chapter ends with a discussion of the implications of the development towards publishing more research in English and less in Danish. Here, we also discuss the question of the responsibility of universities when it comes to publishing research.

The Development in Publication Languages in Denmark from 2010 Onwards

In 2017, 17 out of 20 research publications from Danish universities were published in English.[4] As Fig. 4.1 shows, this number has increased steadily since 2010, where researchers from Danish universities published around 22,000 research publications in English and 6000 in Danish. There were also a small number of publications in third languages such as French and German, equivalent to 3% of the total research publications in 2010. Between 2010 and 2017, the number of English language research publications gradually increased to around 31,000, corresponding to 86% of the total number of research publications. In contrast, both the number and share of research publications in Danish decreased in the same period. In 2010, every fifth research publication from Danish universities was published in Danish. This number had decreased to around every eighth in 2017. The share of third language publications decreased to less than 2% in the same period.

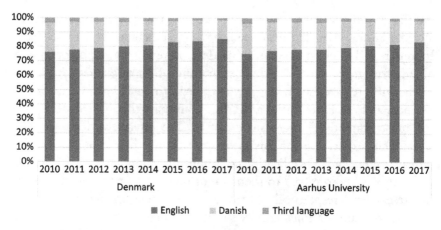

Fig. 4.1 Share of English, Danish and third language research publications, all Danish universities and Aarhus University. *Source*: The national database, "Forskningsdatabasen.dk"

As Fig. 4.1 also shows, a similar change in the publication patterns can be observed at Aarhus University. In 2010, English language research publications accounted for 75% of the more than 7000 research publications. Danish language publications accounted for 21%, and third languages for 4%. The total number of research publications rose to around 9000 in 2017, and the corresponding percentages for research languages were 84% English, 14.5% Danish and 2% third languages.

If we look at the development across main scientific areas at Danish universities, there are huge differences between the different areas in the share of English language research publications (cf. Fig. 4.2).[5] However, all the main areas have experienced a growth in the number and share of English language publications over the period. Science and Technology already had around 90% English language research publications in 2010, but this figure has now increased to more than 96%. In the Humanities, where the majority of research publications were still published in Danish in 2010, more than 55% of all research publications are now published in English. The Social Sciences have likewise experienced a significant increase, from around 59% to 70% over the period, as has Medical Science (from 84% to 92%).

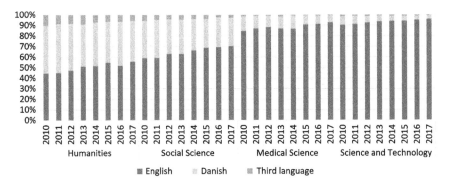

Fig. 4.2 The development in English, Danish and third language research publications across the four main scientific areas in Denmark. *Source*: The national database, "Forskningsdatabasen.dk"

The Development in English Language Publications at Aarhus University

In Fig. 4.3, the development from 2001 onwards within the different main areas at Aarhus University is displayed.[6] The graph clearly shows that significant changes have taken place over the last 17 years within all scientific areas, but especially within the Humanities and the Social Sciences. While only 24% of the research publications from the Humanities were published in English in 2001, this figure had increased to 53% in 2017, and, in the Social Sciences, a similar dramatic change from around 47% to about 80% has taken place.

We further looked into the different academic environments (schools and departments) within the Social Sciences and Humanities to find out, which among them had undergone the most significant transformations. Many of the departments had experienced radical changes in their publication patterns over this period. However, within the Social Sciences the Department of Management had undergone the most substantial changes. In 2001, 58% of the research publications from the Department of Management were in English, whereas this in 2017 had changed to nearly 96%.[7] This means that Danish as well as third languages have more or less disappeared as publication languages for research publications in this department.

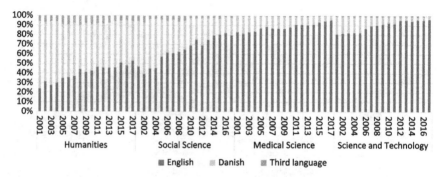

Fig. 4.3 Share of English, Danish and third language research publications across four main areas at Aarhus University. *Source*: The local "PURE" database at Aarhus University

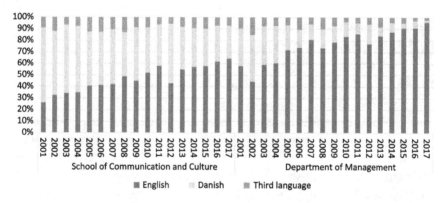

Fig. 4.4 The development in the share of English, Danish and third language research publications at the Department of Management and the School of Communication and Culture at Aarhus University. *Source*: The local "PURE" database at Aarhus University

Within the Humanities, it was the School of Communication and Culture that had undergone the biggest changes.[8] Here, Danish was still the dominating publication language in 2001 with around 64% of the research publications published in Danish. This balance has now tipped, so that most publications now are in English. The share of English language research publications has gone up from about 26% in 2001 to around 64% in 2017. The development in the two scientific environments is shown in Fig. 4.4.

Push and Pull in the Migration to English

In order to better understand these rather dramatic developments, we interviewed eight researchers from these two academic environments about their experiences and understandings of the changes. The eight researchers (three women and five men) are all professors or associate professors at the Department of Management or the School of Communication and Culture. They have also all of them been employed at Aarhus University for most of the monitored period and therefore themselves experienced the changes. In the Department of Management we talked to researchers from the sections Corporate Communication and Organization, Strategy and Accounting. In the School of Communication and Culture, we interviewed researchers from the Department of Art History, Aesthetics and Culture and Museology as well as the Department of Scandinavian Studies and Experience Economy. These sections and departments were likewise chosen based on an analysis of the changes that had taken place, so that we interviewed researchers from the scientific environments, which had seen the most radical changes.

In the following, we report on the findings from the interviews. Our analysis strategy is inspired by migration studies. We examine the shifts in publication language patterns as a form of migration from Danish and other languages to English. One of the most established theories explaining migration is the "push-pull" model (see, for example, Portes and Böröcz 1989; Petersen 1958), which categorizes hardships in the region of origin as push factors and opportunities in the destination region as pull factors. The combination and strengths of the various push and pull factors condition the effects of migration flows. In Table 4.1 the findings from our interviews are categorized according to push and pull factors, followed by an in-depth discussion.

Push Factors

Danish

The concept of push factors, when translated for publication practices, identifies pressures that create an environment that is not conducive to

Table 4.1 Push and pull factors in the migration from Danish to English language research publications

	Danish	English
Push	National publication system	Subject of study
	Funding	Methods and theories
	University policy	Thinking and writing
	Department management	
	Career advancement	
Pull	Identity	Legitimacy and prestige
	Students	Socialization
	Public sphere	Career advancement
	Journals	Cooperation and belonging
	Public accessibility	Audience
		Quality

Danish language publication. Push factors are negatively connoted and reflect a pushing away from something. These push factors also encourage (we might even say that they push towards) English publication, and as we have seen in the previous section the push away from Danish has not led to an increase in publication in other languages than English, nevertheless, the perception of researchers is different for this set of factors than for what we characterize as pull factors. While there are corresponding pull factors of English, they are not just a mirror image of these push factors, but can be better characterized through legitimacy, socialization and career advancement, as we will explain in the section below.

Five main types of push factors come out of our interviews. To some extent they are interconnected, as bibliometrics and the national points system for publications percolates from the top down and has an impact on the university-level pressures as well as the department and individual-level ones. The conditions are set at the highest political levels: "there is a political wish from the government, from parliament, that all research should be international... the legislators tend to think that international is English (6)". This second part of the statement was both a reflection of reality, which is to say that for many of the researchers we spoke with, this was uncontested, but on the other hand, a criticism of the conflation of these two terms. The interpenetration of the national can be seen clearly in this comment: "I think it basically has to do with the signals that have been sent politically. Any young scholar with a minimum of sensitivity could see from the early years of this century that a career in the system would require an orientation towards the English language and publications in international journals (4)".

The national publication points system is perceived as one of the push factors away from Danish:

> *after the bibliometric system was implemented, suddenly it was very difficult getting the best scores for publishing in the Danish journals, so you kind of had to publish in an international journal to get two points [the highest level], so... and I don't necessarily think that people care that much about the points, but there is still this, somehow, pressure. (7)*

The claim that points were not intrinsically valued by researchers was reflected in many of the responses. Despite not wanting to clearly pin down points as the sole cause of this publication shift, there was a clear sense of bibliometrics being central in developing pressure towards publishing in English:

> *The thing about pressure is really difficult, because no one is telling me 'you have to publish in English', and no one is telling me 'you have to publish in Danish', but... but I think the whole structure around publications is becoming more and more inclined to publishing in English, for instance through the bibliometric system. (7)*

Funding also puts pressure on researchers to move away from Danish. "In the early century, just around the university law and the rising pressure towards English language it was almost impossible to get funding from the research foundation to publish anything that was not in English (4)". In this regard however, there was a sense that this pressure was easing up a bit, and that in more recent years it had again become at least possible.

The university policies also favour publications in English, but researchers do not comment strongly on this level as affecting their decisions. They see the university seeking to brand itself internationally and pursuing higher rankings on international lists. What comes through more strongly is the sense that the university is obligated to make this emphasis, but the stronger pressures come from the departmental or School management. In the humanities, the dean's level even appears to play a bit of a buffering role:

the dean of the humanities, not my department, has said explicitly: "Don't bother about the bibliometrics. Don't bother. Publish your things where it makes sense"—in an academic sense of the word. Which is a relief. He did that 2 or 3 years ago. That has in my experience taken a bit of the drama out of this. Up till then, even I had started calculating about what I should do in order to legitimize [my research]. I have published quite a few English language articles because of that consideration. I don't do that anymore. I mean… It is not that I distanced myself from the articles, they were fine, but the reason I did them in English was this pressure existed. (4)

The pressure from department management varied between the two departments we studied. In the social sciences, there was a more formal approach: a list of around 50 journals conscribed the acceptable publication outlets. This list derived not from the national system but from the Financial Times; that said, it does not diverge from the national bibliometric system, as it is a subset of the high impact factor (level 2) publications. All of the publications are in English. The implementation of this system came from a management change in the department:

I think actually the shift from going from Danish to English, it kind of reflected that new management. Suddenly we had a new, actually, we HAD a strategy, an official strategy that we wanted to publish internationally… We have a very, very focused management, who rather want us to publish one high ranked article every year than just have a lot of small publications in minor journals. (2)

Additionally, researchers spoke about the personal interactions between themselves and management, and how that had changed over time, becoming more active in pressuring researchers to achieve specific aims: "Management interferes a lot more in my research work and want to shape my behaviour, also publication behaviour, than was the case 20 years ago (8)". In the humanities department, there is a less formalistic approach and no strict hierarchy of publications, but still management pressure is clear: "when I was interviewed for my position as associated professor, the only thing that the head of the department said was that you have to publish more in English (1)".

Here we can see the close interaction between management pressures and the internal pressures of research for their career. In these terms, the picture presented is stark: "if you want to make a good career at this department you should target these journals [i.e. those on the abovementioned Financial Times list] (8)". It is presented as something that leaves little room for decisions or manoeuvre on the career path:

> when you are in a process where you have not met your final destination so to speak, then it is quite important that you focus on the indicators that matters in order to affect whether or not or how fast you can be promoted. So, from that point of view I don't think English or Danish is really a choice. It's given. (3)

English

There are also push factors away from English, though these tend to situate themselves more at the level of publication, in terms of the choice of subject, methodology and the processes of thinking and writing, which in some ways are more restrictive in English. Subjects of study are not equally interesting to all audiences, and it can be a challenge to take something that is of interest locally or nationally and make it engaging for an international audience. "So perhaps discussions in a publication that would be relevant in a Danish context might be less relevant in an international and global context (8)". There is thus a push away from local knowledge, or stated even more dramatically: "it destroys a lot of the local knowledge (5)". Unless a subject can be made of interest to an international audience, it will not be publishable in English. A researcher who also has journal editorship experience, comments on why that might be the case, and we see that it ties at least in part to what is interesting:

> I have also been doing a lot of case studies. There can be a case that is not only unique but is also based on a very particular regulation that only exist in Denmark. You should probably also ask yourself as a researcher then, is that really interesting? (3)

One of the ways to make a subject interesting internationally is to focus more on theory:

So, you do write in different ways when you address a broader public of literary scholars, you tend to theorize more, you don't do readings as much, you don't [do] history as much. There needs to be some kind of theoretical edge to it in order to go through within this larger audience. (6)

More specifically, and in line with what Lillis and Curry (2010) have argued, the key factor is not just about being interesting to an abstract international audience, rather the definition of what is interesting is shaped by journals and their country of publication. "When we say internationalization at Aarhus University, it is very much in an American, a US context (1)". So having a theoretical focus in the publication is not necessarily enough, it also needs to be a particularly type of theory: "When you have a theoretical interest that is not well represented in the English-speaking world, you end up a little bit alone (4)". In the School of Management, this meant that trends in the US and to a lesser extent the UK steered the type of research being done. In the following example, the researcher talks about the difficulty of getting conceptually based research published in her field:

And some of the strongest within this field have been France and Germany, and Denmark also, in many ways we have had this tradition, but it is very difficult actually to publish anything on that because it is a more rationalistic approach, whereas when you go into the US, then they will just have you look at some much more empirical things... I also think that the US research methods are blind to some social values. (5)

In the humanities, we still find a significant share of publications in Danish, which provides a chance to more fully explore the reasons and trade-offs behind this practice. One issue that came up several times was the choice of examples that get used in an English as opposed to a Danish publication. Several authors describe the challenge of making a theoretical argument relevant by adjusting the examples they use to ones that resonate with an international audience: "I mean... which writers can I write about in the larger international circuit? Only very few, only those who are already well famous (6)". While it is not seen as impossible to undertake the task of introducing lesser known examples, for instance newer writers in literature, it increases the challenge of getting work published. If the main thrust of the article is theoretical then, as one researcher describes it: "you might want to change your examples for Scandinavian/ Danish to examples who are for the U.S., so I have done that… sometimes… then you also change your research subject in some ways (1)". On the other hand, in other sub-fields this is something of a non-issue: "it doesn't necessarily matter what cases I study, it is the theoretical development and then it doesn't matter if it is a Danish or an English case. And a lot of the Danish cases that I study usually have quite a lot of international attention anyway (7)".

So, in terms of both the subject and the methodological approach, there is evidence that English does not only expand possibilities through its large audience but also, in some ways, constrict them. In other words, researchers focusing on local knowledge may be pushed away from English.

A third way in which researchers are pushed away from English has to do directly with language. In this, there are three aspects: concept translation, nuance and thinking. Concepts are determined by the choice of language. While in many (maybe most) cases there are adequate translations, there are times that a particular language expresses an idea more effectively: "there are things you can say and think in Danish and German that are foreign entities in the English language. Concepts and lines of thought that are essential in much of my work has been extremely difficult to transpose into English because there was no translation for them (4)". This in part has to do with the way in which language is constructed: "in Danish you can put words together. Like in German, so… so you build up, sort of conceptually, you can build up systems… for instance I can make a word, within my field in Danish, that probably one word would be more or less a whole line. (Laughter). But I cannot do that [in English] (5)".

All of the interviews were conducted in English, and it was abundantly clear that all the interviewees were fluent and perfectly comfortable in English; however, from their own perspective, writing in English did present challenges that could be seen as push factors. The following passage in which the researcher describes an article he recently wrote in Danish, somewhat ironically with an American colleague based for many years in Denmark, sums up many of the overall themes we heard from others, that is, reflecting both an increased level of confidence and nuance and a sense of enjoyment:

> *about this Danish publication that I did with the American colleague of mine, it was a pleasure to write in your own language. I felt much more competent. I feel more competent when I write in Danish. We are sort of amateurs when it comes to writing in English. We can do it and I think most of us don't have any problem of formulating or getting a message through but of course we don't have the same feel for English as we do for our native [language]. (8)*

What the author means in this case by "feel" was developed further by the other researchers. For many of them it had to do with nuance: "the problem can be to write sentences that are much nuanced. It is not at the level of the terminology but it is perhaps the way you construct your sentences (8)". And nuance can also affect other aspects of writing, like humour or engagingness: "I think my language is better in Danish... I am funnier, I make my arguments more clear... my excellent sense of humour when I speak in Danish, and it is kind of lost when you are speaking English because you don't know all the nuances (2)". Another researcher explains that the text he produces in English "might tend to become more boring to read also... So perhaps native English-speaking researchers have an advantage, they are probably able to make their publications more reader-friendly, more interesting to read (8)".

The issue of language mastery also came up in several interviews, both from the perspective of writing and understanding: "I master the Danish language in a completely different way than I master English... and I actually wonder how many people really master the English language... I am actually quite worried about that, that we don't get the same sense of what language means (5)". Reflecting on the desire of students for texts and teaching materials in Danish, another researcher shifts the question from understanding to time pressure: "I don't know if they understand it better, but it is easier for them to read, and I think it is faster for them to read (2)". Time pressures also play a role in writing in English: "I put a lot of effort into the English articles I think… and it takes much more time to kind of finish those articles than the ones in Danish (1)".

Finally, there is a direct connection between writing and thinking. Interestingly this also affects the local work environment where the language used can change according to the purpose of the discussion: "We speak Danish, but then sometimes we, if we are discussing papers, we switch to English, because it is easier if the article is written in English anyway (7)". This implies that the process of discussion, thinking and writing are deeply intertwined, as we see in this comment: "language is the medium in which I think, so in order to do my thinking as good as possible, I have to write in Danish. I'm simply better in Danish than in English (6)".

Pull Factors

Danish

The push factors described above do not prohibit publication in Danish but make it something that falls outside of normal job expectations, at least in the social sciences. As one researcher explained, you do not publish in Danish "unless you really have your heart in it … REALLY want to". What does pull researchers into publishing in Danish falls into several categories: identity, students, intellectual public sphere and accessibility to the public.

Particularly in the humanities, scholars reflect on their academic identity as a factor in publishing in Danish: "I am still kind of also seeing myself as a Scandinavian scholar so it is important to … to do research in Scandinavian language and publish in Scandinavian peer-reviewed journals and things like that (1)". Connecting to and serving students is another: "A lot of our students, they really like to read the Danish chapters and somehow it makes more sense to them (2)". This suggests that comprehension in Danish is higher, which was a belief also shared by others, but another aspect might be just that the speed and ease of reading is better. The flip side is that with teaching now increasingly (and in the Department of Management entirely) being done in English, this factor also has a pull effect in the opposite direction.

Some variation on the idea of maintaining a public intellectual space in Danish was shared among many of the respondents. Some considered it as valuable in itself: "I think there is a point in keeping Danish as a scholarly language (4)", and this also means supporting Danish journals: "I actually think that there are some pretty good journals in Danish, and I also think that it is, somehow I feel that it is important to keep those journals alive (7)". Others described this as wanting to "engage in the Danish debate (5)", which does not have to be solely academic, but can also cross over into other spheres of society: "where we have scientists discussing literature in English and journalists talking about literature in Danish, we need to have a common space, and that common space must necessarily be in the Danish language (6)". There was an argument made that publishing in Danish was necessary in order to maintain the language itself:

> If we want to insist that we have to speak Danish in the state of Denmark, then somehow we also need to have, we need to continue to develop a language that is nuanced enough to do that. And I think that if we don't continue to publish research articles in Danish, then I think at some point the Danish language will be lacking. (7)

In addition, there is from some researchers' side a desire to be accessible to the Danish public. However, on this there was more division. Not all researchers saw research publications as the proper avenue for this sort of dissemination. Some researchers argued for publication in newspapers, public talks and media appearances as a more appropriate means than research publications; more of a "translation of our research, not only into Danish publications, but also into, you know, make it more appealing, more approachable for a Danish speaking audience (2)". While the need to disseminate is still given lip-service, the pressures to do so are less intense than for publishing in English. Speaking about the change over the past decade this researcher explained: "What I am saying is, previously it was felt more important to also communicate and disseminate the results to practitioners—and they do not read English. So therefore of course I had to publish in Danish also (3)". Now, this person publishes primarily in English.

English

Researchers identified a broad range of pull factors for publishing in English. Legitimacy, socialization and career advancement correspond in many ways with the push factors. Publishing in English is seen to add legitimacy. In one of the studied environments, there was a division between different sub-fields, which resulted in strong internal competition "because we wanted to legitimize our own research area. I think we used the international journals and conferences and networks as, you know, as a means to try to legitimize and show how important this research area really is (2)". Legitimation from publishing in English also was seen to lead towards other benefits, such as being invited to join in grant applications and international projects. Rather than being a concrete pull, one researcher described a "socialization into an international environment" reflecting that: "it is just something that you feel you should do, and you also, you know this again, this doubleness that I feel that it is more rewarding to write in English, mostly, but it also feels like an obligation to maintain this ecosystem (7)". Sometimes it was stated in more direct terms: "it was natural for me to switch to English (2)" or "we were just very eager to, like, become international (1)".

Perhaps the strongest felt pull factors had to do with the audience for one's work and the international interactions, which were facilitated by publishing in English. Researchers described how they were pulled into English publications because they had begun to undertake cooperative research with other international scholars:

I wrote some articles in the late 90's in Danish, which I translated into English, and they were very well received, and that meant that I began to work together with some international scholars, and in particular some English scholars. And I cooperated with them a lot, and that meant that yeah, I went into publishing in English. (5)

More broadly, though, researchers talk in terms of the field and the vastly expanded audience that English language readership provides:

I think sometimes when I publish in Danish, I think 'hmm, this was actually quite interesting, too bad I didn't publish it in English' (laughter). Sometimes that feeling, that it can be maybe a little bit of a waste to write something that is interesting in Danish. (7)

And this is not just about dissemination but also about the quality and amount of feedback that comes: "I am also excited about getting all of these inputs, which is like, I mean if you go into English you have a potentially huge audience and the feedback is much [better] (1)". This in turn leads to an overall improvement in the quality of the publications themselves. Researchers see a direct link between the feedback received through both peer review processes at international journals and less formal interactions with international colleagues and the ultimate quality of an article. So from the level of the conference ("the quality of the conversations that we have on the conferences are better" (2)) to the feedback and perceived higher standards ("we get more high quality reviews and quality feedback when we hand in to high ranked journals, international journals" (2)) to the researcher's self-perception ("it makes you better as a research scholar" (1)), the shift to publishing in English is broadly seen to increase quality.

English publications affect a researcher's prestige and legitimacy and integrate them into the larger international community of their scientific field, "I think for me, it has been important the way that I can get into the international community and get some recognition there (5)" and this is also because one wants to be recognized: "you want to be a part of the field, yeah, you don't want to be overlooked (7)". The choice of publishing in English makes sense because, "of course it gives prestige to publish in the best journal (3)". The national bibliometric system that ranks journals in two levels reinforces this (almost none of the top-level journals are in Danish). One researcher described the efforts they made in their field to push back against the idea that "you can't publish anything that has prestige attached to that, unless you do it in English (7)" by getting some Danish journals included in the level 2 categorization.

In sum, we see that push and pull factors in the migration to English language publication have both positive and negative effects, in terms of what is gained and lost in the migration to English publications (Table 4.2). In the following section, we discuss how a responsible university should both support what is gained and take steps to mitigate against these losses.

Table 4.2 What is gained and what is lost in the migration to English language

Gained	Lost
Quality	Local knowledge
Field relevance/importance	Concepts
Intellectual stimulation	Approaches
Belonging/scientific community	Nuance
Prestige	Humour
Legitimacy	Thinking
Citations	Time
Audience	Dissemination avenues

Conclusion: The Need for a More Responsible Language Policy

As we have shown in this chapter, Danish universities have undergone a massive change in recent decades when it comes to the language in which research publications are published. Today, 86% of all research publications from Danish universities are published in English. Almost all research publications from the Natural, Technical and Medical Sciences are written in English and aimed at the global scientific community. The Social Sciences seem to be moving in the same direction and in the Humanities, more than half of the research publications are today in English.

This development has, according to the interviewees in our study, clear advantages when it comes to enhancing the quality of research and enabling Danish researchers to take part in transnational scientific networks and communities. On an aggregate level, the shift towards publishing in English language journals has further helped to draw attention to research produced in Denmark, making it possible for Danish universities to assert themselves in international competition.

However, as the researchers interviewed in our study made clear, something is also lost in this transition towards English language publications. Some researchers state that they think and write better in Danish. They are, for example, able to express themselves with more nuance and humour. They also from time to time find it hard to translate key concepts into English. English language journals—especially high impact

journals—furthermore seem to be less interested in cases from small countries, in preference for Anglo-Saxon cases, and favour particular theoretical
and methodological approaches over others. Finally, the migration to
English also seems to have had a negative impact on the Danish language
public sphere—according to the interviewees it even may have been a factor in the closing down of Danish language journals like *Grus* and *Kritik*.

An important question related to the context of this book then is, how
a responsible university should respond to the development towards more
English language publications. It is not an easy question to answer.
Universities are on the one hand expected to perform and compete globally, while they on the other hand still have obligations nationally and
locally. This is not least the case for Nordic universities, which primarily
are public entities financed by tax payments. According to the Danish
University Act, Danish universities have an obligation to "… conduct
research and offer research-based education at the highest international
level within its academic fields". The transition to publishing more in
English undoubtedly makes it easier for universities to live up to these
two obligations. However, universities also have a third obligation:

> *The university must collaborate with the external environment and contribute
> to the development of international collaboration. The university's research and
> educational results must contribute to promoting growth, prosperity and the
> development of society. As a central knowledge-based body and cultural reposi-
> tory, the university must exchange knowledge and competences with society and
> encourage its employees to take part in the public debate. (Uddannelses- og
> forskningsministeriet 2011)*

In relation to this third mission, the transition to English language
research publications might be more problematic, because this activity
mostly takes place in the local language which also provides a greater local
absorptive capacity in terms of the local population's ability to make use
of disseminated knowledge. Especially worrying is, as mentioned above,
the closing down of high-quality Danish language journals, which dealt
with local as well as international cases, and helped translate international
debates and issues into a Danish context, contributing in turn to keeping
a Danish language public sphere vibrant.

This chapter shows that there is a need for starting a discussion on what universities, not just in Denmark but everywhere in non-Anglophone countries, can do to battle the negative consequences of the transition to English while at the same time holding on to the benefits of this movement. One place to begin could be to ask if English is, in all cases, better or if more room needs to be given to the national language. Bibliometric systems, reward systems and grant systems together with carrier systems all seem to value English language publications more than national language publications. However, it might be time to start developing more nuanced understandings of English versus national language publications. It should be recognized that the current buzzwords of excellence, impact and relevance are context dependent, and that they can be achieved in local languages albeit with slightly different, though not necessarily less important, results. The responsible university should therefore develop ways to evaluate and recognize quality, impact and relevance in all three of its main missions with consideration given to whether and how language choice reflects and furthers the objectives of the research outputs.

Acknowledgements The authors would like to thank Jens Peter Andersen, senior researcher at the Danish Centre for Studies in Research and Research Policy (CFA), who helped us by making the language algorithm, setting up data and answering questions regarding PURE data. We would also like to thank Henrik Skadhauge Clausen and Nicolaj Veje Pedersen, librarians at Aarhus University Library, who kindly extracted PURE data for us, made comparisons between data in PURE and data from the national database and helped us understand the data. Furthermore, Lotte Faurbæk from the Danish Agency for Science and Higher Education, The Ministry of Higher Education and Science, has been helpful in sending us national bibliometric data. Anna-Kathrine Bendtsen, Astrid Marie Kierkegaard-Schmidt, Anders Møller Jørgensen, Emal Sadeq Aqazadeh, Signe Nygaard and Olivia Hesselholt Dupont Igens, student assistants at CFA, have helped us with various practical tasks such as transcribing interviews, extracting data, validating publication language, and so on. We would also like to thank Anna Kristina Hultgren, Senior Lecturer at the Open University, for her kind and thorough review of our chapter and for her many helpful suggestions for improvements. Finally, our interviewees should also be thanked for helping us making sense of the shift in publication patterns.

Notes

1. John Benjamins Publishing Company ISSN 2590-0994.
2. See Aarhus University's homepage for more information on students, staff and rankings: https://international.au.dk/about/profile/keystatistics/.
3. The interviews were conducted in August and September 2018. We interviewed eight researchers from the two scientific environments. The interviews were transcribed and coded in MAXQDA, using a coding strategy combining both structural and in vivo codes.
4. When we here and in the following refer to research publications, we mean journal articles and review articles, books and book chapters, PhD and doctoral theses, reports and report chapters, and conference papers that have been published and categorized as "scientific" rather than "popular" or "educational".
5. By "main scientific areas" or just "main areas" we here and in the following refer to a division of all the scientific fields represented at Danish universities into four groups: Humanities, Social Sciences, Medical Science, and Natural Science and Technology.
6. At the national level, we only analyse data from 2010 onwards due to data accessibility and data quality. Data at the national level is from "Forskningsdatabasen.dk", which is a publicly available database. At Aarhus University we have received and analysed data reaching back to 2001. The data is from the local PURE (Research Information Management System) database. Within this system, researchers register their publication, including the language of the publication, and librarians validate the registration. The data is not perfect. However, we have checked the validity of the categorization of language with help from an algorithm and by manual coding. Less than 1% of the publications were incorrectly registered, and the errors seem to be random (English language publications registered as Danish or Danish publications registered as English).
7. The Department of Management was established in 2011 as part of several mergers at Aarhus University. When analysing publications at the department level, publications from merged departments are included. For instance publication from the former Department of Marketing and Department of Management are also included. For the history of the mergers, see: http://bss.au.dk/om-aarhus-bss/profil-og-strategi/aarhus-bss-historie/.
8. The School of Communication and Culture is also a result of mergers. As it is the case with the Department of Management, publications from merged departments are included in the analysis.

References

Altbach, P. G. (2013). The Imperial Tongue. In *The International Imperative in Higher Education. Global Perspectives on Higher Education*. Rotterdam: Sense Publishers.

Ammon, U. (2001). *The Dominance of English as a Language of Science: Effects on Other Languages and Language Communities*. New York: Mouton de Gruyter.

Bull, T. (2004). Dagens og gårdagens akademiske Lingua Franca [Today's and Yesterday's Academic Lingua Franca]. In D. F. Simonsen (Ed.), *Språk i kunnskapssamfunnet. Engelsk—eliternes nye latin? [Language in the Knowledge Society. English—The New Latin of the Elites?]*. Oslo: Gyldendal Akademisk.

Flowerdew, J. (1999). Problems in Writing for Scholarly Publication in English: The Case of Hong Kong. *Journal of Second Language Writing, 8*(3), 243–264.

Gazzola, M. (2012). The Linguistic Implications of Academic Performance Indicators: General Trends and Case Study. *International Journal of the Sociology of Language, 216*, 131–156.

Gregersen, F. (Ed.). (2014). *Hvor parallelt. Om parallellspråkighet på Nordens universitet* [How parallel. On parallellingualism at the Nordic university] with contributions by Frans Gregersen, Olle Josephson, Sebastian Godenhjelm, Monica Londen, Jan-Ola Östman, Ari Páll Kristinsson, Haraldur Bernharðsson, Unn Røyneland, Gjert Kristoffersen, Marita Kristiansen, Jacob Thøgersen, Taina Saarinen, Anna Kristina Hultgren og Linus Salö. Nordisk Ministerråd 2014. Denmark: TemaNord 2014:535.

Hanauer, D. I., & Englander, K. (2011). Quantifying the Burden of Writing Research Articles in a Second Language: Data from Mexican Scientists. *Written Communication, 28*(4), 403–416.

Hultgren, A. K. (2014a). Whose Parallellingualism? Overt and Covert Ideologies in Danish University Language Policies. *Multilingua, 33*(1–2), 61–87.

Hultgren, A. K. (2014b). English Language Use at the Internationalised Universities of Northern Europe: Is There a Correlation Between Englishisation and World Rank? *Multilingua, 33*(3–4), 389–411.

Kaplan, R. B. (1993). The Hegemony of English in Science and Technology. *Journal of Multilingual and Multicultural Development, 14*, 151–172.

Kuteeva, M., & McGrath, L. (2014). Taming Tyrannosaurus Rex: English Use in the Research and Publication Practices of Humanities Scholars in Sweden. *Multilingua, 33*(3–4), 365–387.

Lillis, T., & Curry, M. J. (2010). *Academic Writing in a Global Context. The Politics and Practices of Publishing in English*. London and New York: Routledge.

Madsen, M. (2008). *"Der vil altid være brug for dansk". En undersøgelse af 11 naturvidenskabelige forskeres grunde til at vælge henholdsvis dansk og engelsk i deres arbejde ["There will always be a need for Danish". An examination of 11 Natural scientists' reasons for choosing English and Danish respectively in their work].* Københavnerstudier i Tosprogethed, bind 48. Copenhagen: Copenhagen University.

Martín, P., Rey-Rocha, J., Burgess, S., & Moreno, A. I. (2014). Publishing Research in English-Language Journals: Attitudes, Strategies and Difficulties of Multilingual Scholars of Medicine. *Journal of English for Academic Purposes, 16*, 57–67.

Montgomery, S. L. (2013). *Does Science Need a Global Language?: English and the Future of Research.* Chicago: University of Chicago Press.

Mortensen, J., & Haberland, H. (2012). English—The New Latin of Academia? Danish Universities as a Case. *International Journal of the Sociology of Language, 216*, 175–197.

Petersen, W. (1958). A General Typology of Migration. *American Sociological Review, 23*(3), 256–266.

Portes, A., & Böröcz, J. (1989). Contemporary Immigration: Theoretical Perspectives on Its Determinants and Modes of Incorporation. *International Migration Review, 23*(3), 606–630.

Saarinen, T., & Taalas, P. (2017). Nordic Language Policies for Higher Education and Their Multi-layered Motivations. *Higher Education, 73*(4), 597–612.

Sørensen, M. P., & Schneider, J. W. (2017). Studies of National Research Performance: A Case of 'Methodological Nationalism' and 'Zombie Science'? *Science and Public Policy, 44*(1), 132–145.

Sørensen, M. P., Bloch, C., & Young, M. (2016). Excellence in the Knowledge-Based Economy: From Scientific to Research Excellence. *European Journal of Higher Education, 6*(3), 217–236.

Swales, J. M. (1997). English as *Tyrannosaurus Rex. World Englishes, 16*(3), 373–382.

Uddannelses- og forskningsministeriet. (2011). *The Danish University Act.* Retrieved February 14, 2019, from https://ufm.dk/en/legislation/prevailing-laws-and-regulations/education/files/the-danish-university-act.pdf.

Wächter, B., & Maiworm, F. (2014). *English-Taught Programmes in European Higher Education. The State of Play in 2014.* Bonn: Lemmens Medien GmbH.

Wagner, C. S. (2008). *The New Invisible College: Science for Development.* Washington, DC: Brookings Institution Press.

Part III

Innovations in University

5

MOOCs and Responsible University: Implications for Higher Education

Linda Barman, Cormac McGrath, and Christian Stöhr

Introduction

For the past decade, universities around the world have offered a new form of online education that circumvents traditional university admis-

L. Barman (✉)
KTH Royal Institute of Technology, Stockholm, Sweden

Karolinska Institutet, Stockholm, Sweden
e-mail: lbarman@kth.se

C. McGrath
Stockholm University, Stockholm, Sweden

Karolinska Institutet, Stockholm, Sweden
e-mail: cormac.mcgrath@edu.su.se

C. Stöhr
Chalmers University of Technology, Gothenburg, Sweden
e-mail: christian.stohr@chalmers.se

sion processes and provides broad and open access to knowledge from higher education institutions (HEI). These large-scale education initiatives are commonly referred to as MOOCs (Massive Open Online Courses). This chapter addresses MOOCs as an example of how universities in Sweden have responded to a "novel" (non-traditional) way of offering education with the potential of taking a broader responsibility to educate society. We acknowledge that MOOCs may create opportunities for universities to take an active role in educating society and provide affordable pathways to lifelong learning for a wider population, on a global scale. Furthermore, MOOCs potentially offer a way for universities to be accountable actors in society and could, for example, provide means to address issues of diversity and equal opportunities (Barman et al. 2018; Santos et al. 2017). Within the European Union (EU), open education initiatives such as MOOCs are regarded as important drivers of education quality, and their development is stimulated and encouraged through, for example, policy recommendations (Santos et al. 2017) and funding from EU-supported networks like EIT Health (European Institute of Innovation & Technology) (www.eithealth.eu). Today, the higher education sector is the largest public sector in Sweden, and many different stakeholders share an interest in its responsiveness and relevance vis-à-vis societal needs, the quality in its processes and outcomes, and the accountability of the academic institutions (Sadurskis 2018; Barman 2015).

The literature has identified a number of potential benefits of MOOCs, such as extending public outreach and offering free education for all (Henningsohn et al. 2017; Stöhr et al. 2019). MOOCs, given their massive scale and the possibilities to re-use course material, are also argued by some to act as a cost-efficient way of offering higher education (e.g. Ruth 2012). Further, MOOCs could provide higher education students with the opportunity to study courses from universities other than those they are admitted to. MOOCs could be a way to combat the increasing income-related gaps affecting access to higher education which, for example, in the US, continue to increase (Haveman and Smeeding 2006). This potential affordance of MOOCs also brings into focus the option that they may provide a way for universities to practise responsible agency in society, taking responsibility not only for educating for domestic purposes but also demonstrating a global claim to provide education for all. In addition, responsibility with respect to MOOCs may be achieved through the introduction and utilisation of new and emerging technologies. For instance, distance or blended learning approaches create opportunities for non-traditional students, as admission policies can be changed to allow larger groups of students to attend introductory MOOC courses as a way of identifying students with an aptitude for a subject. Moreover, it may be argued that this opening up of education via MOOCs could be a way for Swedish universities to comply with the so-called third mission, which states that, in addition to research and education, universities should engage in public outreach, and the dissemination of knowledge from the university into society at large:

The mandate of higher education institutions shall include third stream activities and the provision of information about their activities, as well as ensuring that benefit is derived from their research findings. (Swedish Higher Education Act, §1, Section 2)

As such, MOOCs may be one way for Swedish universities to extend their public outreach at a global level. Viewed through an outreach perspective, MOOCs appear to be a promising way for Nordic HEIs to embrace the notion of being a responsible stakeholder in society (Kahlroth et al. 2016; Santos et al. 2017). In doing so, MOOCs could act as a vehicle for the delivery of the United Nations Sustainable Development goal number 4, aiming to "Ensure inclusive and quality education for all and promote lifelong learning" (United Nations 2018). Consequently, MOOCs could serve universities to act responsively to the needs of the global society by extending their education offerings to a global public, disseminating their knowledge and provide free education to all.

More sceptical voices, on the other hand, may view MOOC initiatives as little more than costly sales pitches for universities to recruit top students, or even more insidiously, as a way of reinforcing colonial views of knowledge and knowing that run contrary to and risk de-legitimising local knowledge production (Deimann 2015; Bali and Sharma 2017). Those voices question the pedagogical quality of MOOCs (e.g. Vardi

2012; Chafkin 2013). Also, the question of credentialing and quality assurance regarding institutions and MOOCs that offer higher education credits is debated. Evidently, MOOC initiatives come with several, and at times, conflicting expectations.

Universities that have developed MOOCs, as well as public debate surrounding MOOCs, have often emphasised many of the affordances outlined above under the guise of *free education, anywhere, anytime*, evoking near mythical connotations (Pappano 2012; Deimann 2015). Given the tradition of offering tuition-free education in Sweden, in this chapter we discuss how offering MOOCs resonates with the notion of the responsible university from the perspective of Swedish higher education. We reason about which roles MOOC initiatives may play in the Swedish higher education context by describing the response to the MOOC phenomenon in three universities: Karolinska Institutet (KI), Chalmers University of Technology (Chalmers) and KTH Royal Institute of Technology (KTH). To inform the discussion, we analysed *notions of intent* expressed in these three universities' formal MOOC statements, including visions, MOOC project missions, strategies and internal calls for engaging teachers. To discuss the meaning of the MOOC initiatives and the roles these may play, we juxtapose the discourses expressed in these written documentations with an adaptation of a framework by Christensen et al. (2007) on how public organisations negotiate bounded realities and how these discourses may reflect the notion of the responsible university.

The remainder of the chapter is structured as follows: After a short introduction to the history of MOOCs and its major promises that can be connected to the notion of the responsible university, we describe the emergence of MOOCs in the Swedish and the Nordic context and discuss some of the challenges for HEIs in Sweden to offer MOOCs. Finally, we discuss what role MOOC initiatives may play in the Swedish higher education (HE) context, based on a document analysis of the rationalities for offering MOOCs at three Swedish universities. This is followed by some concluding remarks about MOOCs and the responsible university in the Swedish context.

What Are MOOCs and How Have They Developed?

The term 'MOOCs' dates back to Stephen Downes and George Siemens, who developed and ran a course known as CCK08 "Connectivism and Connectivity Knowledge" in 2008 (Siemens 2013). The 25 campus students attending the course were accompanied by 2300 online participants from around the world (Fini 2009). However, the popularisation of MOOCs is typically attributed to Peter Norvig and Sebastian Thrun's MOOC "Introduction to Artificial Intelligence" in 2011: 160,000 learners enrolled and more than 20,000 completed that course (Rodriguez 2012). A few months later, Thrun founded Udacity, the first MOOC repository, followed by Coursera, founded by Stanford professors Andrew Ng and Daphne Koller in April 2012, and edX, a partnership between Harvard University and MIT in May 2012.

The two MOOCs mentioned above applied very different pedagogies and served as the basis for the most established MOOC typology: cMOOCs and xMOOCs. cMOOC refers to the concept of connectivism that stresses the role of distributed knowledge networks. Connectivist MOOCs, such as CCK08, attempt to create many-to-many relations between learners by emphasising learner autonomy, peer-to-peer learning and social networking (Rodriguez 2013). Content is developed collaboratively by participants in smaller communities with a shared interest in a specific phenomenon (Siemens 2013) and spread through various collaborative tools, including blog posts and discussion forums. xMOOCs take a more traditional, tutor-centric approach to learning, establishing a one-to-many relationship. This typically involves a combination of video lectures and automatically graded quizzes and tests. The automated assessment and feedback allow for the inclusion of large (/massive) numbers of learners, as Norvig and Thrun's MOOC demonstrated. Teacher-learner and learner-learner interactions are non-mandatory and often reduced to reading and writing in a discussion forum. In the public discourse, the term MOOC is usually used synonymously with the xMOOC model (Moe 2015).

The *New York Times* named 2012 "The Year of the MOOC" (Pappano 2012). As a potential force in higher education, it was argued that MOOCs have the potential to revolutionise, but also to threaten traditional higher education (Yuan and Powell 2013). Key advantages of MOOCs include (Huang 2015):

- an increased learner flexibility due to the asynchronous studies of a few hours per week over a shorter or longer period, such as 5–15 weeks
- global, free access enabling anyone to "learn on schedule, anytime, anywhere"
- a flexible pedagogy, allowing learners to learn at their own pace and style
- online communities for active learners
- reduced costs through scalability and repeated usage
- various functions to fit the different needs of lifelong learners.

Interest in Massive Open Online Courses has grown tremendously worldwide, and they have become a part of the international educational and education research landscape. Today (December 2018), more than 900 education institutions offer more than 11,000 MOOCs with over 101 million subscribed learners (Shah 2018). Universities are thereby not the only course providers, as companies (e.g. Microsoft and IBM) or other organisations (e.g. the Linux foundation and Amnesty International) increasingly engage in MOOC development as well. Additional MOOC providers, such as FutureLearn, were founded and the major platforms also offer MOOCs in a range of languages, such as Mandarin, Hindi, Korean, French and Spanish, to name a few.

The MOOC landscape has evolved and currently includes a broad selection of course-like offerings in various formats, such as cMOOCs, xMOOCs and mixtures of both. It also inspired the birth of similar concepts such as quasi-MOOCs (e.g. Khan Academy), extremely short Nano Open Online Courses (NOOCs), pop-up MOOCs addressing highly topical issues, as well as somewhat alternative models such as Small Private Online Courses (SPOCS). In recent years, the major MOOC providers have also encouraged universities to bundle their MOOCs into programmes. The MOOC series programmes often target professionals and include highly specialised skills training. Some providers go even further, offering a complete online master's programme, like Coursera (www. coursera.org/degree), or edX's MicroMasters, which is a series of courses at graduate level which, upon successful completion, lead to an own-standing professional certificate and offer a pathway to credit in a regular master's programme in the MOOC-hosting university (Stöhr 2018).

MOOCs and Free Access to Education

A fundamental idea of MOOCs is to provide easily accessible learning materials via the internet that can be free of charge. MOOCs, particularly in the early years, were seen as a way of providing access to high quality education from cutting edge researchers, to a broad audience. A major promise is thereby the provision of education to disadvantaged, underprivileged groups who are without access to established routes to higher education. In this respect, the major platform and course providers have, over the years, shared several success stories about how people with limited access to higher education have improved their lives or living conditions for their societies after gaining new knowledge via MOOCs. Such an example is the story about a small village in Colombia that gained electricity after building a generator utilising solar energy. Other examples include the establishment of a network of women in the Middle East that accessed education as a result of participating in MOOCs from their homes, or how patients have learned to understand illness and sought hospital care as a result of having attended a MOOC on urology.

MOOCs may offer HEIs ways to be responsive and address urgent societal challenges, such as the recent stream of refugees, by contributing with large-scale, accessible education (see e.g. https://kiron.ngo, Kahlroth et al. 2016). However, Swedish universities' options for taking action to meet such urgent national or global social challenges are limited. In Denmark, Norway and Finland, universities may offer and assess individuals in continuing professional development (CPD) at a cost (Kahlroth et al. 2016; Danmarks Akkrediteringsinstitution 2016). In Sweden, however, CPD is restricted by the mandate given to higher education institutions (Higher Education Ordinance, SFS: 2002:760). Currently, the Swedish system allows for contracts between companies and HEIs in the form of commissioned education, but universities cannot in other ways provide higher education credits for individuals outside the regular admission system. In addition, many Swedish universities are legal authorities and as such, are regulated by the administrative law, which makes little room for initiatives outside the mandate provided to legal authorities. Universities that wish to act upon and take responsibility in situations, such as the one we outlined above, need to be appointed a special mission by the government, or collaborate and seek contracts with other organisations.

MOOC Credentials and Business Models

In general, MOOCs that are "open for all" do not provide higher education credentials, but participants that fulfil course requirements may be offered certificates of participation for small handling fees or significantly reduced fees, compared to regular university tuitions. MOOC certificates thus offer proof of skills verified by universities, and according to the major course providers, MOOC certificates are proof of competence development and marketed as career advantages of interest for employers (Santos et al. 2017). However, an increasing trend is seeing MOOC providers offering learners the opportunity to transfer MOOC credits to HE credits (Danmarks Akkrediteringsinstitution 2016, www.coursera.org, www.edx.org). Since MOOC fees in general are significantly lower than regular tuition fees, there may be a strong incentive for potential higher education students to participate in and earn MOOC credits. In line with a broader marketisation of higher education, MOOC initiatives enable universities to adopt business models where student populations can be increased, thus providing revenue via tuition fees. At the same time, universities are visible on the global market and can attract new students. Initially, MOOC providers emphasised the free-for-all dimension of access while highlighting the non-profit dimensions. However, more recently providers have refined their business models to increase the numbers of paying learners. For example, recently edX changed their policy with the consequence that not all learning material is accessed for free, and courses are only open for a limited period of time unless learners pay for verified certificates.

MOOCs and Inclusiveness

In addition to access, MOOCs offer flexibility for learners on several levels. Given the online character of courses and the dominance of asynchronous learning activities, course participants are enabled to learn anywhere, anytime and at their own pace, fostering a global, lifelong learning approach to education. Since the beginning, the major MOOC providers require that all learning material is presented in ways that are accessible to a diverse learner population. Such demands include how material should be presented, for example, the combination of sound and texting provided in all videos, or the increased use of screen readers that aid the visually impaired to access and perceive visual material. MOOCs have the potential to meet the needs of diverse learners in various ways. However, a recent study suggests that teachers involved in MOOCs at a Swedish university held quite naive understandings of inclusiveness. One view was, for example, that by virtue of being openly accessible online, the course is in itself inclusive. Teachers with more sophisticated views on inclusive teaching still found it hard to meet the needs of various learners in practice (Barman et al. 2018). Offering education to all by granting access to online course material may create equal opportunities in theory, but questions like translation of learning material into multiple languages and the possible lack of learners' previous higher education experiences are some of the issues that arise and may be difficult to compensate. A more critical question is that of student demographics. There is considerable empirical evidence suggesting that MOOCs mostly benefit those who are already well-educated and struggle to reach disadvantaged, underprivileged groups (e.g. Emanuel 2013). One observation is that typically, MOOCs require a reasonably high degree of self-regulated learning (Littlejohn et al. 2016).

MOOCs in the Swedish Context

Sweden is well known to be a country in the forefront of technological developments, not least in the context of higher education. For example, Sweden has a long tradition of distance learning (Elf et al. 2015). However, in the European context, Sweden was neither particularly quick nor slow in its response to the global MOOC movement. Independent from the MOOC developments in the US, the first MOOC-like offerings from HEIs in Sweden date back to the beginning of the millennium and targeted a native speaking public. An early collaboration between Stockholm University and KTH (later including several HEIs) aimed to provide math courses (in 2002) to bridge the students' secondary school knowledge of maths with the needs of STEM (Science, Technology, Engineering and Mathematics)-oriented higher education programmes. MOOC-like initiatives primarily targeted towards secondary school pupils were also found in other Nordic countries, such as Finland, that were offering open online courses in Finnish in 2010. In Denmark, three universities partnered and offered MOOCs in English via the global platform Coursera in 2013. Today, a number of MOOCs are offered in Danish from other platforms with less global reach (Kahlroth et al. 2016). Initiatives from Iceland came later, but in 2018, a few MOOCs could be found on edX (www.edx.org). Since the global MOOC hype started, governments in the Nordic countries have in various ways taken action for enabling the universities to offer MOOCs (Kahlroth et al. 2016).

When the first course offerings from Swedish HEIs started to appear on the major global platforms in 2014, it was still unclear to what extent MOOCs could be developed and offered as part of the higher education mission. In Sweden, the initiative started with a few top-ranked research-intensive universities that usually partnered with one of the two major MOOC providers, edX and Coursera. Unlike countries such as France and Norway (Brown et al. 2015), Sweden did not develop a national strategy for addressing MOOCs. In Norway, for example, as early as 2013, a commission was set up to investigate possibilities and challenges with respect to MOOCs (NOU 2014). In Sweden, the lack of national policies and guidelines for MOOC development from HEIs was pointed out in the Swedish Higher Education Authority's report published in 2016 (Kahlroth et al. 2016). Kahlroth et al. (Ibid.) directed attention to a number of challenges related to MOOC offerings from HEIs in Sweden, such as handling of personal data utilised for learning analytics and research. Also considered was whether MOOCs could be offered via funding provided by the state, and if offering MOOCs corresponded to the mandate given to HEIs in Sweden (Ibid.). Since the beginning, the number of HEIs in Sweden that offer MOOCs for global outreach has increased, although the offerings are, to this date, quite modest. We found 60 unique courses from eight different universities in Sweden offered via the major platforms, including Coursera, edX, FutureLearn and Canvas Network between the years 2014 and 2019.

Higher education in Sweden, as in all Nordic countries, has a long tradition of being tuition-free. It has been less than a decade (since 2011) that non-Europeans/or non-EEC members (European Economic Community) are required to pay tuition for their university studies in Sweden. The universities in Sweden are governed by the Higher Education Act (1992:1434) and in addition, the Higher Education Ordinance (1993:100), stipulating that higher education should be non-profitable. These conditions rule out the business models used in many other countries where MOOCs are used as a means to finance, for example, teachers' engagements in public outreach. From September 1, 2018, the Higher Education Ordinance (1993:100, chapter 11) stipulates that public funding can be used to create and offer MOOCs, and that certificates can be issued upon course completion. However, the ordinance states that MOOCs are *open*, which means that HE admission processes do not apply. Consequently, MOOCs are not a part of the higher education offerings in Sweden, and hence the participants are not deemed students in higher education. The HE Ordinance legitimises HEIs in Sweden to offer MOOCs, but still there are a number of "grey areas" that remain, such as the practicalities around issuing of certificates or the validation process for recognising individual students' MOOC certificates as part of their HE studies; these issues have, in our experience, continued to create debate locally. Currently, proof of MOOC completions would follow the same validation process as other testimonials of prior learning made from practice and not be considered higher education credits. In the public debate, the MOOC offering in Sweden is strongly connected to the universities' social responsibility and an increased pressure to offer possibilities for lifelong learning (Universitetskanslerämbetet 2017). Whether the initiatives to engage in MOOCs will lead to new policy in Sweden for offering education to non-enrolled higher education students remains to be seen.

Rationalities for Offering MOOCs at Three Swedish Universities

So far, we have focused this discussion on how MOOCs may be one way for higher education institutions in general, and particularly in Sweden, to broaden its mission by educating society at large and how this reflects on HEIs as being a responsible agent. In this passage, we discuss what role

MOOC initiatives may play in the Swedish HE context from the perspective of how three HE institutions have positioned their initiatives to engage in and offer MOOCs. We have chosen to inform this discussion by examining the intentions with their respective MOOC initiatives expressed by three universities, each with a strong profile on taking social responsibility in their research and education fields of medicine and health (Karolinska Institutet), and technology and engineering (Chalmers University of Technology and KTH Royal Institute of Technology). Furthermore, Karolinska Institutet was the first Swedish university to provide free, globally available MOOCs in October 2014. Between 2015 and 2019, Chalmers and KTH offered the highest number of MOOCs through the major global platforms, including two varieties of MOOC programmes: MicroMasters and the Professional Certificate programme. Our discussion about the role that MOOC initiatives may play for universities in Sweden is based on the analysis of key MOOC-related documents outlining the vision, mission and strategy at the three universities. We choose to include documents in the public domain, such as overall university strategies, and internal documents identified as being central to MOOC initiatives within each university. These include the universities' calls for teachers to engage in MOOCs and the MOOC mission or project statements. Although the overall university strategies do not address the MOOCs as a central theme, these documents were of interest as they include digital learning visions and strategies during the development of MOOCs at the respective universities (2014–2018). First, we provide a brief introduction to the universities and their respective MOOC initiatives.

Karolinska Institutet (KI)

Karolinska Institutet (KI) offers a broad range of education in medicine and health sciences at both undergraduate and graduate levels and accounts for over 40 per cent of the medical academic research conducted in Sweden. Since 1901, the Nobel Assembly at Karolinska Institutet has selected the Nobel laureates in Physiology or Medicine. In 2013, KI was the first university in Sweden to join edX as a charter member, with the outspoken ambition to offer MOOCs that represent a broad spectrum of KI life science education and to share the knowledge generated at KI with a broad and global audience. KI claims that the MOOCs are further expected to contribute to a commitment to quality education that can lead to an improvement of human health. To date, KI offers 12 unique MOOCs on edX. The courses run as tutored courses with staff on hand or as self-paced courses where the course activities, materials and assessments are available without active engagement from staff members.

Chalmers University of Technology (Chalmers)

Chalmers University of Technology is a research-intensive university that offers education in technology, science, shipping and architecture, with a sustainable future as its global vision. Unlike many other Swedish universities, Chalmers has the status of a private foundation university making it somewhat less dependent on Swedish regulation for public universities. Chalmers started its engagement with MOOCs in 2014. During a three-year pilot project, eight MOOCs were produced and conducted, addressing different engineering and sustainability-related topics from introductory up to advanced level. As part of Chalmers "lifelong learning" strategy, the project was followed by a second MOOC project that aims at developing a MicroMasters programme in "Emerging Automotive Technologies." The MicroMasters programme is a series of seven MOOCs that, when completed, provides learners with a company-endorsed certificate and potential accreditation for students that are admitted through the regular system to study at Chalmers.

KTH Royal Institute of Technology (KTH)

KTH is the largest technical research and learning institution in Sweden that offers study programmes in engineering, teaching and architecture. KTH positions itself as an innovative European university working with industry and society in the pursuit of sustainable solutions to some of humanity's greatest challenges, such as climate change and future energy supply. KTH joined as a contributing member of edX in 2015 with the ambition to develop capacity for offering MOOCs with global outreach within engineering and related subjects. Up to this date, 16 unique courses and several re-runs have been developed, as well as two Professional Certificate Programmes targeting industry professionals. At KTH, the course material from several MOOCs has been transferred to the regular campus courses.

The MOOCs offered by KI, Chalmers and KTH are all in English and targeted towards the general public, professionals within certain fields, or are suitable for higher education students or even graduates at masters or doctoral levels. Table 5.1 presents a brief overview of the courses offered by the three universities, focusing on the main intended audience and levels of specialisation.

MOOC and Discourses of Change

A recurring theme in the MOOC rhetoric is the notion of global outreach (Deimann 2015). MOOCs are used to enable the universities a place in the global higher education arena, and thus provide an opportunity to market the institution and its research and education, while strengthening their profile as being socially responsible. Both these affordances could be expected to drive the MOOC initiatives at the three universities discussed here, and these rationalities are part of the universities' intentions with their respective MOOC initiatives (see overview in Table 5.2). However, by examining how the three universities express their respective *notions of intent* related to MOOCs, another discourse also stands out: namely, how universities are using the MOOC initiatives to drive change within each institution. To better understand the role that MOOC initiatives may play at these universities, we performed a content analysis (Graneheim and Lundman 2004) of the overall university's vision and MOOC-related mission statements, teaching and learning strategies (where MOOCs are mentioned) and internal calls related to the MOOC initiatives at KI, Chalmers and KTH. The analysis showed two very different motives where the MOOC initiatives aim for *external recognition and social responsibility*, but at the same time

Table 5.1 MOOC offerings 2014–2019

Main target group	Karolinska Institutet	Chalmers	KTH
General public *Anyone without prior knowledge in the area.*	Behavioural medicine Introduction to global health eHealth	Sustainability in everyday life Sensing planet earth—from core to outer space Sensing planet earth—water and ice	Sustainable development for engineers and problem solvers I–II Human spaceflight
Students or professionals *Enhance knowledge/skills in specific areas of working-life or undergraduate studies.*	Statistics with R Life science innovation Physical examination and history taking Introduction to urology CARE I–V, series targeted caregiving for elderly	Computer systems design for energy efficiency System design for supply chain management and logistics Master control in supply chain management and logistics	Proficiency in risk management of manual handling proactively I–III/*Prof. Certificate Programme* Digital transformation I–IV/*Prof. Certificate Programme* Philosophy of science for engineers and scientists
Highly advanced courses *Students or professionals with sufficient knowledge for masters/doctoral-level courses.*	Pragmatic randomised controlled trials	Emerging automotive technologies I–VII *MicroMasters programme* Graphene science and technology Advanced concepts of microprocessors	High performance finite element modelling I–II Reliable distributed algorithms I–II Cyber physical networks

Table 5.2 MOOC rationalities at Karolinska Institutet, Chalmers and KTH

Intentions include the aim to strengthen	Examples from documents
MOOC initiatives as EXTERNAL recognition and social responsibility	
Marketing, including display of strong research areas and attracting new students	"Brand profiling where Chalmers increases its visibility with regard to its vision of sustainable development both through content and the target groups' ability to change their environment and future." (*aim in the MOOC project directive Chalmers*) "The objectives of the activities of MOOCs are to: [...] contribute to making KI's educational programmes and research more widely known." (*KI MOOC strategy*) "The purpose of this cooperation agreement is to [...] broaden the opportunities for student recruitment [...]." (*KTH agreement for cooperation with edX*)
Offering of lifelong learning, including contribution to educate professionals in defined fields	"Lifelong learning. The Micromasters program should provide a qualification in line with the needs of at least one company." (*aim in the resolution MicroMasters Chalmers*) "The objectives of the activities of MOOCs are to disseminate and make available knowledge on medicine and health issues globally." (*KI MOOC strategy*)
Internationalisation and collaborations	"E-learning is developed in order to facilitate collaboration with other leading universities and to strengthen the internationalisation of KTH." (*Vision for e-learning KTH*) "The purpose of this cooperation agreement is to better meet the future challenges and developments through collaborations with other leading member universities around the world [...]." (*KTH agreement for cooperation with edX*)
MOOC initiatives as INTERNAL development of processes	
Digitalisation and improved education for on-campus students	"Chalmers needs to set even more focus on quality and modernisation that meet the expectations on individualized education; to develop the pedagogy of existing courses by utilizing IT-technology from MOOCs." (*MOOC project directive Chalmers*) "An important purpose of KTHs MOOC investment is to strengthen and develop the current campus education." (*KTH offer*)

(continued)

Table 5.2 (continued)

Intentions include the aim to strengthen	Examples from documents
Scholarly work on flexible/ scalable teaching and learning	"KTH's main goal with entering into this collaboration agreement can be summarized as such that KTH's MOOCs should enhance research and development regarding the pedagogy of online learning." (*decision MOOC steering group KTH*)
Internal competence development	"Contribute to the fulfilment of KI's need of knowledge within general skills such as, for example, sustainable development, equal conditions and ethics." (*KI MOOC strategy*)

Analysis of MOOC intentions expressed in the vision, mission and strategy documents and MOOC calls at Chalmers, Karolinska Institutet and KTH, 2014–2018

are intended to *drive the development of various internal processes* (see Table 5.2).

To understand the prevailing notions of what purpose the MOOCs may serve, we adapted Christensen et al.'s (2007) conceptual framework for explaining how public organisations are formed, maintained and governed. The framework suggests three perspectives: one instrumental (the instrumental perspective) and two institutional (the mythical and cultural perspectives) (Christensen et al. 2007). The different perspectives offer a way of understanding how public organisations negotiate a bounded rationality where the universities' statements of goals, strategies and policies are to a large extent based on a rationalist perspective, but where the enactment of these statements takes place in an ever-changing environment. The consequence of this is that the outcomes of various governing statements are highly contingent on uncontrollable and external factors, but also on internal cultural factors. As such, the instrumental and mythical perspectives provide a sort of push/pull effect on the organisation with the purpose of stipulating key performance outcomes (instrumental), while simultaneously providing rhetoric of change (mythical). In this chapter, we have modified the framework outlined above, and argue that the discourses expressed in the various 'goal documents' may serve a number of purposes, both instrumental and mythical, aimed at internal and external audiences at the same time, as shown in Table 5.2.

At all three universities, the MOOC initiatives were initially set up as projects where an experimental approach was encouraged. The idea to experiment relates to one key element expressed in the universities' rationales for offering MOOCs, which is the discourse of change and development of internal university processes. The discourses expressed in various goal documents are used to build a narrative around the change, which is reflected in what Christensen et al. (2007) refer to as the mythical perspective. This perspective offers insight into the different notions that the universities wish to convey during the process of change, for example, the ways in which hype regarding the MOOC suggests that education is free for anyone. The mythical perspective as an analytical tool also reveals how universities position themselves as key stakeholders in society, and this may be used to comment on the purpose the university plays when engaging with broader society. Here, we argue that the rhetoric used in these narratives show the current myths that universities strive to cultivate. Universities across the globe are using similar rhetoric in the face of innovation and emerging technologies in relation to MOOCs, and one may suspect a degree of institutional isomorphism. The mythical perspective, we argue, is meant to appeal to both external and internal stakeholders. For example, when KI writes that MOOCs will: *satisfy global knowledge requirements and the demand within medicine and health*, and also *meet national and international demand within subject-specific fields of competence which exist at KI*, it is clear that KI is talking to an external audience, and making claims that position KI as a responsible actor in a global context whose offering of MOOCs may, in some capacity, contribute to addressing global needs for "knowledge requirements." Similarly, Chalmers justified the MOOC initiative among other things with the need to *strengthen its trademark as a modern, progressive, technical university with a strong sustainability vision, and a global view on education and open access*. The documents also point to the role of MOOCs to adapt to the *changing needs of companies for customised professional education* that is offered by Chalmers. In contrast, the mythical perspective also plays a role for creating meaning and rationalising MOOCs within the university.

Analysis of the documents provided input regarding how myths are brought to the fore. In relation to the three universities discussed here, the documents provide more clarity for internal stakeholders, such as university management or educational leaders. For example, the MOOCs are expected to fulfil a wide range of needs, including; *contribute to the fulfilment of KI's need of knowledge within general skills such as, for example, sustainable development, equal conditions and ethics.* Hence, this statement suggests that the choice of courses would rather be based on internal competence development needs, albeit with a strong social responsibility dimension, than the dissemination of knowledge. Further, the MOOC format and its continuous development as a way of digitalising higher education and increasing capacity for teaching scalability are intended to revolutionise, or at least develop, the internal support for digitalisation of education. For example, KTH motivates teachers to develop MOOCs in saying that it: *aims to strengthen and develop the current campus education, for example in the development of digital educational resources that can be used in MOOCs as well as in regular campus courses.* Chalmers makes a more visionary claim in one document that reads: *MOOCs are a part of a paradigm shift, where we see education through new lenses; where concepts such as "connected learning,", individualised and customised knowledge appear as increasingly important.*

All three universities connect their respective MOOC initiatives to the development of internal processes related to the digitalisation of educa-tion. For example, there is a focus on re-usability and transfer of course material created for MOOCs to campus education to ensure an efficient use of resources. In addition, engaging in MOOCs aims to increase knowledge about teaching and learning which, it could be argued, offers a form of rationalised myth (Christensen et al. 2007). In this way costs could perhaps be legitimised, but it also brings the MOOC initiatives closer to the universities' core of doing scholarly work. For example, the MOOC initiative at KTH aims to *increase the knowledge of how digital learning resources can be created and used for scalable teaching-learning and educational innovation.* In relation to the universities' drive for innova-tion, MOOCs provide unique research opportunities through detailed documentation of thousands of learners' online activities. Globally, MOOCs have fed data into the emerging fields, such as learning analytics or big data in education, with the promise to utilise massive amounts of click-stream data and provide insights about the unique learning paths of the participants and their performances (e.g. Zhua et al. 2018). We argue that using massive amounts of data to provide an evidence-based rationale for innovation and enhancement serves as an attractive myth to strengthen the self-perception of research-intensive universities. However, there are also opposing arguments that stress the difference between measuring learners' behaviour on platforms and facilitating learning processes that, for example, depend on the learners' intentions and needs (Ross et al. 2014; Barman et al. 2018). Apart from gaining knowledge about learners' behaviour in online environments, the MOOC initiatives are also expected to result in the possibility of adapting learning resources to individual students' needs and fostering a student-centred, personalised approach to education. For example, Chalmers states their desire to: *set even more focus on quality and modernisation that meet the expectations on individualised education.*

Various types of goal documents may act as specific instruments of governance, indicating the direction in which an organisation aims to strive, where the words and concepts used reverberate through the different stages of implementation. Such a rational form of instrumentalisation offers a tool for governing large-scale change initiatives or for controlling implementation of major reforms. The instrumental perspective also affords tools for quality control and accountability, where the key words used in various goal documents may then form the basis for checks and balances. In the case of MOOC, such tools for accountability could include outreach in terms of number of individuals, countries and other demographic information. In the documents we see how the instrumental perspective is articulated by pointing out the many ways in which MOOCs could be used internally within the university. For example, MOOC should *be able to be used as educational modules in existing courses,* but also *contribute to the development of digital teaching at KI's educational programmes.* Similarly, Chalmers attempts *to develop the pedagogy of existing courses by utilising IT technology from MOOCs.* In addition, the instrumental dimension there also includes the generation of *indirect income through a strengthened trademark, higher application rates to campus programmes and possible income from administrative fees.*

The MOOC Phenomenon and the Responsible University

The public discussion about MOOCs so far has focused on the extent to which MOOCs could be a disruptive force in the higher education setting. Broadly, questions have been raised as to whether MOOCs undermine traditional pathways through higher education, thus enabling a change in the demographics where non-traditional students gain access to higher education. Concerns have also been raised that Ivy League universities may threaten the very existence of a diverse HE arena around the world. Others have acknowledged that MOOCs could bring about a change in the certification of higher education credit, with some examples of this already starting to appear (McKenzie 2018).

Given that the MOOCs are rather limited in content and design, and costly to develop, we argue that it is unlikely that MOOCs will replace regular higher education, at least in the near future. In this chapter, we have shown that MOOCs in the Swedish context are not considered to be higher education, even though HEIs are, since fall 2018, mandated to offer MOOCs and use state funding for that purpose. However, given that the course content in the MOOC offerings from the universities illustrated in this chapter are fairly advanced (see Table 5.1), individuals' learning outcomes gained via MOOCs can be equivalent to knowledge acquired in higher education, and sometimes even at research level. Clearly, offering MOOCs enables universities to take a social responsibility to educate on a global scale and share knowledge that contributes to sustainable development in important areas such as energy and health. In this chapter, we have outlined a number of those affordances that MOOCs potentially provide, including access to knowledge from HEIs to diversified and unprivileged groups, flexibility and customisable learning trajectories. However, from the perspective of Swedish HE, we have also identified potentially conflicting rationalities that arise between maintaining strong norms of free, state-funded education and the developing business models of the MOOC platform providers that restricts the presumed openness of MOOCs.

Besides the obvious and somewhat mythical rationale for offering MOOCs that allow universities to engage in social responsibility, we argue that for HEIs to be frugal it depends on how well they develop and integrate the processes and lessons learned from engaging in MOOC initiatives that will ultimately show responsibility. From the three university examples used in this chapter, we have seen how the initiatives to engage in MOOCs are, among other things, intended for capacity-building and digitalising education. Examples of such spill-over effects from MOOCs to regular university education could be to implement requirements on inclusive teaching that are currently connected to MOOCs; this would meet the needs of diverse students and benefit higher education at large. At the same time, the capacity of the universities to offer, and thereby meet, an increasing need for flexible forms of lifelong learning to private and public organisations, is also likely to be strengthened. In the long term, in order to meet the needs of graduates concerning re-skilling and up-skilling, MOOCs could facilitate collaborations by offering education between universities nationally and internationally, as well as between universities and organisations. In Sweden, this means that new policy or clarification regarding credentialing and credit transfer is needed.

In light of the changing MOOC arena, we believe claims that MOOCs are one way of universities being responsible needs further scrutiny. For example, universities might attempt to adapt to the business models currently implemented by the major MOOC providers. This may be a cost-efficient way of providing outreach, but it is likely to create a conflict with the ideas of openness and providing MOOCs for free, as well as contrast with strong norms in the Swedish and Nordic contexts that HEIs should provide tuition-free education. The 'openness' in MOOCs provided by the major platforms, and thus many of the worlds' most prestigious universities, seems to be on the decline. Therefore, we see the potential for the Swedish and Nordic HEIs to take responsibility in continuing to provide free access to MOOCs. This ambition seems particularly important in an era when information is easily spread and almost anyone can claim to provide facts about important issues in society. Universities in Sweden and in the Nordic context are in a position where, at least to some extent, information that is provided by universities to the public does not have to create revenue or be politically managed and, from those perspectives can be considered trustworthy. The private sector may invest in and offer online courses for skills training that is related to their business offerings, such as specific computer applications; whereas universities can potentially provide more advanced topics based on the idea of continuing to foster academic and critical approaches in activities for lifelong learning and global outreach. MOOCs developed at Swedish universities in the future, we speculate, are likely to offer lifelong learning opportunities for graduates and highly skilled professionals or otherwise, serve as a complement to HE studies. MOOCs based on the tradition of "folk-bildung" that rhymes with notions of public outreach and education for all, we believe, will only be offered to a limited extent.

Acknowledgements We wish to express our gratitude to colleagues at the department of Learning, KTH, and, to Cathrine Tømte at the University of Agder, as well as to the editors of this book for insightful comments on this chapter. Also, we wish to thank all participants in the Workshop series who made this book happen!

References

Bali, M. A., & Sharma, S. (2017). Envisioning Post-Colonial MOOCs: Critiques and Ways Forward. In R. Bennett & M. Kent (Eds.), *Massive Open Online Courses and Higher Education: What Went Right, What Went Wrong and Where to Next?* (pp. 26–44). New York: Routledge.

Barman, L. (2015). *Striving for Autonomy. Health Sciences Teachers' Enactment of Policy.* Thesis for Doctoral Degree. Stockholm: Karolinska Institutet.

Barman, L., Naimi-Akbar, I., McGrath, C., & Weurlander, M. (2018). *Engineering Teachers' Approaches to Design and Deliver Teaching in Flexible Learning Spaces.* Paper presented at the Frontiers in education 2018. Fostering Innovation Through Diversity, San Jose, California, USA.

Brown, M., Costello, E., Donlon, E., & Giolla-Mhichil, M. N. (2015). A Strategic Response to MOOCs: How One European University Is Approaching the Challenge. *The International Review of Research in Open and Distributed Learning, 16*(6), 98–115. https://doi.org/10.19173/irrodl.v16i6.2151.

Chafkin, M. (2013). Udacity's Sebastian Thrun, Godfather of Free Online Education, Changes Course. *Tech Forecast.* Retrieved December 10, 2018, from http://www.fastcompany.com/3021473/udacity-sebastian-thrun-uphill-climb.

Christensen, T., Lægreid, P., Roness, P. G., & Røvik, K. A. (2007). *Organization Theory and the Public Sector: Instrument, Culture and Myth. Organization Theory and the Public Sector: Instrument, Culture and Myth.* London: Routledge. https://doi.org/10.4324/9780203929216.

Danmarks Akkrediteringsinstitution. (2016). *MOOCs kvalitet og perspektiver.* Rapport, Danmarks Akkrediteringsinstitution Köpenhamn, Danmark.

Deimann, M. (2015). The Dark Side of the MOOC-A Critical Inquiry on Their Claims and Realities. *Current Issues in Emerging eLearning, 2*, 1. https:// scholarworks.umb.edu/ciee/vol2/iss1/3/.

EIT Health. (2018). EIT Health Home. Retrieved December 8, 2018, from https://www.eithealth.eu/.

Elf, M., Ossiannilsson, E., Neljesjö, M., & Jansson, M. (2015). Implementation of Open Educational Resources in a Nursing Programme: Experiences and Reflections. *Open Learning: The Journal of Open, Distance and e-Learning, 30*(3), 252–266.

Emanuel, E. J. (2013). Online Education: MOOCs Taken by Educated Few. *Nature, 503*, 342–342. https://doi.org/10.1038/503342a.

Fini, A. (2009). The Technological Dimension of a Massive Open Online Course: The Case of the CCK08 Course Tools. *The International Review of Research in Open and Distributed Learning, 10*(5). https://doi.org/10.19173/ irrodl.v10i5.643.

Graneheim, U. H., & Lundman, B. (2004). Qualitative Content Analysis in Nursing Research: Concepts, Procedures and Measures to Achieve Trustworthiness. *Nurse Education Today, 24*(2), 105–112.

Haveman, R., & Smeeding, T. (2006). The Role of Higher Education in Social Mobility. *The Future of Children, 16*, 125–150.

Henningsohn, L., Dastaviz, N., Stathakarou, N., & McGrath, C. (2017). KIUrologyX: Urology As You Like It—A Massive Open Online Course for Medical Students, Professionals, Patients, and Laypeople Alike. *European Urology, 72*(3), 321–322. https://doi.org/10.1016/j.eururo.2017.02.034.

Higher Education Act (SFS 1992:1434) Ministry of Research and Education. Stockholm, Sweden.

Higher Education Ordinance (SFS 1993:100). *Swedish Higher Education Ordinance.* Stockholm: Government offices of Sweden. (regulations on con-tract education SFS 2002:760. Retrieved from http://rkrattsbaser.gov.se/ sfst?bet=2002:760).

Huang, C.-L. (2015). MOOCs for Lifelong Learning. *Chengren Ji Zhongshen Jiaoyu = Journal of Adult and Lifelong Education; Taipei, 25*, 1–35. https://doi. org/10.3966/181880012015120025001.

Kahlroth, M., Ejsing, C., Herjevik, M., & Karlsson, N. (2016). *Öppna nätbase-rade kurser (MOOCs) i svensk högskola– Redovisning av ett regeringsuppdrag.* Report 2016:1. Stockholm: Universitetskanslersämbetet.

Littlejohn, A., Hood, N., Milligan, C., & Mustain, P. (2016). Learning in MOOCs: Motivations and Self-Regulated Learning in MOOCs. *The Internet and Higher Education, 29,* 40–48. https://doi.org/10.1016/j.iheduc.2015.12.003.

McKenzie, L. (2018). Online, Cheap—And Elite. *Inside Higher Ed.* Retrieved December 10, 2018, from https://www.insidehighered.com/digital-learning/article/2018/03/20/analysis-shows-georgia-techs-online-masters-computer-science.

Moe, R. (2015). The Brief & Expansive History (and Future) of the MOOC: Why Two Divergent Models Share the Same Name. *Current Issues in Emerging ELearning, 2,* 1. https://scholarworks.umb.edu/ciee/vol2/iss1/2.

NOUn Norges offentlige utredninger. (2014). *MOOCs for Norway New Digital Learning Methods in Higher Education.* Official Norwegian Reports NOU 2014:5. Retrieved December 3, 2018, from https://www.regjeringen.no/contentassets/ff86edace9874505a3381b5daf6848e6/en-gb/pdfs/nou 201420140005000en_pdfs.pdf.

Pappano, L. (2012). The Year of the MOOC. *The New York Times.* Retrieved December 10, 2018, from https://www.nytimes.com/2012/11/04/education/edlife/massive-open-online-courses-are-multiplying-at-a-rapid-pace.html.

Rodriguez, C. O. (2012). MOOCs and the AI-Stanford Like Courses: Two Successful and Distinct Course Formats for Massive Open Online Courses. *European Journal of Open, Distance and E-Learning.* Retrieved December 10, 2018, from https://eric.ed.gov/?id=EJ982976.

Rodriguez, O. (2013). The Concept of Openness Behind c and x-MOOCs (Massive Open Online Courses). *Open Praxis, 5*(1), 67–73.

Ross, J., Sinclair, C., Knox, J., Bayne, S., & Macleod, H. (2014). Teacher Experiences and Academic Identity: The Missing Components of MOOC Pedagogy. *Journal of Online Learning and Teaching, 10*(1), 57–69.

Ruth, S. (2012). *Can MOOC's and Existing E-Learning Efficiency Paradigms Help Reduce College Costs?* SSRN Scholarly Paper No. ID 2086689. Rochester, NY: Social Science Research Network.

Sadurskis, A. (2018). Higher Education in Sweden. *Status Report 2018:10.* Stockholm: Swedish Higher Education Authority.

Santos, A. I. d., YvesPunie, Scheller, K. (2017). Going Open: Policy Recommendations on Open Education in Europe (OpenEdu Policies). *EUR—Scientific and Technical Research Reports*. https://doi.org/10.2760/111707.

Shah, D. (2018). By The Numbers: MOOCS in 2018. Retrieved February 22, 2019, from https://www.class-central.com/report/mooc-stats-2018.

Siemens, G. (2013). Massive Open Online Courses: Innovation in Education? In T. McNamara, R. McGreal, W. Kinuthia, & S. Marshall (Eds.), *Open Educational Resources: Innovation, Research and Practice*. Vancouver: Commonwealth of Learning and Athabasca University.

Stöhr, C. (2018). The MicroMasters Concept as Mixed Blessing—First Experiences from Developing a MOOC Program in "Emerging Automotive Technologies". *EDULEARN18 Proceedings* (pp. 6572–6580). https://doi.org/10.21125/edulearn.2018.1565.

Stöhr, C., Stathakarou, N., Mueller, F., Nifakos, S., & McGrath, C. (2019). Videos as Learning Objects in MOOCs: A Study of Specialist and Non-Specialist Participants' Video Activity in MOOCs. *British Journal of Educational Technology, 50*(1), 166–177.

Universitetskanslersämbetet, UKÄ. (2017). Retrieved December 10, 2018, from http://www.uka.se/om-oss/konferenser%2D%2Dseminarier/konferenser%2D%2Dseminarier/2017-12-04-hogskoleforum.html.

United Nations. (2018). Sustainable Development Goal 4: Quality Education. Retrieved November 11, 2018, from https://www.un.org/sustainabledevelopment/education/.

Vardi, M. Y. (2012). Will MOOCs Destroy Academia? *Communications of the ACM, 55*(11), 5–5. https://doi.org/10.1145/2366316.2366317.

Yuan L., & Powell, S. (2013). *MOOCs and Open Education: Implications for Higher Education, 2013*. JISC CETIS white paper. Retrieved December 10, 2018, from http://publications.cetis.org.uk/2013/667.

Zhua, M., Saria, A., & Miyoung Leeb, M. (2018). A Systematic Review of Research Methods and Topics of the Empirical MOOC Literature (2014–2016). *The Internet and Higher Education, 37*, 31–39.

6

Responsibility of Universities and Co-Creation

Kirsi Pulkkinen and Antti Hautamäki

Introduction: Problems and Solutions in Co-creation

Exploring the meaning of co-creation follows the idea of the entrepreneurial university (Etzkowitz et al. 2008; Clarke 1998). This resembles the idea of searching innovative approaches and embracing renewal of practices to solve problems, without turning universities into business (Lyytinen 2018). Yet, rather than focusing on the variety of possibilities universities could offer, the discussions have centered on the regional and economic impacts (Trencher et al. 2014). The market logic has dominated discussions on the development of universities and their role in society, and largely ignored that the positive economic impact of universities are based on long-standing research efforts that follow the science logic (Berman 2012).

K. Pulkkinen (✉)
University of Lapland, Rovaniemi, Finland
e-mail: Kirsi.pulkkinen@ulapland.fi

A. Hautamäki
University of Jyväskylä, Jyväskylä, Finland

This chapter explores the following research question: *how does co-creation between universities and companies enhance the responsibility of universities?* The responsibility of universities manifests itself on issues how universities help companies and public organizations to adopt and apply new knowledge in solving local and global wicked problems. Co-creation is an effective way to meet this challenge. We are guided by an interest to understand what elements are needed for co-creation to occur, and why and how this form of collaboration is pursued in universities. We approach the research question through an experimental project and place it in a broader context of the changing academic working environment. While the experiment provides a micro-level view into the thinking of researchers and businesses, it allows us to explore the sense-making (Weick and Sutcliffe 2005) of two groups of participants in a live setting.

The major reason for developing co-creation models is the failure of a linear model of knowledge transfer (Trencher et al. 2014). Conventional academic dissemination is one-sided and ignores the capability of knowledge users to understand and apply the knowledge. Hence, interest has grown toward identifying more effective ways to improve adaptation of new knowledge during the knowledge creation process. This entails a double-change in mindsets: firstly, that participation in knowledge creation supports *learning by promoting sharing* and, secondly, that in order to access the knowledge of others all actors (including academic researchers) need to open up to have *discussions already during the process of knowledge creation.* Co-creation is a process where the lines between knowledge producers and knowledge users become muddled, and they discuss and work together in solving shared concrete problems. This is the essence of co-creation.

Co-creation in the Evolution of Science-Society Relations

Co-creation is a reflection of European evolution of science-society relations. The status of researchers and universities as the dominant producers and disseminators of knowledge has changed gradually while consultancy companies, think tanks and so on have entered the field. The goal of the modern university to spread knowledge in society has transformed, but continues to connect to the attainment of educated citizenship (Delanty 2001). Mode 1 introduced the linear understanding of technology transfer (Regeer and Bunders 2009; Gibbons et al. 1994). Moving to a co-productive mode 2 presented a more constitutive change, as the operating models of both science and other institutions began a transformation toward joint knowledge creation (Nowotny et al. 2003). Universities started to be envisioned as societal actors among others and the separation of knowledge creators and problem solvers blurred.

In the current situation, societal interaction is increasingly realized through collaboration in a mutually beneficial process (e.g. see Prahalad and Ramaswamy 2004; Ramaswamy and Gouillart 2010; Trencher et al. 2014). The change is seen also in policy developments, such as changing EU's funding instruments from "Science and Society" to "Science in Society" and further to "Science with and for Society" and has pushed to formalize the new working environment. Governmental steering functions are increasingly used to legitimize the existence of universities and use of public funds (Välimaa 2004). As with governance, a policy convergence process seems to appear also in relation to the pressure to increase societal interaction (Pulkkinen et al. 2019). Governments are changing the discourse, rules and policies of knowledge transfer and interaction. These are adapted to local level as the concepts that govern our understanding of science-society relations change, leading ultimately to behavioral changes in research communities (Moisio 2018). The Finnish Strategic Research Council funding instrument (Aarrevaara and Pulkkinen 2016) is a case in point.

Societal interaction is part of the social contract and accountability of universities (de Jong et al. 2016). However, the internal tensions of science communities and the contradictory expectations posed on universities also surface. Open science and the push to commercialize research have raised questions about intellectual property rights and the need to verify scientific quality through expose to counter-argument and conventional peer review (Nowotny et al. 2003). This balancing act between research integrity (Banks 2018) and economics-driven interaction is reality for researchers. Policy-makers and university managers have marketed co-creation with external arguments but failed to tackle the practical need for tools to manage the contradiction. Understanding the dynamics and underlying assumptions of research-company co-creation has thus become a crucial element in the process of developing working mechanisms for researchers, universities and companies alike.

Co-creation

We approach co-creation as a transformative path that consists of several steps. The aims of the collaborators define which format is relevant and feasible in a given context. In this chapter, we focus on *bridging co-creation*, which aims at creating connections between two sets of differently thinking and acting participants who share certain interests. Bridging co-creation produces solution proposals for problems that are identified in cooperation between equals rather than in a master-servant setting. This could continue to *experimental co-creation* or co-development, which aims to find solutions to a company's problem by experimenting with options. *Co-research* refers to research that is conducted by a university and company together, and aims to create new knowledge. The work is then more abstract in nature and less focused on solving a particular problem (Hautamäki et al. 2018).

Co-creation is not only collaboration but particularly a mutual learning process (Guile 2010; Hakkarainen et al. 2004). There are no external stakeholders in the co-creating group of participants. Instead, all participants have a stake in the identification and framing of a problem as well as the knowledge creation process. Their stakes vary due to different personal backgrounds and professional roles, but the weight of their stakes is of equal value. This is akin to communities of practice that agree on their shared code of excellence through direct collaboration (Brown and Duguid 2001). Managing the boundary work with science ethical principles intact requires, however, that researchers recognize high-quality science from low-quality and non-science (Vuolanto 2014).

Problem and Solution in Co-creation

Co-creation is analogous to the open innovation paradigm (Chesbrough 2003). The problems to be solved are not defined beforehand by one party, but rather identified through discussions. Co-creation provides a way to tackle unstructured problems, which are difficult to specify and require unconventional approaches. Knowledge production is tightly intertwined with problem solving, making scientific knowledge function side by side with social and experiential knowledge (Regeer and Bunders 2009). Co-creative problem solving thus follows a Schumpeterian idea that solutions are innovations by combining existing know-how and resources (Schumpeter 1934) and build a coherent system of complementary knowledge. The interaction process and the learning open innovation entails is itself a valuable solution as it leads the participants on a path (Spaapen and van Drooge 2011). The solution may not be measurable with indicators. A solution is not expected to be a prototype of a product or service, but rather steps that are necessary to reach a concrete solution. They can also be properly defined and well-targeted questions for new collaborative projects, seeds for an organizational transformation or new applications of existing data.

Conceptual Framework: Dialogue as a Tool for Sharing and Creating Knowledge

We approach co-creation as a phenomenon in a rapidly changing research environment. University institutions and individual researchers operate between multiple pressures (Stilgoe et al. 2013) and respond to external pressure. One of these is connected to finding ways to interact proactively with other actors, and managing to create new knowledge-based value. Responsibility is not portrayed in the number of interactions but rather their quality. As such, responsibility implies actions beyond communication and focuses on creating processes where universities tackle societal challenges. They do not only produce new knowledge but also participate in finding solutions.

Co-creation provides an avenue for this as it is inherently inter-specialist interaction (Karvonen 2014) where researchers need to uphold high scientific quality and integrity, and develop their skillset in order to remain relevant. Inter-specialist interaction is not just academic expertise but rather created through action, which is based on extensive knowledge within a particular field. As such it is a dimension of co-generated learning and knowledge creation (Klev and Levin 2012), but with an essential difference in understanding of inclusion. While co-generated learning and knowledge creation differentiate between insiders and outsiders, our approach to co-creation considers such a separation superfluous and harmful to the building of shared visions. Instead, all stakeholders (Kazadi et al. 2016) are insiders in a shared process. Experts from different fields communicate ideas to each other with the intention of learning, but their language, interaction styles and perspectives differ. Participants are required to acknowledge their own and others' strengths and limitations, while being aware of the differences in use of language. Moving beyond this communicative challenge and further to the process of mixing different expertise to create new knowledge is where co-creative practices serve a purpose.

The SECI model of Nonaka et al. (Nonaka and Konno 1998; Nonaka et al. 2001) provides a structure for conceptualizing co-creation in the academic world. This model (see Fig. 6.1) focuses on converging tacit and explicit knowledge dimensions. Tacit knowledge is internalized in experiences, values and ideals and difficult to formalize, which makes it hard to communicate to others explicitly in words or graphs. It is experiential knowledge, something we know but cannot verbalize (Polanyi 1966). Explicit knowledge, on the other hand, is expressed in words and numbers. It can be communicated through data, formulae, manuals and so on and "be readily transmitted between individuals formally and systematically" (Nonaka and Konno 1998, 42).

In the SECI model, knowledge creation starts with the socialization (S) of discussants and their tacit knowledge. Because tacit knowledge is highly context-specific and difficult to verbalize, its transfer to others requires shared experiences, joint activities and physical proximity (Nonaka et al. 2001). During the externalization (E) phase, the individual participants fuse their ideas to form a new dynamic whole. Participants articulate their own and interpret others' tacit knowledge, which has been translated to understandable forms using metaphors, examples, diagrams and so on (Nonaka et al. 2001). These are utilized to enable reflection between the participants as tacit knowledge is activated, marked as "dialogue" in Fig. 6.1.

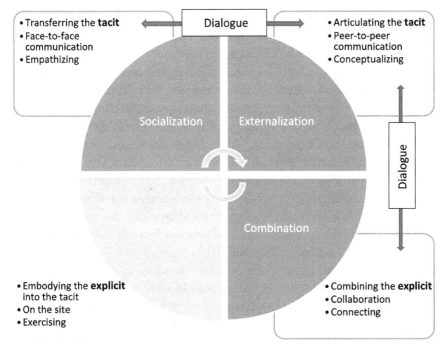

Fig. 6.1 The SECI model, adapted from Nonaka and Konno (1998) and Nonaka et al. (2001)

In the combination (C) phase, the pools of explicit knowledge start to converge into more complex and systematic explicit knowledge. Participants communicate them through documents, meetings and conversations. In the process of sorting, combining and categorizing existing knowledge, the participants reconfigure it to create new knowledge (Nonaka and Konno 1998). The logic is akin to innovative knowledge communities (IKC) developed by Hakkarainen et al. (2004) whose purpose is to create new knowledge by combining different types of expertise into a new whole. Finally, in the internalization (I) phase, the new explicit knowledge is embodied into tacit knowledge. It transforms through a process where individuals share new knowledge throughout an organization, and use it to broaden and reframe tacit knowledge and understanding (Nonaka et al. 2001). Seen in the context of the three types of co-creation described in section "Co-creation in the Evolution of

Science-Society Relations", this phase extends beyond bridging co-creation and is thus outside the scope of this study.

In order to apply the SECI model into university-company co-creation, an understanding of the difficulties of bridging scientific disciplines is needed. Discussion in the academic world rests on critiquing the work of others and testing them through counter-arguments. The conventional peer-review process follows this format, which Myra Strober (Strober 2010) calls the "doubting game." Here competition and rivalry between researchers, their frameworks and results form the basis. This makes trust an inherently difficult feature to gain (Elbow 1973). While this style of discussion is justified in an academic context consisting of experts from similar fields, it is ill-suited for interdisciplinary and multi-professional contexts. To achieve constructive and solution-oriented discussion, the "believing game" is needed (Strober 2010). In such a setting, participants follow and develop, rather than criticize the ideas and approaches that others present in dialogue. In order to build trust and gain new understanding, participants need to have confidence in others' expertise and show this in their communication by allowing the crossing of (disciplinary) boundaries (Hakkarainen et al. 2004). Practicing the believing game for a longer period may lead the participant to discover new creative potential and avenues of thought that they would not have found in their conventional setting (Strober 2010). This, in turn, facilitates a move toward connecting their own specialized, disciplinary knowledge to that of others, for example, by forming and testing hypotheses (Hakkarainen et al. 2004). A synthesis that follows is a result of the mixing of separate worlds. It is not likely to be found without verbalization of thoughts and trust in other discussants.

The essence of Strober's interdisciplinary discussion format ties closely with Nonaka's SECI model, leaning heavily on articulation of hidden knowledge and value structures. Furthermore, both are built on the premise of dialogue (Alhanen 2013; Bohm 1996) between different types of expertise. They aim at understanding others rather than convincing them of the primacy of one's own argument, and rest on the belief that the mixing of different types of expertise has the potential to produce creative solutions.

Data and Method

The data for this chapter is derived from an experimental project that took place in 2017 and was funded by the Finnish agency for innovation Tekes, now Business Finland. The project is here referred to as COHU ("CO-creation model of Helsinki University").

The project was led by the Research Services' Business Collaboration Team at the University of Helsinki. In addition, the core team included Helsinki Innovation Services as well as an experienced external facilitator. The team was transdisciplinary and consisted of experts with backgrounds in biology, physics, engineering, anthropology, philosophy and political science. As the project was part of a larger Innovation Scout (iScout) program aiming at supporting research-based innovation, its target was to develop and pilot a functional model for co-creation. In order to make the model sustainable, the project also included a research component focusing on two things in particular: (1) what are the core characteristics that differentiate co-creation from conventional collaboration, and (2) which formats or tools work in researcher-company co-creation.

The selection of participants for the project was done with purposive sampling in order to allow for the experimental character of the project. This project did not aim at generalizability but followed co-creation principles (Regeer and Bunders 2009) where participants are purposefully selected from different backgrounds to complement existing knowledge (Hakkarainen et al. 2004). Five companies and seven post-doc or associate professor-level researchers from the humanities and social sciences (SSH) at the University of Helsinki participated in the project. SSH fields were selected because there is less tradition of business collaboration and because they play an integral role in solving complex issues related to wicked problems. The researcher participants represented communications, philosophy, sociology, social psychology and social policy and were selected to represent a broad spectrum of views: while some were positive or neutral to business collaboration, there were also those who held prejudged, critical views. The companies were selected through negotiations with diverse actors in the broad networks of the facilitator. The companies ranged from small start-ups to multinational corporations, and represented the fields of housing, IT, law, health and the metal industry.

The project ran six facilitated half-day workshops that were held fortnightly during March–May 2017. Each workshop began with an informal breakfast, followed by an intensive three-hour session where participants sat in a circle with no physical obstacles between them. Participants were requested to refrain from using laptops and other digital devices.

The facilitator of the process was a professor emeritus of innovation studies who, in addition to academic expertise, had experience of working in companies and public foundations. His background and extensive experience from different kinds of developing processes gave him authority as well as capabilities to facilitate the dialogue. As part of the workshop facilitation, he wrote a report for all companies about the problem they presented and the results reached in the dialogue process.

Two researchers, an anthropologist and a political scientist, specialized in societal interaction of science, observed the project with a combination of participatory action research principles (Reason and Bradbury 2008). They recorded the workshop discussions without participating in the discussions of the sessions. In the workshops, attention was given to the verbal communication as well as body language, gestures, tones and style of speaking.

The workshops followed a structure, despite the experimental nature of the project. Discussions were held with the facilitator and the project team between the workshops to evaluate the situation and to adjust plans. Adjustments concerned the order in which cases were discussed, length and style of presentation, and constructive ways of managing conflicts. The team made decisions to adjust plans collectively.

Representatives of companies initially proposed problems for discussion but the final formulation was defined jointly by all participants. This helped start the discussions but allowed the problems to be formulated so that they were deemed interesting and relevant for all. This key premise was made clear to participants prior to the workshops, and it was re-iterated at the beginning of the workshop series. They worked toward defining potential solutions that in most cases were intangible in character or service-centered. A dialogue method (e.g. Bohm 1996; Senge 1990) based on equality was used in the workshop sessions. The idea of the "believing game" (Strober 2010) was explained in the first workshop.

A systematic content analysis was performed with the data, using the NVivo software. A conceptual hierarchy was formed based on combining the SECI model with Strober's interdisciplinary conversations model. The analysis followed four main dimensions which were based on Strober's model, with the role of facilitation being treated as a cross-cutting issue under each. The dimensions listed below were then placed in the different phases of the SECI model in order to follow progression of co-creation through the process.

- Defining goals, interests and visions
- Shared language
- Defining forms of collaboration
- Working logic

Analysis

In the workshop, the expectations of all participants—including the project team—were openly presented to boost transparency and trust. Each came to the experiment as professionals in their own fields. Combining researchers and companies whose fields did not match was an intentional choice aimed at allowing the discussions to focus on building understanding rather than sticking to familiar jargon. The researcher participants received no remuneration for their efforts and companies paid no fees. Their involvement was voluntary, but all participants committed to all workshops. In order to support the confidentiality of discussions and required trust between participants, a non-disclosure agreement was signed.

Defining Goals, Interests and Visions

There was a specific effort during the first two workshops to build an environment of equality. Companies presented initial problem ideas, while researchers put forth a brief portrayal of their academic background. While most followed standard, even stereotypical styles, one skillfully broke the pattern using story-telling techniques to capture others' attention. Beginning with *"communication is the telling of a love story"* (researcher R1), she defied the expectation of a conventional researcher and managed to lure all participants to listen as she explained what this meant. She talked in layman's terms through live examples. The move followed throughout the workshop sessions as an example of surprise made possible by open minds of the listeners, and the courage of the presenter to break habits. It set the stage for exploring uniting angles. Yet, the speech also embodied the early sharing which remained removed from others, and resembled thinking aloud to themselves rather than actually delving into dialogue.

Strober's "believing game" was set as an overall wish for all discussions and a premise for interaction. By opening up to new perspectives, the participants began to understand the limitations of their original ones. Demands of the process itself provided a concrete enough link, and so stepping to unfamiliar territory and facing prejudices connected the participants before any issues of substance. Realizing the vastness that lay beyond their own perspectives seemed to inspire participants, especially company representatives, to share their own interests and visions. The tension that first existed in the room was eased once the participants dared expose their own preconceptions through light-hearted jokes.

> One thing that disturbed the discussion in the beginning were unexpected prejudices. The way people related to those who came from another background. It opened up little by little when we got to understand each other's thoughts. But this is a problem in all new teams. Here the format was different. No table except for the first session. An empty space in between, it had to be filled with something. We had to create something to get away. (Company, C1)

Development of the discussions followed Strober's pattern of interdisciplinarity. Trust is a prerequisite for productive conversations (Strober 2010), but this accentuated the facilitator's role in two ways. Firstly, the facilitator acts as a guarantor of equality between participants, regardless of their background. Trust in this fairness precedes trust between participants. Secondly, in order to avoid development of restraining factions, the facilitator must be able to pay attention to the complex feelings of participants. The SECI socialization phase stresses a similar focus on empathy. In COHU, reoccurring confusion was created by co-facilitators unclear roles. This led to inconsistencies in their reactions in discussions as they revealed lack of understanding for different speech community rules by demanding styles closer to their own. The main facilitator's skill in mediating such situations, however, helped restore and strengthen trust in the process and highlighted the importance of facilitation.

Regarding the goals for cooperation with researchers, companies emphasized the role of scientific knowledge challenging their usual thinking frames: companies were not after "quick-fixes" to concrete problems. They sought partnerships with researchers to find solution paths to wicked problems, not everyday problems.

> If we need solutions to everyday problems, we turn to consultancy companies. Companies don't want to steer universities to become consultancies. We want cooperation based on researchers' research work. All we want is to work with researchers on what they're already doing. It's what they know. (Company, C2)

> Researchers, why do you hold back? There're think tanks, we need to develop do tanks. We need talk tanks so we can really talk about issues. (Company, C3)

For the researchers involved in the COHU project, co-creation was a way of showing they are willing to face the claims of responsibility, also for their own sake.

> As a researcher you feel, well, a little dead at times, because research work is so slow and you can't concentrate on it because the university processes take so much time. This has been lovely, there's been time to think. I feel like I've found whole new empirical dimensions to my research. (Researcher, R1)

Both companies and researchers communicated visions of wanting to serve a purpose. While in the beginning these were separate and based strongly on assumptions, the visions began to converge through the facilitator's efforts to uphold a proper structure. As Strober (2010) notes, a specific commitment is needed for exploration of syntheses. It was clearly the role of the facilitator to make room for observation and the voicing of all ideas. This meant that presentations were shortened so that enough time was available for reflection in the group.

Deeper dialogue emerged as the participants could verbalize their underlying hesitations and confusions. This made their value structures more visible. Participants started to reflect more critically, which led to questioning the basis of the experimentation itself.

> *Collaboration between researchers and those outside academic circles is in a wild state. The formats that break borders of science are muddled. What is the kind of cooperation where the focus is on co-creation? The terminology of co-creation is so confusing and diverse that you can't grab it.* (Researcher, R3)

Strober (2010), following March (1991), emphasizes the importance of distinguishing between exploration and exploitation as a means to balance portfolios. In tackling the efforts to find shared visions, this distinction came to fore. Exploitation is action that utilizes existing knowledge, while exploration is action that takes peoples outside that, which is already known to look for something new. The effort meant that participants needed to look at their own perspectives through the lenses of others. This is in line with the SECI externation phase; it is important to recognize and analyze new perspectives and to perceive their value.

> *I didn't always think about where the ideas came from. It is good that there's enough diversity. If all the companies were similar we'd go straightforwardly somewhere. When we're really lost, we're actually getting somewhere. There's no pondering about the destination. If someone thinks they know where the finish line is it's too easy to just head straight there. With so many types of experts here the discussion was balanced. We took the time to think about possibilities.* (Company, C1)

Throwing ideas led the participants to realize they weren't as far from each other in their thinking as they thought. This became apparent only after the participants had started to discuss the basic assumptions behind their interests, visions and fears, that is, able to articulate their tacit knowledge in the externalization phase.

Shared Language

Prior to the workshop sessions, the project team had expectations on use of concepts and professional jargon. During the first workshop, it was clarified that participants should all pay attention to avoiding use of jargon as it splits rather than unites the group. Efforts were instead needed to use non-technical language, yet without losing or hiding the professional expertise. The team, however, realized during the workshops that they had themselves fallen victim to generally held notions of companies not being interested in hearing conceptual talk. Somewhat surprisingly, companies were positive about the coining of new terms, and requested more specific and pointed use of words.

> *Why would we automatically dilute the specific language? Why would we need to create a new language to discuss these things when we already have a language that can manage complexity—the scientific one.* (Company, C1)

Another pattern emerged in relation to discussing internal issues of relevance only to similar actors. This had the same effect as using jargon but in a more explicit sense.

> *A small, slightly disturbing, issue is the occasionally occurring academic talk that bypasses companies. I understand that there's too little space to have such big discussions across scientific borders. Universities are like big corporations where you run into surprising new dimensions and want to discuss them. But in the future when you include companies in co-creation, it's worth considering whether falling to academic talk here is a good idea.* (Company, C5)

Several researcher participants followed similar patterns of thought. This was interesting as concepts lie at the heart of the scientific communities. Managing a multitude of concepts within the open-minded process played a major role in the planning of the COHU dialogue process, despite several science communication guides urging researchers to avoid conceptual talk. Instead of pushing them apart, the use of concepts seemed to bind the participants together. Being clear about the meanings of terms or phrases encouraged participants to challenge others, while giving an opportunity to take a deeper look at the tacit processes of their own professions. The issue of using concepts to tackle problems appeared when discussion turned to the pace at which (consultancy) companies brand new terminology.

> *The operative logic is different. Consultants needed to create revenue, and coining new concepts serves this purpose. Good concepts continue to live. I agree with [company C4], communication and operative actions must be in line.* (Researcher, R7)

> *An opinion is just an opinion. Science brings perspective to discussions that companies would otherwise be lost in. We need that perspective.* (Company, C5)

> *If it's a good process it'll be adopted and used. It makes all the difference how the concept is brought in.* (Company, C1)

As the discussion around problems unfolded, the debate about use and meaning of concepts such as what constitutes a problem became more specific. The pieces of explicit knowledge brought forward by individual participants were being molded to create new knowledge, shared understandings of the concepts and why they were so complex, following the principles of the SECI combination phase. While some continued to defend their original standpoints, many of the participants realized that they could only provide a partial view of the issue and that the other parts were needed to find feasible solutions. Strober (2010) discusses such patterns from the viewpoint of creativity. To increase creativity, it's necessary for discussants to diversify the idea *categories*, not the quantity of ideas. By producing more categories through the utilization of multiple perspectives, it is possible to generate more flexible and original ideas and solutions.

One of the key roles of the facilitator was to ensure that spoken language was understandable to all. However, the more tedious and central task consisted of getting participants to understand how the others *think*: their assumptions, methods, evaluating and reporting "truth," that is, their habits of mind (Strober 2010) or tacit knowledge particularly in the socialization-externalization interface of the SECI model. As shown in the quotes above, language is strongly embedded in socio-linguistic systems and the underlying speech communities. The COHU facilitator nurtured even negative viewpoints, including toward co-creation/design/development and so on, in order to support the translation between the different linguistic systems. This demanded tolerance for frustration in discussions but resulted in collective realizations on how others made sense of issues and sought solutions.

Defining Forms of Collaboration

Co-creation means solving problems in cooperation with people with diverse backgrounds and different competence profiles. The problem can be a simple concern that needs to be clarified or solved, a phenomenon, occurrence, task, product and so forth. At the beginning of the COHU project the problems could be vague and complex, such as unsuccessful communication or dysfunctional division of work in the company. The problems could also be a new phenomenon, such as the impact of artificial intelligence on specialists' work. Some problems were extremely challenging, for example, measuring service impact or the role of emotions in digital communication.

Over the course of the workshops, the problem definitions changed in several ways. A participant who had presented a solution and was in need of a problem ended up realizing that what seemed an obvious solution would instead entail multiple ethical problems that the company could not accept. Another participant frustrated by personnel management issues realized that the problem was instead in the communication style that unintentionally signaled disrespect toward the employees. Participants stated that the reason they could come to such realizations was the completely different perspectives brought by experts, which they would normally not have thought to consult. For a social psychologist, the dialogue sessions had been an eye opener to new possibilities.

> *I've noticed that my own research fields are relevant to companies. Shared emotions can be utilized in a group to develop internal solidarity. There could be practical applications for these. This knowledge could actually have other uses than just writing.* (Researcher R4)

Researchers' expectations of and responses to co-creation vary. Some worry about losing their scientific autonomy and integrity, and about becoming mere commissioned researchers who serve the needs of non-academic groups. Others are frustrated over not feeling appreciated as professionals for their research efforts. However, many also found opportunities in being challenged.

> *Managing the change requires broader skills, action and impact from universities. There's a huge risk involved if researchers only focus on publication when the probability of getting a permanent position is so small. Globally we recognize the political pressure towards universities and researchers. It's up to us how we react to it. We risk running ourselves into a corner.* (Researcher, R1)

Scientific curiosity and the process of interaction drive this group. They have an interest in broadening their skillset, which resembles the thinking of life-long learning. For them co-creation provides new employment opportunities. They view co-creation as a function that supports also their "purely" scientific endeavors as interaction with non-academics challenges their mindsets and pushes their scientific thinking forward. From a knowledge production perspective, the difference reflects both the externalization and the combination phase of the SECI model. As noted by Strober (2010), the clashes are understandable and finding common ground is only possible once participants can move beyond the externalization and reflect on the meanings that others bring to the table.

> *I'm interested in how services are built. [CompanyC5] problem helped me structure my interest and specify what I want to do next. I approach research problems through thinking what I can methodologically learn from them. I now got concrete ideas about the problems that companies have. The feeling of academic detachment is eased.* (Researcher R6)

The forms of collaboration also tie to what can be gained financially from the cooperation. For companies, it seemed obvious that they should pay for the services that co-creative collaboration can provide for them. It was even understood as a way to show that universities value the intellectual property they possess. For companies, problems and solutions entail economic, technological and commercial aspects. They realize the potential data, equipment and infrastructure they can provide to research processes. For researchers, the opportunities were only partly visible at the start of the process, but the exchange of thoughts helped clarify the situation. The "rules" of collaboration were clearly in line with the SECI combination phase where discussions were concrete and highlighted the value of their own and others' knowledge and work. It seemed that in order to collaborate properly, both companies and researchers wanted the other party also to recognize their own value so as to strengthen the connection in a balanced manner.

> *I got lots of concreteness from the companies. Data from [Company C3], enthusiasm. We've already started. From [Company C1] an entirely new idea to pedagogical development, which is also very conceptual and theoretical. In listening to you I understood how a particular model could be supplemented. I've now pushed that forward. It's possible this idea never would've surfaced without these discussions.* (Researcher R1)

Finding genuine new solutions in cooperation with like-minded people is demanding. With participants coming from different organizations and disciplines, issues appearing as "self-evident" needed to be unraveled and clarified. By playing "the believing game," the co-creation process managed to highlight deficiencies in existing operating methods and in alleged truths. This realization led to re-evaluations of the problems or finding new, unanticipated solutions as the participants began to converge their thinking in the combination phase. In the combination phase, the participants played "the believing game," as noted by Strober (2010) and Elbow (1973), to the fullest as they tried to understand the interpretations that were foreign to themselves but implied opportunities to succeed.

Working Logic

Collective learning proved necessary for the knowledge exchange and the SECI process to function. It occurred systematically in response to conflicts and clashes in the discussions. At times, these originated among researchers, for example, on the meaning of a concept or an academic working habit. This confused companies but they seemed to try to follow the thread and built bridges. The "believing game" proved tricky to uphold, but discussants fought to keep dialogue going, with coherent support by the facilitator.

> *So many insignificant administrative events. A lot of consultancy talk. You create a nice conceptual construction for the audience and then lead them to recognize something there. The foundations or substance is never elaborated. This is tricky for researchers.* (Researcher R3)

> *I recognise this from the company world. A lot of speeches that are accepted as opinions, but no one explains why things are the way they are claimed to be. The substance and meaning is missing.* (Company C5)

> *What is inside and what outside? I'm intrigued. Is there a fundamental difference in the working logic?* (Company C1)

The clashes exacerbated differences in underlying value and ideal structures. Critically minded researchers could frustrate others but managed to push for the biggest breakthroughs. In the end, the dialogues brought researchers critical to co-creation to realize that companies were not trying to dismantle science ethical principles, but rather looking for ways to find mutually functional working models.

> *I feel like I'm from the wrong field. It seems the most I can do is to help question concepts.* (Researcher R3)

The main facilitator interrupts, offering support. "But this is an academic virtue."

> *I would so like to get my hands dirty and do more than just question. It's nice to hear that others have gained more. I could perhaps offer something to solve your [project team's] problems, that's my expertise. I could be of use there.* (Researcher R3)

Advancing research-company co-creation is only possible if universities understand the logic of co-creation and, in particular, the coupling to scientifically viable arguments. The COHU project showed that instead of an external demand, researchers need evidence of how co-creation fits with the scientific community and supports career development. There was a shared curiosity to understand the dynamics of co-creation in order to be able to apply them in teaching and research consortia. Similarly, there was an interest to understand how facilitation works, with the specific intention of developing skills on facilitation of societally linked knowledge production. This result follows the learning curve from the conventional academic "doubting game" to a more cooperatively minded "believing game." Over the length of the workshops, researchers and company representatives had learned to understand the others' thinking patterns better through dialogue. Their conceptualization of problems and potential solutions had evolved from a superficial communication of own thoughts to peer communication in the externalization phase and further to explicating concrete collaboration in the combination phase on their own merit.

Concluding Discussion

Returning to the research question "how does co-creation between universities and companies enhance the responsibility of universities?" we find that co-creation is a *goal-oriented tool*—not an end result. It is a tool to demonstrate responsibility in a manner that cuts across all functions at universities. It is not merely a part of the so-called third mission but rather a feature that is, or could be, integrated into all parts of action, be they teaching, research, management or societal relations. First and foremost, co-creation that serves a purpose in a university setting is a cross-cutting operational mode, which facilitates learning individually as well as between actors.

In the piloted bridging co-creation model, dialogue was considered a tool for co-creation, not the aim as such. The real target was co-creative knowledge production between researchers and companies, and approaching co-creation with the SECI model allowed an exploration into sub-processes of knowledge production. The analysis shows that dialogue holds a *core* position in the learning that constitutes the essence of co-creation (Fig. 6.2). Its role is highlighted especially in the intersections where tacit knowledge is externalized to open discussion and complementary knowledge from different participants is combined into new knowledge (innovations and solutions). In bridging co-creation, externalization and combination phases dominate, that is, the more social levels of the process, where also the sharing of experience (and skills) happens. It is also learning process, in which explicit knowledge is internalized at a personal level. These two last phases of SECI model are operating in full effect in co-development and co-research, where the interaction between researchers and companies is long-standing and intensive. All elements are present even in bridging co-creation.

Bridging co-creation between researchers and companies provides a limited outlook to co-creative options. However, analysis of the experiment showed that such a focused format already included the essential parts for productive co-creation: problem definition, composition of questions, perspectives, learning through exposure, the meaning of trust and reciprocity. The role of dialogue proved to be particularly essential in the enabling of several perspectives, building of trust between participants and reciprocity of sharing. These produce the central building blocks of the externalization and combination phases of the SECI model.

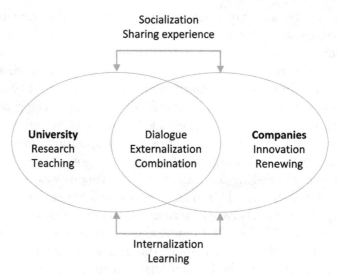

Fig. 6.2   The SECI Model in Co-creation

This leaned strongly on the facilitator, who acted as a knowledge broker. As such, the facilitator performed translation tasks (Hakkarainen et al. 2004), in micro-format, as independent activities aimed at supporting knowledge production in a rapidly changing environment.

Bridging co-creation seems to lean on the idea of epistemic communities (Haas 1992). These consist of knowledge-driven actors who share similar goals, cognitive frameworks and an understanding of their roles in a system. Such communities exist in the academic as well as other expert contexts. It is in the meeting of these epistemic communities where new knowledge can emerge if suitable dynamics for co-creation exist. Understanding the importance of personal responsibility is a premise for the participants to be able to verbalize their tacit knowledge in a way that is understandable to discussants from other disciplines and professions. This is necessary to move from the externalization phase to the combination phase of the SECI model.

As with the centrality of dialogue in the same phases, the COHU project showed that the knowledge production process does not follow a straight path. Instead, it moves in multiple directions and builds opportunities for learning by allowing the participants to move between phases naturally and even simultaneously. Here, the role of an experienced, broadly trusted facilitator, who provides the necessary support structure for the goal-oriented process, is highlighted. The advancing of co-creative practices entails facilitation tasks (Regeer and Bunders 2009) which are generally not included in conventional research training. This has led to a need to develop capacity and competencies for facilitation that promotes credibility broadly.

While the COHU project used an external facilitator, it would not provide a sustainable or particularly responsible practice in the long run. In order to ensure that both scientific integrity and societal interaction are upheld, facilitation should be managed by the university in the long run. If the role was understood in a narrow sense as a communication issue, the risk of breaking science ethical principles could be jeopardized. Discussions about the meaning and importance of research integrity and researchers' virtues (Banks 2018) are necessary for the building of such trust. They include not only application of reliable methods of research but being curious and critically minded, conscientious, open, honest and willing to listen to other researchers. Researchers' personal epistemic responsibility is central in research and knowledge creation (Code 1987). If virtues and personalities of researchers are stressed, then integrity is a crucial issue in co-creation, also with companies. To uphold this, universities could invest in the development of facilitation skills as a form of specialization for researchers who have an interest in dynamic forms of knowledge production. Such training could also provide a skillset that boosts employability of researchers outside academia.

So, is co-creation a reflection of the responsible university? It is a way to implement and strengthen the societal responsibility of universities, a phenomenon that can build bridges and deepen the understanding of what makes universities unique institutions in society. However, it can also set the ideals of modern science (such as open science) on a crash-course with the practices of business (e.g. IPR) (Stilgoe et al. 2013) if universities encourage the use of co-creation without considering its implications and preconditions. The engagement intensity of co-creation concretizes the clash of science and market logics (Berman 2012), and forces researchers to contextualize the meaning of research integrity in a new light. However, this should not only be seen as a threat but rather a chance to deepen the understanding of what the role of scientific research is in modern society. Sharing tacit and explicit knowledge with companies allows researchers to appreciate the practices that make their research work significant if they choose to create new, scientifically and societally valuable explicit knowledge jointly with, for example, companies. In the COHU project such crystallizations appeared through realizations that while universities have lost their dominant positions as producers of knowledge, they remain the most capable institutions to link needs of industries, public sectors and informed citizenship (Delanty 2001) in a systematic and analytical manner.

Finally, the COHU project provides practical lessons that warrant further investigation. The COHU project showed that company interests in co-creation with universities lies in gaining access to scientific knowledge. Companies are willing to trade their experiential and practice-related skills and data in order to build a mutually beneficial setting. The building of a safe and respectful context requires that rules for the bridging of different worlds are defined and meeting dynamics led (Haynes 2011).

Essentially, what is needed are consultancy-skilled researchers who have expertise not only in their field of substance and recognizing the boundaries of science (Vuolanto 2014) but also in dialogical techniques.

Responsibility is not only about production of knowledge and "pouring" it on others. It can be a goal-oriented mix of problem and solution-centered action. This is what makes co-creation meaningful for all participants. Co-creation is epistemic responsibility (Code 1987), that is, responsibility to scientific communities as well as to society. It is one way of applying the corporate social responsibility mode of thinking into a university environment. University citizenship responsibilities entail the furthering of shared societal goals, supporting societal development (including but not limited to the economic) and working for the common good. Co-creation is based on equality between participants, rather than a master-servant setting, and as such a platform for in-depth learning that has the ability to produce change.

Acknowledgments We would like to extend special thanks to Emmi Holm for her efforts in collecting the data from the COHU project, and for valuable discussions with the COHU project leader Dr. Maarit Haataja on the role of co-creation in university context and Dr. Leena Ripatti-Torniainen on the possibilities of co-creation in developing university pedagogics. A further thanks is owed to James Tommy Karlsen and Miren Larrea for valuable comments to an earlier version of this chapter. We also kindly acknowledge the generous iScout funding to the COHU project from former Tekes (now Business Finland), project number 4870/31/2016.

References

Aarrevaara, T., & Pulkkinen, K. (2016). *Societal Interaction of Science in Strategic Research Council Funded Projects*. Project report for Public Engagement Innovations for Horizon 2020. Retrieved from https://pe2020.eu/wp-content/uploads/2014/02/Soc-interaction-at-SRC_160916_valmis.pdf.

Alhanen, K. (2013). *John Deweyn kokemusfilosofia [The Experiential Philosophy of John Dewey]*. Helsinki: Gaudeamus.

Banks, S. (2018). Cultivating Researcher INtegrity: Virtue-Based Approaches to Research Ethics. In N. Emmerich (Ed.), *Virtue Ethics in the Condusct and Governance of Social Science Research* (pp. 21–44). Emerald Publishing Limited.

Berman, E. O. (2012). *Creating the Market University. How Academic Science Became an Economic Engine.* Princeton, NJ: Princeton University Press.

Bohm, D. (1996). *On Dialogue.* New York: Routledge.

Brown, J. S., & Duguid, P. (2001). Knowledge and Organization: A Social-Practice Perspective. *Organization Science, 12*(2), 198–213.

Chesbrough, H. (2003). *Open Innovation, The New Imperative for Creating and Profiting from Technology.* Boston, MA: Harvard Business School Press.

Clarke, B. R. (1998). *Creating Entrepreneurial Universities: Organizational Pathways of Transformation.* Oxford: Pergamon.

Code, L. (1987). *Epistemic Responsibility.* Hannover: University of New England.

de Jong, S. P. L., Smit, J., & van Drooge, L. (2016). Scientists' Response to Societal Impact Policy. *Science and Public Policy, 43*(1), 102–114.

Delanty, G. (2001). *Challenging Knowledge. The University in the Knowledge Society.* Buckingham: Open University Press.

Elbow, P. (1973). *Writing Without Teachers.* New York: Oxford University Press.

Etzkowitz, H., Ranga, M., Benner, M., Guaranys, L., Maculan, A. M., & Kneller, R. (2008). Pathways to the Entrepreneurial University: Towards a Global Convergence. *Science and Public Policy, 35*(9), 681–695. https://doi.org/10.3152/030234208X389701.

Gibbons, M., Limoges, C., Nowotny, H., Schwartzman, S., Scott, P., & Trow, M. (1994). *The New Production of Knowledge.* London: Sage Publications.

Guile, D. (2010). *The Learning Challenge of the Knowledge Economy.* Rotterdam: Sense Publishers.

Haas, P. M. (1992). Epistemic Communities and International Policy Coordination. *International Organization, 46*(1), 1–35.

Hakkarainen, K., Palonen, T., Paavola, S., & Lehtinen, E. (2004). *Communities of Networked Expertise. Professional and Educational Perspectives.* Amsterdam-Tokio: Elsevier.

Hautamäki, A., Haataja, M., Holm, E., Pulkkinen, K., & Suni, T. (2018). *Co-creation. A Guide to Enhancing the Collaboration Between Universities and Companies.* Helsinki: University of Helsinki.

Haynes, C. (2011). Interdisciplinary Conversations: Challenging Habits of Thought (Review). *The Journal of Higher Education, 82*(6), 803–805.

Karvonen, E. (2014). Tiede tuottaa todellisuutta – Kenen etujen mukaan ja kuinka eettisesti? In R. Muhonen & H.-M. Puuska (Eds.), *Tutkimuksen kansallinen tehtävä* (pp. 53–86). Tampere, Finland: Vastapaino.

Kazadi, K., Lievens, A., & Mahr, D. (2016). Stakeholder Co-creation During the Innovation Process: Identifying Capabilities for Knowledge Creation Among Multiple Stakeholders. *Journal of Business Research, 69*(2), 525–540.

Klev, R., & Levin, M. (2012). *Participative Transformation Learning and Development in Practising Change*. Farnham: Gower.

Lyytinen, A. (2018). The Concept of the Entrepreneurial University for Analysing the Organisational Transformation of Higher Education Institutions. In E. Pekkola, J. Kivistö, V. Kohtamäki, Y. Cai, & A. Lyytinen (Eds.), *Theoretical and Methodological Perspectives on Higher Education Management and Transformation. An advanced reader for PhD students* (pp. 105–118). Tampere: Tampere University Press.

March, J. G. (1991). Exploration and Exploitation in Organizational Learning. *Organization Science, 2*(1), 71–87.

Moisio, J. (2018). Policy Transfer in Higher Education Policy Formation. In E. Pekkola, J. Kivistö, V. Kohtamäki, Y. Cai, & A. Lyytinen (Eds.), *Theoretical and Methodological Perspectives on Higher Education Management and Transformation. An Advanced Reader for PhD Students* (pp. 67–86). Tampere: Tampere University Press.

Nonaka, I., & Konno, N. (1998). The Concept of "Ba". Building a Foundation for Knowledge Creation. *California Management Review, 40*(3), 40–54.

Nonaka, I., Konno, N., & Toyama, R. (2001). Emergence of "Ba". A Conceptual Framework for the Continuous and Self-Transcending Process of Knowledge Creation. In I. Nonaka & T. Nishiguchi (Eds.), *Knowledge Emergence* (pp. 13–29). New York: Oxford University Press.

Nowotny, H., Scott, P., & Gibbons, M. (2003). Introduction. 'Mode 2 Revisited: The New Production of Knowledge'. *Minerva, 41*, 179–194.

Polanyi, M. (1966). *The Tacit Dimension*. New York: Doubleday & Company, Inc.

Prahalad, C. K., & Ramaswamy, V. (2004). Co-creation Experiences: The Next Practice in Value Creation. *Journal of Interactive Marketing, 18*(3), 5–14.

Pulkkinen, K., Timo Aarrevaara, T., Nordstrand Berg, L., Geschwind, L., Foss Hansen, H., Hernes, H., Kivistö, J., et al. (2019). Does It Really Matter? Assessing the Performance Effects of Changes in Leadership and Management Structures in Nordic Higher Education. In R. Pinheiro, L. Geschwind, H. F. Hansen, & K. Pulkkinen (Eds.), *Reforms, Organizational Change and Performance in Higher Education. A Comparative Account from the Nordic Countries* (pp. 3–36). Cham: Palgrave Macmillan.

Ramaswamy, V., & Gouillart, F. (2010). Building the Co-creative Enterprise. Harvard Business Review, Issue Oct 2010.

Reason, P., & Bradbury, H. (Eds.). (2008). *The Sage Handbook of Action Research: Participatory Inquiry and Practice*. Thousand Oaks, CA: Sage.

Regeer, B. J., & Bunders, J. F. G. (2009). *Knowledge Co-creation: Interaction Between Science and Society*. Den Haag: RMNO.

Schumpeter, J. (1934). *The Theory of Economic Development*. Cambridge, MA: Harvard University Press.

Senge, P. M. (1990). *The Fifth Discipline: The Art & Practice of the Learning Organization*. New York: Doubleday Business.

Spaapen, J., & van Drooge, L. (2011). Introducing 'Productive Interactions' in Social Impact Assessment. *Research Evaluation, 20*(3), 211–218.

Stilgoe, J., Owen, R., & Macnaghten, P. (2013). Developing a Framework for Responsible Innovation. *Research Policy, 42*, 1568–1580.

Strober, M. H. (2010). *Interdisciplinary Conversations. Challenging Habits of Thought*. Stanford, CA: Stanford University Press.

Trencher, G., Yarime, M., McCormick, K., Doll, C., Kraines, S., & Kharrazi, A. (2014). Beyond the Third Mission: Exploring the Emerging University Function of Co-creation for Sustainability. *Science and Public Policy, 41*(2), 151–179.

Välimaa, J. (2004). Kolmas tehtävä korkeakoulutuksessa: tavoitteena joustavuus ja yhteistyö. In K. Kari, K. Erkki, K. Pirjo, L. Tarmo, N. Mika, & J. Välimaa (Eds.), *Yliopistojen kolmas tehtävä?* (pp. 43–68). Helsinki, Finland: Sitra.

Vuolanto, P. (2014). Hyvän tieteen määrittely ja rajanvetokiistat. In R. Muhonen & H.-M. Puuska (Eds.), *Tutkimuksen kansallinen tehtävä* (pp. 259–270). Tampere: Vastapaino.

Weick, K. E., & Sutcliffe, K. M. (2005). Organizing and the Process of Sensemaking. *Organization Science, 16*(4), 409–421.

7

Universities and Regional Development

James Karlsen and Miren Larrea

Introduction

Over the last two decades, the discourse on the role of universities and higher education institutions in innovation, economic growth, social change and regional development has expanded. Universities have been urged to become more socially accountable and to contribute directly to local, regional and national economic development (e.g. Dunning 2002; Laredo 2007; OECD 2009). Various models of the socially responsible university have been developed, such as the entrepreneurial university (Clark 1998, 2004), the Mode 2 university (Nowotny et al. 2001), the triple helix model (Etzkowitz and Leydesdorff 1995), the engaged university (Boyer 1990) and the civic university (Goddard et al. 2016). For

J. Karlsen (✉)
University of Agder, Grimstad, Norway
e-mail: james.karlsen@uia.no

M. Larrea
Orkestra-Basque Institute of Competitiveness, University of Deusto,
San Sebastian, Spain
e-mail: miren.larrea@orkestra.deusto.es

the sake of the argument about the regional role of the university, we distinguish between two university models, the add-on model and the integrated model, and we begin with the former model. It has been argued that regional development represents a new *third* mission for universities, in addition to the first (teaching) and the second (research) missions (Perkmann et al. 2013). The third mission is a general concept that covers all kind of university activities outside academic environments (Molas-Gallart and Castro-Martínez 2007). It is an *add-on* to the traditional activities of universities and is organised separately from the first two missions. The concept of the entrepreneurial university (Clark 1998; Etzkowitz 1983) focuses on the addition of a range of knowledge transfer and market-oriented activities, such as the incubation of start-up firms, the commercialisation of knowledge, the development of knowledge transfer partnerships and the delivery of entrepreneurship courses.

The university models that employ the integrated approach include the Mode 2 university (Nowotny et al. 2001) and the civic university (Goddard 2009; Goddard et al. 2016). The authors of these models argue that the third mission should be integrated into all university activities and practices, that is, into the first and second missions. They claim that this would engage the entire university as a knowledge institution in social and regional development. The authors of the Mode 2 university model argue that the mode of knowledge production in society has changed and that the university must adapt to this new mode of knowledge production (Mode 2) to survive.

The aforementioned models present challenges for universities. Rothaermel et al. (2007) argue that the entrepreneurial university represents the next logical step of the development of the university. Goddard (2011) claims that universities must be more rigorously managed to meet strategic priorities regarding entrepreneurship and knowledge-based development. Pinheiro et al. (2012b) argue that such an approach assumes that a university is an organisation that can orientate teaching and research resources towards regional development processes. However, if the university is not such an organisation, that is, an organisation that cannot be managed rigorously, how can it then integrate the third mission (regional development) into the two other missions? Moreover, what kind of organisation is the university?

This chapter aims to contribute to the literature on universities' role in regional development. First, in the theoretical section, we address the question of what kind of organisation a university is. We distinguish between the university as a homogeneous (tightly coupled) organisation and as a heterogeneous (loosely coupled) organisation. Second, we connect the concept of regional development to a responsible research and innovation approach. The main topic of the book is the Responsible University and our argument is that universities should take a responsible approach to regional development. Our approach to responsibility departs from the theory of responsible research and innovation (Stilgoe et al. 2013) and especially the dimension of care (Bardone and Lind 2016; Wilford 2015). The responsible research and innovation approach does not distinguish the institutional from the personal and requires that individuals take personal responsibility for their own actions while also reinforcing institutional responsibility for setting policy and providing redress (Wilford 2018, 541). Responsibility concerns how researchers practice their work and relate to external actors. It describes a type of active engagement in the world that entails researchers becoming part of their own practice.[1] An example of responsibility is that we, the authors, write in the first person and that we are explicit about our engagement in the case we present and our aim for change. As researchers, we must choose whether we write about the university in a detached manner, as if we were not part of the university, or whether we act and write responsibly and, thus, take responsibility for the change process. In this chapter, we cast light on regional responsibility from the positions of different groups within universities, such as researchers, teachers, students and management.

Third, we respond to the lack of in-depth studies of universities engagement with regional actors conducted from the inside and out. It is time to open the black box of universities and study micro-engagement between university actors and external actors. We present an action research case between master students, their teachers and external actors in a university city over one semester. Action research is a methodology that involves working together with actors. It entails co-generating knowledge with actors through action and reflection cycles (Greenwood and Levin 2007). Action research can adopt a process approach or both a process and product approach. The former is usually referred to as reflection-in-action while the latter is reflection-on-action (Schön 1983). This chapter takes a process approach. The case presented is that of the University of Agder, Norway, which is a relatively young public university. The question we explore is: *Does a responsible university need a third mission?*

Theoretical Framework

In this chapter, we introduce two theoretical discussions that frame the case study and discussion. One examines whether universities are homogeneous or heterogeneous in nature, and the other addresses the interactions between the individual and organisational levels in third mission strategies. At the end of this section, we integrate them both into an analytical framework.

The Homogeneous or Heterogeneous Nature of Universities

We find the previous discourses on universities and their engagement with external actors challenging for a discussion at the micro level because they are abstract and use generic concepts. What kind of higher education are we talking about? The discourses on universities do not always distinguish between different types of universities. As Greenwood and Levin (2016, 22) argue:

> There are community colleges, for-profit colleges and universities, vocational schools, liberal arts colleges, regional colleges, private universities, flagship public universities, land-grant universities, state university and colleges systems and national public university systems in Europe.

However, we not only have to consider differences between universities but also within universities. Greenwood and Levin (2016) describe the university as a collection of different systems that interact and consider administration, students and faculty as three different groups in these interactions.

The methodological problem is that by abstracting, homogenising and analysing universities, we treat them as the same type of university, and by interpreting the university as a homogeneous organisation without considering the complexity inside each university, we have a 'one-size-fits-all' university model. Moreover, we run the risk of making analytical errors, which also can have consequences for the future policies of universities if policy-makers use the analysis. As Greenwood and Levin (2016) demonstrate, universities differ and they are internally complex. Therefore, there is a need for more precision and for a nuanced debate on universities that considers questions such as what kind of universities we are talking about, how they are configured and the context in which are they located.

In recent years, scholarly discourse has begun to question the basic assumption that universities are organisations with homogeneous and uniform capacities to perform and contribute to social engagement (Kitagawa et al. 2016; Pinheiro et al. 2012a; Sánchez-Barrioluengo 2014). Empirical studies show that universities are extremely diverse and that they tend to respond differently to external opportunities and challenges. A comparative case study of universities in the United Kingdom, Austria and Sweden shows that policies in these different countries tend to favour different models of university third mission engagement (Trippl et al. 2015). Numerous studies have shown that universities are heterogeneous organisations in their third mission activities (Charles et al. 2014; Hewitt-Dundas 2012; Huggins et al. 2012; Kitagawa et al. 2016). It seems that each university develops its approach to the third mission by targeting different areas of activities (Kitagawa et al. 2016, 736). This paper contributes to this literature by following the path initiated by Greenwood and Levin (2016) and proposing action research as a research strategy that helps integrate the internal specificities of universities into the research process.

The central problem that this theoretical framework addresses is that, with exceptions such as those previously cited, most approaches seem to involve an implicit assumption that a one-size-fits-all model can be applied to universities and that a university is an organisation with homogeneous and uniform capacities to perform and contribute to social and regional engagement.

In this chapter, we propose an interpretation of university and regions as loosely coupled systems in which different actors interact from different positions and with different interests. In this context, regional engagement is the result of such interactions, which include learning and negotiation across groups. These activities of learning and negotiation sometimes happen inside the university between the different actors that form the university and sometimes between university actors and regional actors.

The idea that universities are heterogeneous and loosely coupled organisations is inspired by Weich (1976). This idea implies that the connections between the various internal subsystems may be infrequent, circumscribed, weak in mutual effects, unimportant or slow (Weich 1976). By contrast, a homogenous organisation is a tightly coupled organisation.

Regional Responsibility

It is with the previous discussion in mind that we approach the issue of responsibility, which is the thread that runs through the different chapters in this book. Our approach builds on the responsible research and innovation approach (Spruit et al. 2015; Stilgoe et al. 2013) and especially on the new dimension of *care* (Bardone and Lind 2016; Burget et al. 2017; Wilford 2015). Stilgoe et al. (2013, 1570) define responsible research and innovation as 'taking care of the future through collective stewardship of science and innovation in the present'. The dimension of care stresses the importance of personal responsibility (Wilford 2015) in addition to a collective approach to the research and innovation process. Care is a process through which people collaboratively develop abilities to perceive, act and judge (Burget et al. 2017; Groves 2009). Care is not a set of normative rules on how to act but rather the decisions and actions of an individual, such as a researcher, teacher or student. It is a 'way to bring together people's high objectives and day-to-day practices' (Burget et al. 2017, 13).

Responsibility as care concerns the concrete behaviour of individuals and organisations and on how care is embodied in their daily activities. This means that, in this chapter, formal documents on university missions with regard to regional engagement and normative discourses are relevant but not central. The approach of responsibility as care is mainly observable in an individual's actions. It is a type of active engagement in the world, which means that researchers cannot be separated from their practice and are, therefore, embodied in practice. This brings researchers' agency to the forefront and contrasts with the vision of responsibility as a set of guidelines imposed externally to obtain funding or to engage in specific modes of behaviour with the broader society and regional actors to be a responsible university. Regional responsibility is about care for the region in which the university is located, both on the institutional (collective) level and the personal level and in the connections between these levels.

An Analytical Model

Based on the points discussed above, we have constructed an analytical framework (see Table 7.1). The first dimension in the model is the

Table 7.1 Regional responsibility in tightly and loosely coupled organisations

| | | View of regional responsibility as | |
		Organisational rules	Individual practice
Interpretation of the university as a	Tightly coupled organisation (homogeneous)	A set of codified guidelines for responsible regional development	Following established rules for responsible regional development
	Loosely coupled organisation (heterogeneous)	A set of norms and values developed by each unit for regional responsibility based on individual and shared experiences	Space for individual responsibility adapted to the regional context

perception of the university as either a tightly coupled organisation (homogeneous) or a loosely coupled organisation. We use the term 'perception' because, although we have made clear in the previous sections that we build on literature that regards universities as heterogeneous entities, we also consider that some university processes are defined based on the assumption that universities are homogeneous entities and some processes are built on the assumption that universities are heterogeneous entities. The coexistence of these processes is one of the main challenges in the development of third mission strategies today, and we want the analytical framework to reflect that.

The second dimension is responsibility as either a set of codified organisational rules or individual responsible practice. In a university, there are different types of individuals, such as teachers, researchers and students, who engage in different practices. Management practices, such as those of the university director, managers at different levels in the university and project leaders, are also included in these individual practices with external actors. We interpret the university as a tightly coupled organisation when there is a set of codified rules for regional engagement. This does not necessarily imply a restricted space for individual practice and adaptation to the external context either within the university or with regional actors.[2] Generally, however, when the focus is on codified rules to guide individual action, little attention is given, and few resources are allocated, to such individual practices. With a strategy that conceives the university as a loosely coupled organisation, each unit, such as a department, develops a set of informal norms and values for engagement with regional actors, and individual practices are at the core of those norms and values. This also implies that there some units may have no, or almost no, engagement with regional actors, while other units may allow space for individual engagement with regional actors. Furthermore, in each unit, there might be highly engaged individuals and individuals with no engagement at all. In a loosely coupled organisation, there is space for individual practice and adaptation to the regional context. This space exists if individuals want to avail of it, but there is also space for not engaging with regional actors.

In proposing the aforementioned framework, we do not mean to suggest that there are only two models for universities' positions on regional responsibility. There are many nuanced models and they depend on the type of university. We want to discuss that how these two analytical types can be combined by adopting multiple approaches. We argue that third mission strategies often assume that universities are tightly coupled organisations and that such strategies can be difficult to implement if universities are not tightly coupled. At the same time, individuals or units within the university that feel responsible for the region may implement initiatives and engage with regional actors in their daily endeavours, and these initiatives and endeavours may not be considered part of the third mission strategy. We want to use our framework to argue that a responsible strategy for the third mission is one that considers both individual initiatives and codified guidelines as part of the third mission.

Methodology

Our methodological approach is based on action research. Action research is considered the most appropriate meta-methodology for exploring lived practical knowledge that informs a community of practice (Guba and Lincoln 2005). The case we present in this chapter was designed as an action research process. Action research is concerned with praxis, a concept that integrates practice and theory. It is a research strategy that integrates action, reflection and participation with various actors through a cyclic, dialogical process aimed at change (Greenwood and Levin 2007; Reason and Bradbury 2008), such as for territorial development (Karlsen and Larrea 2014, 2018). Action research is designed for working with change processes in real time and from both inside and outside the university since it involves cycles of reflection and action. It involves participation and engagement with regional actors, where the action researcher is considered both an insider and an equal regional actor with other regional actors, such as industry actors and policy-makers (Karlsen and Larrea 2014, 2018). When we refer to actors, we might refer to individuals (e.g. specific firm representatives, policy-makers, politicians, researchers) or the organisations they represent in their interactions (e.g. firms, governments, universities).

Context, Method and Data

The data presented is from an action research process with university actors from the University of Agder and actors from Grimstad municipality, which is the host region of one of the University of Agder's two campuses in the Agder region in Norway. The Agder region is the most southern region in Norway and consists of the two counties, that is, Aust-Agder County and Vest-Agder County. It has 305,000 inhabitants, which is 5.8% of the population of Norway. The University of Agder is a public university with approximately 13,000 students and 1300 employees (2019). Grimstad has approximately 23,000 inhabitants, and there are around 3500 students on the Grimstad campus, mainly engineering and nursing students but also innovation students from the Department of Working Life and Innovation, which belongs to the School of Business and Law. The students and the staff from that department are the university actors in this case.

The case was conducted from early spring 2017 to the end of 2018. Collaborative activities generated data, which were codified in field notes. In addition to field notes, data were generated from qualitative interviews, two quantitative surveys and analysis of documents detailing strategic plans for the University of Agder beginning in 2004, and in Karlsen (2007).[3]

The positionality of researchers is a relevant issue in action research processes. In this case, we distinguish between two positionalities: an insider and an outsider. One of the authors, Karlsen, is an insider to the process as he has actively participated in the process in collaboration with university managers and is responsible for the course the case is based on. The other author, Larrea, participated as a lecturer for the first two weeks of the course. Her positionality is that of an outsider who helps insiders reflect on the processes that are happening. We consider that the main positionality in the chapter is that of insiders. Larrea's experience as an action researcher was mainly developed through praxis in Gipuzkoa, Basque Country (Spain) as part of a programme named the Territorial Development Laboratory, previously known as *Gipuzkoa Sarean* (Gipuzkoa Networked in the Basque language). The programme was initiated in 2009 to develop new governance modes in this region (Karlsen and Larrea 2018). Karlsen has worked as an outsider on this programme since 2009.

Case

The case study is from an ordinary course at the School of Business and Law at the University of Agder. We use the term 'case study' (Yin 2013). The case involves university actors and other regional actors. In this section, we provide a thick description (Geertz 1973) of the case. First, we address the origins of the case. Although the case focuses on developments made in Agder in 2017–2018, it is difficult to understand without framing it within processes that have underway for several years. Second, we briefly describe the third mission initiative and, finally, the design and development of the course.

The Knowledge Sources and the Institutional Conditions for the Case

There are several knowledge sources that inspired the case. One such source was a 2007 PhD thesis on the regional role of the University by one of the authors of this chapter (Karlsen 2007). In the thesis, the concept of the co-generation of knowledge between the university and the region is discussed. At the time, this work did not have any concrete influence at the University of Agder. However, the opportunity to work with these ideas arose in the Basque Country, where attempts were being made to create the conditions for action research and, consequently, for the co-generation of knowledge between research organisations and regional actors. In 2009, the framework inspired the initial steps of the *Gipuzkoa Sarean* project, which later became the Territorial Development Laboratory.

The theoretical concepts developed from the work in the Basque Country and the experience of collaborating with territorial development practitioners have recently been brought back to Norway and the Agder region.[4] The institutional conditions for conducting action research on territorial development were established with the University of Agder's 2016 strategic plan, which set out a vision for the *co-creation of knowledge*. One of the aims of the strategic plan was to

> develop further and establish new arenas and forms of interaction and co-creation and that both University of Agder and the community must have the courage to experiment and try out new solutions and forms of cooperation. (University of Agder 2016, 6)

The aim of experimenting and testing out new forms of collaboration with external actors resonated well with the action research for territorial development developed in the Basque Country and was influential for the further development of the case. The strategic plan provided the necessary support to collaborate with regional actors. The case was initiated as a result of a request from the economic development director in Grimstad municipality for a meeting with researchers from the Department of Working Life and Innovation. This department is well known for its long tradition of collaboration with regional actors from industry and the public sector. The purpose of the meeting was to obtain support for the establishment of a strategic industrial development plan for Grimstad. The proposal to collaborate on this plan was made to Karlsen and another colleague, a professor and an expert in the regional innovation system approach. The meeting began in a traditional manner with the delivery of a report to the municipality with recommendations for action. However, during the meeting, the dialogue shifted to a discussion about engagement and co-generation of knowledge between the University of Agder and various types of actors from Grimstad, such as industry and tourism professionals, policy-makers and politicians from the municipality. Both the economic development director and the researchers thought this was a good idea. We had all had experience of reports that ended up on bookshelves collecting dust and that had little real impact. Since Karlsen had recently taken over responsibility for a 7.5 credit course (Innovation in the Public Sector) in the master's programme Innovation and Knowledge Development, the course, which had 14 students, became the arena for experimenting with an action research process with actors in Grimstad municipality.

The Third Mission Initiative—The Co-creation Lab

When we had reached agreed with Grimstad municipality about the process, we decided to initiate collaboration with the Co-Creation Lab (*Samskapingsverkstedet*) at the university. At that time, the Co-Creation Lab was the official organisation for implementing the co-creation vision with regional actors. It was established as a third mission initiative, as an add-on to the teaching and research missions, at the level of the university director's office. During our collaboration with the Co-Creation Lab, we obtained information about the challenges of reaching the academic core of researchers and teachers, that is, of finding academics to collaborate with. We were also informed it was much easier to find actors in the region that were interested in collaborating with the University of Agder. We invited the leader of the Co-Creation Lab to participate in our events, and the lab used our students to promote their project during external events they organised. This gave us access to communication resources that we used to promote our course internally within the university system. The Co-Creation Lab also funded co-creation projects in the university, and, since the course was promoted as one of the pilot projects of the Co-Creation Lab, we requested funding to contract Larrea to teach at the beginning of the course. We never received the funding but decided to fund the teaching through a project we were involved with in the department at that time. The connection between us and the Co-Creation Lab can be characterised as loose and was mainly through Karlsen.

Design of the Course

The authors of this chapter designed the course together with the professor mentioned above, an associate professor from another department at the Faculty of Social Sciences and a policy-maker (the economic development director) from Grimstad. It was designed with three phases:

teaching, co-generation and a shared reflection on the results of the co-generation process.

The teaching phase began with a presentation of the challenge the students were to work with by the economic development director from Grimstad municipality. This was followed by a series of teaching sessions involving actors such as university managers and municipality representatives. In these sessions, traditional linear transfer of knowledge in the form of lectures was combined with co-generative methods. The co-generative process took place over an intensive week that began with an introduction to action research for territorial development followed by group work where the students were challenged to discuss what co-generation meant for them individually and as a group.

The second phase was the co-generation phase. The students were divided into three groups based on the challenge posed by Grimstad municipality, and each group had one supervisor from the University of Agder. The students were given the responsibility to design their engagement with actors in Grimstad. Therefore, the first part of the co-generative phase involved students and their supervisors as it enabled them to agree on the process and the approach to co-generation that they wanted to adopt to experiment with actors. Students were given a chance to choose between different approaches. The two main approaches discussed were interviews and workshops. Due to the distinction between the roles of interviewees and interviewers, interviews focus mainly on the change process of those interviewed. Workshops allow for a more discussion of roles, including the roles of university actors. Two of the groups decided on a mixed design entailing qualitative interviews with key persons and a workshop, while the last group decided on only qualitative interviews. In total, 50 regional actors participated in the process. After the interviews and workshops, the students analysed the outcomes and discussed their analysis with the economic development director and the teachers. Students met supervisors weekly to discuss the challenges they faced during this phase. During the third phase, the outcomes of the second phase were presented to the politicians and administrators from Grimstad municipality and representatives from industry and the university. The group presentation was one part of the examination for the course, and the other part was an individual exam paper on the engagement process.

Discussion

In this section, we connect the discussion back to the introduction, the analytical model and the previous thick description of the case and address the theoretical implications of the case, that is, what we can learn from the case.

From Liner Knowledge Transfer to Co-generation of Knowledge

Our main aim in our role as lecturers on the course was to enable the students to learn enough from the co-generation part of the process between students and lecturers in the classroom to co-generate knowledge in collaboration with actors in Grimstad. To achieve this aim, we avoided the linear approach of telling the students what co-generation is during the intensive week. Of course, we shared our concepts and frameworks but only as part of the construction process. Co-generation is a dialogic process (Greenwood and Levin 2007) involving actors that construct the meaning of the key concepts themselves. It is a sense-making process, not a sense-giving process (Weich 1995). We worked with concepts such as action research, the co-generative model, conflict and co-creation. For this discussion, we focus on the construction of the students' concept of co-creation (*samskaping*), which is the vision of the University of Agder.

To begin the reflection, we used the framework on action research for territorial development (Karlsen and Larrea 2014). The main challenge was to enable students to develop an awareness (Freire 1996) of the need for a different approach than the traditional linear approach whereby university members reflect on the problems of the region, identify what they think the solutions are and write a report with recommendations for the other territorial actors. We wanted the students to assume personal responsibility for their own knowledge development process with the regional actors. But how could we use this approach to work with the students? Since most of them had never participated in such a process, we created a dialogical learning process in the classroom, which we combined with a series of short linear lectures as an introduction to the main action research concepts. In the classroom, the students discussed the concepts and what they meant for each student. We then challenged them to attempt to generate a shared, collective understanding of the concepts. We decided to allow them to choose their own approach after a discussion on the advantages and disadvantages of different approaches. We presented them with a scenario where they could interview the actors and write a report with recommendations for them; we called this a product perspective. But we also allowed them to decide to move away from this towards more co-generative approaches where the solutions would not be recommended by students to the actor but constructed together with the actor. We named this the process perspective. We aimed to advance from a product perspective to a process perspective slowly, but this also had to be co-generated.

Constructing a Shared Understanding of Co-creation

The Co-Creation Lab, which was responsible for the implementation of the third mission strategy, had no official definition of what co-creation (*samskaping*) meant or any guidelines for how co-creation should be implemented with regional actors. Therefore, there was a need to discuss the meaning of the concept since the students' were going to use it. To frame this process, students were given an opportunity to work with their own definitions of co-creation. First, the students reflected individually on the concepts discussed in the sessions. Then, they were organised into groups in which they began to share their understanding of the concepts. When they had reached a shared understanding, they presented it in a plenary session, and a discussion was initiated with the aim of arriving at a shared definition for the whole class. Reaching a shared understanding was an intense process with much negotiation about which words to choose for the definition. The co-generation process created an awareness in the students about the importance and the necessity of using the time available to discuss the meaning of the concepts and achieve what had to be achieved collaboratively. By reflecting on the process, they realised the challenge of moving from an individual understanding to a shared understanding in a small group to a common understanding as a class. Thus, they were able to develop an awareness of what the process of constructing solutions in collaboration with other territorial actors might be like. The following is the co-generated definition:

> Co-creation is the process of working together towards a solution that is based on the exchange of ideas in a social process, where the goal is that the process should generate some form of action, change and development. (Developed by students at the University of Agder, 6 September 2017)

Co-generation Is Context Specific and Complex

The students' definition of co-creation differs from others that are not so explicit about the elements of process and change, such as the Macmillan dictionary definition:

> [A] way of working together where people from different backgrounds are invited to jointly produce a product or service that will benefit all of them. (Macmillandictionary 2018)

It is reasonable to think that since the students were in a course in which action research was the dominant methodology, their definition emphasises, first, that co-creation is a social process and, second, that the process should generate some form of action, change and development. This means not only that different universities can have different approaches to regional engagement but also that, in university conceived as a loosely coupled organisation, several definitions of regional engagement will co-exist in the same environment. This does not mean that it is worthless for academics to try to develop shared definitions to take the discussion further or that regional engagement can mean anything or that it cannot be measured or evaluated. Rather, it means that approaches to regional engagement must deal with complexity, and complexity includes the fact that different actors in a territory will have different interpretations on what the regional challenges are and what the solutions should be.

Co-generation of Knowledge Is Challenging

There are multiple types of actors within the university who are responsible for the third mission, and we have mentioned three: administrators, academics and students. One of the lessons learnt from the case is that research and teaching can be arenas for regional development. However, not all approaches to teaching and research fit with the idea of co-generation. The transformation of research in the Basque case and the transformation of teaching in the Innovation in the Public Sector course show that integrating the first two missions into regional development is challenging. Research and teaching must integrate process perspectives with product perspectives when addressing regional development. This means taking a step away from the idea that the university should transfer knowledge and solutions to other actors and embracing co-generation.

Despite devoting the initial phase of the course to introducing students to co-generative and process-oriented methods, when students made their own decisions on how to design their approaches, one group chose exclusively to use interviews, and the other two, who decided to organise workshops, did so as a complement to interviews.

Interviews can be part of a co-generative process. However, they are typically a tool of linear approaches where researchers obtain data from practitioners and then interpret the data in non-dialogic ways. Afterwards, the interpretations are presented back to the practitioners in the form of recommendations. In our initial sessions, we attempted to encourage students to try co-generative approaches. Still, none of the groups used these approaches exclusively. We interpret that this as due to existing assumptions not only of the students but also of academics, managers and policy-makers involved in the process. The linear approach is deeply rooted in the traditional understanding of the role of the university in the region and on how scientific or rigorous knowledge is constructed. The interpretation of the role of the responsible university in the region through co-generative processes is based on an interpretation of responsibility as care, which includes an interpretation of the university as part of the problems of the region and part of its solutions and as caring for the shared problems because they are its own. This makes it impossible for universities to position themselves as external observers of the regional problems. They must collaborate and co-generate knowledge with regional actors.

The construction of rigorous knowledge through co-generative processes and the positionality of university actors as insiders to the region requires the initiation of an epistemological discussion on the responsible regional university.

The Need for an Internal Dialogue on Regional Development Within the University

Together with students and academics, university managers play a principal role in the development of regional responsibility. The case shows that their main challenge relates to our previous argument about the separation of the first, second and third roles of the university. Interpreting the third role as separate from the first and second roles makes it easier to manage as it means that managers do not need to initiate the process of transforming the status quo through actual teaching and research. As the case demonstrates, the eagerness to engage too much with us from the Co-Creation Lab was not present. They wanted to create something new, which initially created excitement and energy. An interpretation of the third role as one that integrates the first and second roles within it would mean that university managers would need to engage in processes to make teaching and research more sensitive to the needs of the region. However, the university is an environment in which different actors have a high level of autonomy, and management can do little to transform teaching and research without the cooperation of academics. An interpretation of the third mission that includes teaching and research is more transformative than one that considers the third mission as a separate mission.

Conclusion

To conclude, we connect the discussion back to the introduction and the research question. In the previous thick description and the discussion of the case, we have shown how we integrated the regional development role into our teaching. The case resulted from a combination of circumstances. Through a coincidence, it was developed with Grimstad municipality. If someone from another municipality had approached us with a similar idea, the cases tried have been developed with that municipality. The conditions for such a project were present in the university, which had a new strategy with a vision for the co-creation of knowledge and the third mission initiative (the Co-Creation Lab). The conditions were also present in the academic core at the Department of Working Life and Innovation. Academics from that department had both theoretical knowledge about how to co-generate knowledge with regional actors and knowledge of how to do so in practice. They also assumed personal responsibility for engaging in regional development. The course was established with the aim of facilitating the co-generation of knowledge between students and actors in the region. We believed this could contribute to the University of Agder's vision. Thus, the case is not exclusively about the official third mission strategy nor is it only about administrators at the university taking responsibility for implementing the strategy. It is also a bottom-up initiative implemented by researchers who wanted to test knowledge generated in one context (the Basque Country) in another context (teaching in the Agder region). Abstracting from the case, we can argue that regional development is about connections in the myriad of spaces in which university actors and regional actors interact.

The official third mission strategy at the University of Agder was established as a temporary project and did not play an important or necessary role in our course. The challenge of the project was to reach into the academic core of teaching and research with the third mission initiative of co-creation. There had to be someone that was personally interested in collaborating both with the administration at university and also with regional actors. Viewed from the perspective of the academic core, it is much easier to choose to collaborate directly with regional actors without involving university administrators. The case shows that the existence of an official strategy developed by the university administration does not necessarily mean that the organisation is tightly coupled and that the strategy will be implemented from the top down. Such a strategy can be considered as one element of regional development that interlinks with other initiatives initiated by academics and students. A loosely coupled organisation provides flexibility for the development of initiatives like the one described. The case demonstrates that regional development cannot be solely in the form of a strategy or solely in the form of personal engagement. It must involve both institutional and personal responsibility.

As discussed in the chapter, responsibility is embodied in the practice of the individuals in universities when they act to contribute to improving the situation of the region. We define a responsible university as one in which individuals and communities who participate in any of the three missions consider the challenges of the region as constituents of their routine activities. Taking this step away from normative approaches to responsibility embodied in actions means facing complexity and participating in dialogue both inside the university (between managers, academics and students) and outside the university (with other regional actors).

If a university is a responsible university, does it need a third mission? Reflecting on the case discussed here, our argument is that a formal third mission strategy developed by the management of a university can be a useful vehicle for persons and communities in the university administration to contribute to improving the situation of the region. But, when it comes to academics and students, the first and second missions may have greater potential to make such a contribution as their daily activities, energy and innovative ideas focus on teaching and research. Consequently, we want to avoid an interpretation of regional responsibility that is exclusively connected to the third mission as this would disregard much of the practice of academics and students. If we connect responsibility to all three missions, most persons in universities would be involved in responsibility through their daily work, which would improve these processes.

Thus, the discussion of the case brings us closer to authors that argue that the third mission should be connected to teaching and research

(Goddard et al. 2016; Karlsen et al. 2017; Uyarra 2010). However, by considering universities as loosely coupled organisations, we propose a more nuanced approach that distinguishes between different types of actors inside the university and considers that they can be involved to different extents in the three missions. While third mission strategies that are not directly integrated into teaching and research, such as sitting on boards, participating in strategic processes or organising shared events for furthering the socialisation of knowledge, can be effective vehicles for engaging universities managers in regional issues, we consider that, for academics and students, the development of responsible first and second missions has unexplored potential. The challenge is that such a transformation requires changes in teaching and research methodologies (Greenwood and Levin 2016), which is a topic to be explored in the future.

Acknowledgements We want to thank the editors for inviting us to participate in this writing process. Thanks to Patrica Canto who inspired us to work with the concept of responsible research and innovation and especially responsibility as care. Thanks to Kirsi Pulkkinen and the other editors for their valuable comments and suggestions on an earlier version of the manuscript. Any remaining errors or omissions are our own.

Notes

1. Canto, P. (2019). *Research institutes as change agents in territorial development. An analytical framework on responsible research communication.* (PhD thesis). Deusto University, San Sebastian.

2. By the term 'external context', we mean the environment outside the university as an organisation. The external context can be an administration region, such as the host region of a university. The same applies to the term 'external actors'. An external actor can be an actor in the host region of a university, that is, a regional actor, or an actor outside the host region. In an empirical study, the external context and external actors must be defined.

3. Karlsen, J. (2007). *The regional role of the university: A study of knowledge creation in the agora between Agder University College and regional actors in Agder.* Norwegian University of Science and Technology, Trondheim.

4. For more information about the action research project in the Basque Country and concepts see, for example, Aranguren et al. (2012) and Karlsen and Larrea (2012, 2014, 2016, 2017, 2018).

References

Aranguren, M. J., Karlsen, J., & Larrea, M. (2012). Regional Collaboration – The Glue That Makes Innovation Happen? In H. C. G. Johnsen & R. Ennals (Eds.), *Creating Collaborative Advantage: Innovation and Knowledge Creation in Regional Economies* (pp. 113–122). Surrey: Gower.

Bardone, E., & Lind, M. (2016). Towards a Phronetic Space for Responsible Research (and Innovation). *Life Sciences, Society and Policy, 12*, 5. https://doi.org/10.1186/s40504-016-0040-8.

Boyer, E. L. (1990). *Scholarship Reconsidered: The Priorities of the Professoriate.* Carnegie Foundation for the Advancement of Teaching.

Burget, M., Bardone, E., & Pedaste, M. (2017). Definitions and Conceptual Dimensions of Responsible Research and Innovation: A Literature Review. *Science and Engineering Ethics, 23*(1), 1–19. https://doi.org/10.1007/s11948-016-9782-1.

Charles, D., Kitagawa, F., & Uyarra, E. (2014). Universities in Crisis? New Challenges and Strategies in Two English City-Regions. *Cambridge Journal of Regions, Economy and Society, 7*, 327–348.

Clark, B. R. (1998). *Creating Entrepreneurial Universities: Organizational Pathways of Transformation.* Oxford: IAU Press and Pergamon.

Clark, B. R. (2004). *Sustaining Change in Universities: Continuities in Case Studies and Concepts.* Berkshire: Society for Research into Higher Education and Open University Press.

Dunning, J. H. (2002). *Regions, Globalization, and the Knowledge-Based Economy.* Oxford: Oxford University Press.

Etzkowitz, H. (1983). Entrepreneurial Scientists and Entrepreneurial Universities in American Academic Science. *Minerva, 21*(2), 198–233.

Etzkowitz, H., & Leydesdorff, L. (1995). The Triple Helix – University-Industry-Government Relations: A Laboratory for Knowledge Based Economic Development. *EASST Review, 14*(1), 14–19.

Freire, P. (1996). *Pedagogy of the Oppressed*. Harmondsworth: Penguin Books.

Geertz, C. (1973). *The Interpretation of Cultures: Selected Essays*. New York: Basic Books.

Goddard, J. (2009). *Re-inventing the Civic University*. London: NESTA.

Goddard, J. (2011). *Connecting Universities to Regional Growth: A Practical Guide*. Sevilla, Spain IPTS JRC. http://ec.europa.eu/regional_policy/sources/docgener/presenta/universities2011/universities2011_en.pdf.

Goddard, J., Hazelkorn, E., Kempton, L., & Vallance, P. (2016). Introduction: Why the Civic University? In J. Goddard, E. Hazelkorn, L. Kempton, & P. Vallance (Eds.), *The Civic University: The Policy and Leadership Challenges* (pp. 3–15). Croydon: Edwar Elgar.

Greenwood, D., & Levin, M. (2007). *Introduction to Action Research* (2nd ed.). Thousand Oaks, CA: Sage.

Greenwood, D., & Levin, M. (2016). *Creating a New Public University and Reviving Democracy: Action Research in Higher Education*. New York: Berghahn.

Groves, C. (2009). Future Ethics: Risk, Care and Non-reciprocal Responsibility. *Journal of Global Ethics, 5*(1), 17–31. https://doi.org/10.1080/17449620902765286.

Guba, E. G., & Lincoln, Y. S. (2005). Paradigmatic Controversies, Contradictions, and Emerging Confluences. In N. K. Denzin & Y. S. Lincoln (Eds.), *The Sage Handbook of Qualitative Research* (3rd ed., pp. 191–215). Thousand Oaks, London, New Delhi: Sage Publications.

Hewitt-Dundas, N. (2012). Research Intensity and Knowledge Transfer Activity in UK Universities. *Research Policy, 41*, 262–275.

Huggins, R., Johnston, A., & Stride, C. (2012). Knowledge Networks and Universities: Locational and Organisational Aspects of Knowledge Transfer Interactions. *Entrepreneurship and Regional Development, 24*, 475–502.

Karlsen, J. (2007). *The Regional Role of the University: A Study of Knowledge Creation in the Agora between Agder University College and Regional Actors in Agder Norwegian University of Science and Technology, Trondheim*.

Karlsen, J., & Larrea, M. (2012). Emergence of Shared Leadership in the Basque Country. In M. Sotarauta, I. Horlings, & J. Liddle (Eds.), *Leadership and Change in Sustainable Regional Development* (pp. 212–233). London: Routledge.

Karlsen, J., & Larrea, M. (2014). *Territorial Development and Action Research: Innovation Through Dialogue*. Farnham: Routledge.

Karlsen, J., & Larrea, M. (2016). Collective Knowing. In H. Johnsen, E. S. Hauge, M. Magnussen, & R. Ennals (Eds.), *Applied Social Science Research in a Regional Knowledge System* (pp. 75–89). London: Routledge.

Karlsen, J., & Larrea, M. (2017). Moving Context from the Background to the Forefront of Policy Learning: Reflections on a Case in Gipuzkoa, Basque Country. *Environment and Planning C: Government and Policy, 35*(4), 721–736. https://doi.org/10.1177/0263774X16642442.

Karlsen, J., & Larrea, M. (2018). Regional Innovation System as a Framework for the Co-generation of Policy: An Action Research Approach. In A. Isaksen, R. Martin, & M. Trippl (Eds.), *New Avenues for Regional Innovation Systems: Theoretical Advances, Empirical Cases and Policy Lessons* (pp. 257–274). New York: Springer.

Karlsen, J., Beseda, J., Šima, K., & Zyzak, B. (2017). Outsiders or Leaders? The Role of Higher Education Institutions in the Development of Peripheral Regions. *Higher Education Policy, 30*(4), 463–479. https://doi.org/10.1057/s41307-017-0065-5.

Kitagawa, F., Sánchez-Barrioluengo, M., & Uyarra, E. (2016). Third Mission as Institutional Strategies: Between Isomorphic Forces and Heterogeneous Pathways. *Science and Public Policy, 43*(6), 736–750. https://doi.org/10.1093/scipol/scw015.

Laredo, P. (2007). Revisiting the Third Mission of Universities: Toward a Renewed Categorization of University Activities? *Higher Education Policy, 20*(4), 441–456.

Macmillandictionary. (2018). Co-creation. Retrieved from https://www.macmillandictionary.com/dictionary/british/co-creation.

Molas-Gallart, J., & Castro-Martínez, E. (2007). Ambiguity and Conflict in the Development of 'Third Mission' Indicators. *Research Evaluation, 16*(4), 321–330. https://doi.org/10.3152/095820207X263592.

Nowotny, H., Scott, P., & Gibbons, M. (2001). *Re-thinking Science: Knowledge and the Public in an Age of Uncertainty*. Cambridge: Polity Press.

OECD. (2009). *OECD Regions at a Glance*. Paris: The Organisation for Economic Co-operation and Development. http://www.oecd.org/document/9/0,3746,en_2649_37429_42396233_1_1_1_37429,00.html.

Perkmann, M., Tartari, V., McKelvey, M., Autio, E., Brostrom, A., D'Este, P., … Sobrero, M. (2013). Academic Engagement and Commercialisation: A Review of the Literature on University–Industry Relations. *Research Policy, 42*, 423–442. https://doi.org/10.1016/j.respol.2012.09.007.

Pinheiro, R., Benneworth, P., & Jones, G. A. (2012a). Introduction. In R. Pinheiro, P. Benneworth, & G. A. Jones (Eds.), *Universities and Regional Development: A Critical Assessment of Tensions and Contradictions* (pp. 1–8). London: Routledge.

Pinheiro, R., Benneworth, P., & Jones, G. A. (Eds.). (2012b). *Universities and Regional Development: A Critical Assessment of Tensions and Contradictions.* Milton Park and New York: Routledge.

Reason, P., & Bradbury, H. (2008). *The SAGE Handbook of Action Research Participative Inquiry and Practice* (2nd ed.). London: SAGE.

Rothaermel, F. T., Jiang, L., & Agung, S. D. (2007). University Entrepreneurship: A Taxonomy of the Literature. *Industrial and Corporate Change, 16*(4), 691–791. https://doi.org/10.1093/icc/dtm023.

Sánchez-Barrioluengo. (2014). Articulating the 'Three Missions' in Spanish Universities. *Research Policy, 43*, 1760–1773.

Schön, D. A. (1983). *The Reflective Practitioner – How Professionals Think in Action.* New York: Basic Books.

Spruit, S. L., Hoople, G. D., & Rolfe, D. A. (2015). Just a Cog in the Machine? The Individual Responsibility of Researchers in Nanotechnology Is a Duty to Collectivize. *Science and Engineering Ethics, 11*(1), 1–17. https://doi.org/10.1007/s11948-015-9718-1.

Stilgoe, J., Owen, R., & Macnaghten, P. (2013). Developing a Framework for Responsible Innovation. *Research Policy, 42*, 1568–1580.

Trippl, M., Sinozic, T., & Smith, H. L. (2015). The Role of Universities in Regional Development: Conceptual Models and Policy Institutions in the UK, Sweden and Austria. *European Planning Studies, 23*(9), 1722–1740. https://doi.org/10.1080/09654313.2015.1052782.

University of Agder. (2016). *Strategy 2016–2020.* Kristiansand: University of Agder.

Uyarra, E. (2010). Conceptualizing the Regional Roles of Universities: Implications and Contradictions. *European Planning Studies, 18*(8), 1227–1246. https://doi.org/10.1080/09654311003791275.

Weich, K. (1976). Educational Organizations as Loosely Coupled Systems. *Administrative Science Quarterly, 21*(1), 1–19.

Weich, K. (1995). *Sensemaking in Organizations.* Thousand Oaks, CA: Sage.

Wilford, S. H. (2015). What Is Required of Requirements? A First Stage Process Towards Developing Guidelines for Responsible Research and Innovation. *SIGCAS Computers and Society, 45*(3), 348–355.

Wilford, S. H. (2018). First Line Steps in Requirements Identification for Guidelines Development in Responsible Research and Innovation (RRI). *Systemic Practice Actionion Research, 31*, 539–556. https://doi.org/10.1007/s11213-018-9445-z.

Yin, R. K. (2013). *Case Study Research: Design and Methods.* Thousand Oaks, CA: Sage.

Part IV

Role of Organising in Achieving Responsible Universities

8

Merger of Universities and Interdisciplinarity

Tea Vellamo, Elias Pekkola, and Taru Siekkinen

Introduction

The biggest challenges facing our society today are the so-called wicked problems, which, according to the United Nations, are "related to poverty, inequality, climate, environmental degradation, prosperity, and peace and justice" (The UN Sustainable Development Goals 2015). These global societal problems have also been introduced into the higher education arena through global rankings, such as Times Higher Education, which assesses universities' performance against the UN Sustainable Development Goals.

Universities, which have a key position within societies to produce new knowledge and innovations (Välimaa et al. 2016), answer wicked problems by forming new interdisciplinary structures. Indeed, increased

T. Vellamo (✉) • E. Pekkola
Tampere University, Tampere, Finland
e-mail: tea.vellamo@tuni.fi; elias.pekkola@tuni.fi

T. Siekkinen
University of Jyväskylä, Jyväskylä, Finland
e-mail: taru.siekkinen@jyu.fi

societal complexity, divergent stakeholder needs and conflicting political values make it impossible to solve these problems solely through rational–technical (Head and Alford 2015) or other discipline-based approaches. Instead of expert-driven rational planning and engineering, wicked problems require collaboration involving different actors and organisations (Head and Alford 2015; Ferlie et al. 2011).

In higher education, interdisciplinarity, which entails breaking down disciplinary boundaries, building on different experiences and perspectives and involving new participants, has been promoted as a means to address wicked problems and produce social innovations (Brown et al. 2010). Educational institutions establish interdisciplinary infrastructures to foster new kinds of collaboration outside the traditional disciplinary fields (Ramaley 2014). University mergers are also used to challenge the traditional disciplinary structures and encourage new innovative epistemological approaches by forming larger and more complex interdisciplinary higher education institutions. In addition, institutions create interdisciplinary units through organisational restructuring (Geschwind 2018).

Technical disciplines and engineering are crucial to solving many wicked problems. According to critics of rational–technical approaches, a paradigm shift is needed in technical education. Along with external stakeholders and other disciplines, technical education could eschew tradition and find better ways to tackle these wicked problems (Head and Alford 2015, 712).

In this chapter, we analyse a multidisciplinary, sector-breaking merger of three higher education institutions in the Tampere City region. The strategy of this new university consortium is to combine education and research on technology, society and health to create an interdisciplinary approach for solving wicked problems. The three institutions, which merged in 2019, include a single field technical university, Tampere University of Technology (TUT), and a comprehensive university, the University of Tampere (UTa), forming a new university, Tampere University. The new university owns the Tampere University of Applied Sciences (TAMK), thus forming a university consortium.

The new university adopts a "multidisciplinary approach [which] will not only deliver more effective responses to global challenges but also open up new opportunities for science and its applications" (Tampere University web page—https://www.tuni.fi/en/news/together-we-are-greater). Interdisciplinarity has been chosen as a transformation strategy in the university's organisational reform. Tampere University strategy states, "[w]e recognise and know how to systematically anticipate the most demanding global, national and regional phenomena, challenges and opportunities." This occurs through "[c]lose and well-organised interaction with stakeholders and multidisciplinary research and development platforms and programmes that combine different disciplines ..." (Tampere3 strategy 2 Feb 2018). In practice, this includes establishing new interdisciplinary faculty structures to increase interaction between different fields. Multiple disciplinary views and boundary-crossing cooperation should increase the social relevance of technical education and enhance its capacity to address wicked problems. However, this may challenge the identity of technical education and affect its role in the eyes of stakeholders.

Here, we analyse the new university's interdisciplinary faculty structure plans and their justifications and examine them from the perspective of technical education. The empirical data consist of three subsequent proposals for the new faculty structure by the University Consortium Transitionary Board, the official statements of different internal organs of technical education and open feedback from the higher education institutions' staff and students collected through an electronic questionnaire. The Transitionary Board members represent the highest level of domestic and international expertise in the fields of science and the arts at the university and in industry. According to the Board, the interdisciplinary faculty structure arises from the new university's strategy and educational needs, as interdisciplinary approaches are better for addressing wicked problems. Staff and students commented on the effects they thought the new interdisciplinary structure would have on technical education and its responsiveness to its stakeholders. To identify the anticipated effects of the interdisciplinary organisational structure on technical education, we asked the following question:

- How are the potential benefits and risks of the new interdisciplinary faculty structure for the different stakeholders of technical education represented in the feedback?

First, we identify the different stakeholders presented in the feedback. After which, we examine how the interdisciplinary structure is considered to affect the stakeholders and the university's responsibilities towards them. There is a tension between the aims of the new structure and how representatives of the technical fields think the university should be responsible to its stakeholders from a disciplinary perspective. Since the rhetoric and supporting theories extol the virtues of an interdisciplinary approach, we are interested in the possible threats this new structure creates for technical education. We seek to determine whether the proposed interdisciplinary structure is perceived to jeopardise the identity, responsiveness to stakeholders and social relevance of technical education.

Data Collection and Analysis

The Transitional Board of Tampere University is an external and independent organ comprising representatives with academic backgrounds in the university's disciplines and major industrial stakeholders. According to the Board, the faculty structure was meant to be ground-breaking by combining the focus areas of the new university in an interdisciplinary way and based on the needs of teaching. In addition, the Board aimed to produce a well-balanced, administratively functional faculty structure (slides on the first proposal 24 Nov 2017).

During the process, the Board made two proposals for the faculty structure, receiving 700 and 400 comments, respectively (see Appendix 2). We received permission from the Tampere3 project organisation to use the proposals, the official comments and the staff and student comments collected through online questionnaires. The questionnaires were completed anonymously, so it is impossible to determine whether they are from students or staff or from which institution.

The data were analysed using two methods of qualitative analysis. First, a conventional content analysis was performed, which is appropriate when the aim of the study is to describe the phenomenon and where the categories arise from the data (Hsieh and Shannon 2005). In addition, we employed the ideas of thinking with theory, where qualitative data are analysed based on prior research (Jackson and Mazzei 2012). In practice, employing these two methods meant that the categories arose from the data, although the researchers also applied their previous knowledge of the subject and theories during the analysis process. The relevant theories included university social responsibility and stakeholder theory and theories of disciplinarity. These theories were selected because university social responsibility is related to the aims of sustainability and addressing wicked problems while acknowledging the responsibility of higher education to its different stakeholders. Disciplinarity and the different disciplinary approaches illuminate the chosen interdisciplinary structure and its underlying theoretical implications. In addition, disciplinary theories are a basis for academic identities (Becher and Trowler 2001; Ylijoki and Ursin 2013).

Social Responsibility of Universities

The requirement for social relevance is one of the biggest challenges in higher education (Kogan and Teichler 2007). The function of universities in society is related to creating knowledge, fostering innovations and producing a skilled workforce to meet the needs of society. Knowledge creation is emphasised to be collaborative, breaking down institutional and disciplinary boundaries, and universities have a central function in this regard (Gibbons et al. 1994; Välimaa et al. 2016). Higher education should increasingly involve external stakeholders in research and teaching activities and higher education institutions and their larger communities engage in beneficial knowledge exchange and the reciprocal exchange of resources (Van de Ven 2007; Ramaley 2014). However, as Van de Ven (2007) argues, there is a relevance gap between the theoretical academic research produced in universities and the needs of stakeholders in society for applicable knowledge. New models for collaboration between educational institutions and broader society also have different implications for research, teaching, learning, curricula and the structure of institutions (Ramaley 2014). Accordingly, the academic disciplinary approach may be inadequate for meeting stakeholders' needs for applicable knowledge.

Responsibility in higher education is an elusive concept. Vasilescu et al. (2010, 4177) view universities' social responsibility as "part of the debate about competitiveness and sustainability in the globalization context." Universities strive to become responsible because of moral and legal requirements or to gain competitive edge in marketing the university brand and to maintain their institutional legitimacy and funding (Wan Saiful 2006). The concept of university social responsibility is also closely tied to the concept of stakeholder (Tetrevova and Sabolova 2010). When discussing responsibility and its different aspects, we ask to whom the university is responsible and how. There are multiple stakeholders with either complimentary or conflicting interests in the university. Based on the literature on higher education stakeholder theories (Esfijani et al. 2013; Chapleo and Simms 2010; Tetrevova and Sabolova 2010; Benneworth and Jongbloed 2010; Lyytinen et al. 2017), we can summarise and group actual or potential university stakeholders as follows:

- Students, applicants, graduates
- Staff, employees, academics or non-academics
- Industry, business
- Government on central, regional and local levels
- Other (higher education) institutions as competitors or partners
- Society
- Community
- Funders, grant agencies, sponsors, suppliers
- Environmental groups, consumer groups
- General public, taxpayers

There are different views on the most important stakeholders in public universities. Benneworth and Jongbloed (2010) see government as the most important stakeholder, as it is the major funder of public higher education. However, due to changed funding mechanisms and increased demand for societal impact, external stakeholders have gained importance. Universities are responsible to companies and industry for research and development cooperation and for providing workforce with the needed skills and knowledge; to students, for providing them with relevant degree education; and more generally, to the whole academic community (staff, academics, employees), for providing the conditions and resources for teaching and research as well as institutional reputation and acclaim. Maintaining the university's rank and prestige is not only an intra-institutional responsibility but also an aspect of national and international competitiveness. Environmental responsibility is also important, as universities are indispensable producers of knowledge for solving serious ecological problems. The ways in which a university strives to be responsible to its different stakeholders affect not only its education, research and other actions but also its strategy and organisational structure. Chapleo and Simms (2010, 6) state "a stakeholder group's impact on funding and policies of the university were consistently highlighted as key" as well as "their ability to make demands on the university by their expectations." Thus, universities respond to the needs of the stakeholders, while stakeholders also influence university strategies, policies and structures.

The Transition Beyond Disciplinarity

The Transitionary Board of Tampere University states that the aim of the new university is to form new, bold and broader combinations that transgress traditional disciplinary borders. The Board also states that the structure is based on the needs of teaching and its responsiveness to stakeholders. Research activities will be organised separately through research groups. The justification for interdisciplinary education is to produce relevant knowledge that graduates will need in working life as well as an approach to a sustainable future solving wicked problems. The suggested organisational structure is based on the transition from disciplinarity to interdisciplinarity.

To understand the different concepts related to more than one discipline interacting in education or research, we need to examine the concepts of disciplinarity, crossdisciplinarity, interdisciplinarity, multidisciplinarity and transdisciplinarity (Tress et al. 2005; Stember 1991). A discipline may be defined as a particular academic area of study which has particular identifiable characteristics. Within an academic discipline, there are generally believed to be shared goals and a set of theories and epistemologies but relatively little cooperation with other disciplines (Becher and Trowler 2001). Through their research activities, disciplines are "orientated towards one specific goal, looking for an answer to a specific research question" (Tress et al. 2005, 15). Disciplines are often the basis for forming institutional structures, such as faculties, but they may also be constituents of an academic's identity since they form their own cultures. The identities of academics are based on disciplines rather than on organisations (Becher and Trowler 2001).

The disciplinary tradition has been criticised as restrictive, normative and unable to address the multifaceted aspects of real-world problems (Tress et al. 2005; Chettiparamb 2007). Attempts to overcome disciplinary limits, integrate different disciplinary approaches or even transcend the boundaries of the university are seen as viable solutions. Research and education that is not restrained to a particular discipline may be cross-, inter-, multi- or transdisciplinary. These terms have different meanings, although they are often confused or used interchangeably.

Crossdisciplinarity involves at least two different disciplines and viewing one discipline from the perspectives of others (Stember 1991). Meanwhile, multidisciplinarity involves "several different academic disciplines researching one theme or problem, but with multiple disciplinary goals" in loose cooperation, which does not cross subject boundaries to create new knowledge and theory (Tress et al. 2005, 15–16). Multidisciplinarity is the combination of multiple disciplines with a shared or common goal. The cooperation consists mostly of knowledge exchange, but theory development is still disciplinary based. Multidisciplinarity involves several researchers working together from their own disciplinary viewpoints (Stember 1991). Interdisciplinarity takes the multidisciplinary approach further by crossing disciplinary boundaries and uniting them with common goal-setting. Interdisciplinarity encompasses the development of integrated theories and epistemologies. Transdisciplinary is similar to interdisciplinarity, but it extends the disciplinary, scientific and academic boundaries, integrating both academic disciplines and non-academic stakeholders. Knowledge and theories are developed through cooperation between academia and society, with common goal-setting by actors from different disciplinary and organisational backgrounds, which may be academic or non-academic (Tress et al. 2005).

Recent research has questioned the social relevance of traditional engineering education, especially in addressing wicked problems (Edström 2017; Lönngren 2017). According to Lönngren (2017, 32) "the existence of a strong engineering paradigm seems to create a disciplinary culture in which diversity of perspectives and worldviews is not highly valued." Moreover, engineering education has been criticised for a lack of social relevance and ignoring social, political and environmental issues or real-life problems (Denis and Heap 2012, 265). Thus, the aim of breaking down disciplinary cultures and introducing other disciplinary perspectives would seem fruitful in increasing the social relevance of technical education. A new multidisciplinary university with interdisciplinary faculties would enable technical education to increase beneficial interactions with other disciplines. Both terms "multidisciplinarity" and "interdisciplinarity" are used in relation to the Tampere University merger, and it is not always clear if a distinction is made between these. In our discussion, we have chosen to use the term "interdisciplinary." However, despite the term used, an approach that transgresses the disciplinary boundaries is advocated in the new university and its organisational structure.

Interdisciplinarity in Higher Education Mergers in Finland

Higher education mergers in Western Europe and Nordic countries in particular have been used as policy instruments for restructuring higher education systems and meeting the goals of higher education policies (Pinheiro et al. 2016). Mergers may also be motivated by the need to increase responsiveness to environmental changes and the expectations of societal stakeholder groups. In practice, these demands have called for increased size and enhanced internal diversity, for example, by exploring interdisciplinary synergies (Pinheiro et al. 2016). In previous studies, the concept of discipline has been seen as integral for the success of a merger process. Previous research (Harman and Harman 2003; Pinheiro et al. 2016) indicate that institutions with similar disciplinary structures tend to be culturally more difficult to merge than institutions that are from different disciplinary backgrounds or merged across higher education sectors. Nevertheless, disciplinary structure plays an important role in the merger process, where the aim can be the consolidation of similar types of academic portfolios or creating synergies by combining different types of disciplinary profiles.

Although increasing interdisciplinarity seems to be a "typical suspect" in justifying merger processes, it has not been the most common one in restructuring the Finnish higher education landscape. The Finnish government has initiated a series of mergers since the mid-2000s, termed "the structural development of the Finnish higher education system," with the premise of making Finnish higher education more reactive to global changes (Välimaa et al. 2014). Aarrevaara and Dobson (2016) analysed the main goals of the Finnish merger processes until 2015 in universities of applied sciences (five mergers) and universities (five mergers). Interdisciplinarity was only a stated goal in two out of ten mergers—Aalto University and Tampere University of Applied Sciences. In the latest 2019 merger, the Tampere3 merger, interdisciplinarity is a central aim.

The most significant forerunner is the Aalto University merger, which involved the Helsinki School of Economics, Helsinki University of Technology and the University of Arts and Design Helsinki. This combination of three distinctive fields was intended to create an innovative interdisciplinary and responsive university. Aalto has been an initiator in building a bridge between interdisciplinarity and excellence. As Aula and Tienari (2011) note, since the outset of the Aalto branding campaign, coincidentally or not, other universities in Finland have also branded themselves as "leading multidisciplinary international institutions." Aalto has become a showcase of Finnish innovative knowledge society and practical interdisciplinary industry–university collaboration (Aula and Tienari 2011). This leads to the hypothesis that a multidisciplinary merger with increased interdisciplinarity should increase the relevance, innovativeness and international competitiveness of all fields, including technical education. This also implies that external stakeholders expect mergers to enhance knowledge production and meet the needs of industry and regional stakeholders (Välimaa et al. 2014, 42).

In our other research, we discovered that education and research at Tampere University of Technology were already perceived as interdisciplinary by academics in the university (Vellamo et al. forthcoming). In the new university structure, technical education will not form one or several separate faculties but will be dispersed in five faculties with other disciplines of the comprehensive university. Administratively, this could lead to large faculties, with varied degree programmes (e.g., theatre studies and computer science) being led by one dean. As the stated aim also includes educational cooperation, this has raised questions about identifying shared educational content that will be relevant to disciplines as different as arts and engineering. An interdisciplinary organisational structure was chosen to increase the relevance of educational programmes from the perspective of stakeholders and to strive to become a socially responsible university (see also Chap. 6). This presupposes that the disciplinary-based organisational structure of the merging universities has not contributed to interdisciplinarity and that the new multidisciplinary structure would stimulate cooperation between different disciplines. This would also lead the faculties to provide education better suited to addressing wicked problems and more responsible to higher education stakeholders.

Defining the Stakeholders

The faculty structure of the new university combines different disciplines into faculties based on the needs of educational development and shared themes. However, from the proposals, it is unclear how and by whom these themes have been defined. According to the feedback, neither the academics nor the students of these fields were consulted, and the shared themes did not arise from previous cooperation between the fields. In the plan, no particular resources or other instruments for increasing interdisciplinarity are mentioned; it appears that simply placing different disciplines into the same organisational units is expected to lead to interdisciplinarity in education.

When we examined both the justifications of the faculty structure proposal and the feedback on it, we anticipated that several different stakeholders would be mentioned. We were able to identify five main stakeholders: students, academics, institution, industry and region/nation (cf. Esfijani et al. 2013; Tetrevova and Sabolova 2010). The staff provided most of the feedback, and even though they do not mention themselves as a stakeholder group, it is clear that their interests are important and that the university is responsible to them. The university itself was referred to as a stakeholder several times, although this can often be traced back to the academics. We have labelled one of the stakeholders as the nation/region; however, based on empirical analysis, a nation is defined primarily from the viewpoint of the national economy rather than from a social or legal perspective. This refers to economic and innovative competitiveness at the local, national and global levels, for which technical education is responsible. The stakeholders, the university's responsibility towards them and the possible benefits if the disciplinary approach is transgressed are presented in the following table. Interdisciplinarity has become a normative perspective in higher education policy, and many stakeholders, such as national and international funding bodies, research councils and ministries, are pushing towards interdisciplinarity through financial steering.

In sum, it seems that a more interdisciplinary approach should be beneficial to all stakeholders by increasing the university's responsibility to each stakeholder in different positive ways. In the following sub-chapters, we look at the different aspects of university responsibility to different stakeholders and the effects the new interdisciplinary organisational structure is expected to have on these stakeholders, as perceived by the students and faculty. However, while Table 8.1 presents interdisciplinarity as positive for these stakeholders, the reality might be different. In addition, the stakeholders themselves are presented as monolithic entities with a set of well-defined interests, although they have different views, conflicting interests and multiple stakeholders are represented as a single group. In many ways, we are simplifying the stakeholders, the university's responsibility towards them and their idealised disciplinary stance. With stakeholders such as institutions, we are referring to the meso level of the organisation, acknowledging that this does not actually represent the different parts and levels or members of the organisation.

Table 8.1 Summary of the main stakeholders, university responsibilities towards them and what interdisciplinarity could provide for them

Stakeholder	University responsibility	Idealised interdisciplinarity
Students	Applicable knowledge	Different (inter)disciplinary perspectives
	Skills for working life	
	Relevant degree	Transferrable soft skills
	Employability	New attractive interdisciplinary degree programmes for students
	Attractive study choice for prospective students	
Academics	Attractive workplace for top academics	Interdisciplinary teaching cooperation
	Good resources for teaching and research	Cooperating across disciplines in interdisciplinary research groups
Institution	Institutionally high-ranked university	Attractive and competitive, new and innovative interdisciplinary university
	Other institutions as partners and competitors	
Industry	Providing highly skilled workforce	Involved in teaching and research
	Cooperation in teaching and research	Crossing university boundaries
	Social innovations	
Region/ nation	Local to global competitiveness	Innovation system crossing the university boundaries
	Innovations	
	National economy	

Responsibility Towards Students

The staff and student responses indicate that the primary responsibility of the university and technical education is to students and prospective students or applicants. Technical education, as carried out by the technical university, is described as attractive to applicants and having high-quality teaching. These aspects may be threatened in the new university because of the new faculty structure or because the proposed names of the faculties may be misleading. The following quotes highlight concerns about the attractiveness of technical education in Tampere for future students:

> [H]ow well will the engineering degree programs placed in different faculties fare in the national student applications? They might, no doubt, inter-

est new applicant groups, but most likely not the traditional applicants. (Comments on the second proposal)

If this new faculty structure is carried out, it is certain that Tampere3 remains a second option for [Information and Communication Technology] ICT students compared to the universities of Helsinki and Aalto paddling way ahead. (Comments on the first proposal)

For the fields of engineering, the new structure will make it difficult for applicants to choose which program to apply to, and make Tampere3 a less attractive place. (Comments on the first proposal)

From the above feedbacks, it appears the applicants may not recognise or appreciate technical education in the new university because of the organisational structure. It is surprising that applicants would emphasise the organisational structure and faculty names rather that the content and names of the degree programmes. According to these responses, there is a risk that applicants may choose another (technical) university in Finland (e.g., Aalto), where technical education is perceived as more traditionally or visibly present. In the quotes, information and communication technology (ICT) is a field where there is thought be competition between Tampere and other universities offering technical education. These arguments suggest that future students find a traditional disciplinary structure more appealing and prestigious and would not appreciate a more interdisciplinary organisational structure.

Based on the comments, the current and future students' identities as technical students and their trust in the quality of their education may also be in jeopardy: "We believe the proposed structure will dilute the requirements for study attainments because of the disparity between the fields in the proposed faculty on evaluating credit points and to the degradation of the technical identity of students" (Statement of the Student Guild Indecs and Manager). Here, technical education is presented as demanding and requiring rigorous study, whereas other fields are implicitly less demanding and thus do not have the same prestige. Hence, a more interdisciplinary education might dilute the content and value of technical degree programmes.

Responsibility Towards Industry

Several passages highlight the responsibility of technical education to industry stakeholders and companies. This responsibility of working life relevance seems particular to technical education, as this aspect was not raised in the feedback relating to other fields.

According to the responses, grouping the technical degree programmes into the same faculties with degree programmes from other fields may put the responsibility to industry at risk. The respondents fear that the inclusion of common courses might dilute the content of the technical degree, and graduates would no longer have the technical skills demanded by industry. Another concern is that the perception that companies have of the reputation and brand of the current technical degrees might be diminished, therefore making companies unwilling to hire graduates or to cooperate with the faculty in research or teaching. For example, companies will not cooperate with faculties that do not appear technical enough and will not hire Masters of Science graduates from a "faculty of humanities" (comments on the first proposal). According to one respondent, "The appreciation of industrial management and knowledge management in the working market needs to be secured by keeping the brand of these degree programs focused on technology" (comments on the first proposal). Hence, it seems that industry primarily appreciates technological knowledge, not interdisciplinary degrees or soft transferrable skills. However, this represents the view the respondents, academics and students have on industry stakeholders. The respondents worry that the faculty structures are planned without knowledge of the industry stakeholders' needs. Indeed, there were requests to ask stakeholders what they expect from technical education and how the teaching of these skills should be organised: "please contact local industry like Valmet, Insta, Cargotec, Sandvik and ask what type of M.Sc. students they need" (comments on the first proposal).

Those commenting on the proposed faculty structure do not see the interdisciplinary combination of technical degree programmes with degree programmes from other non-technical fields as a positive development. They fear that industry stakeholders will not recognise this kind of technical degree. In addition, there are worries that the content of the degrees might become less technology-focused. Overall, the respondents are concerned that these changes might result in such a drastic transformation that graduates would no longer constitute a suitable workforce for companies, thereby risking the competitiveness of the whole nation: "This way Tech industry will disappear from Finland" (comments on the first proposal).

The Transitionary Board that prepared the new faculty structure did not ask comments from external stakeholders (e.g., companies). The Board wrote the proposal and then asked for comments from the faculty and students and internal bodies of the three merging institutions. The Board itself is supposed to represent external stakeholders, with members from companies and other investors such as the city of Tampere. However, in the comments on the faculty proposal, the Board is criticised for not knowing what external stakeholders want. The respondents do not consider the Transitionary Board a well-known and respected stakeholder and thus do not consider its proposals legitimate (cf. Geschwind 2018).

Institutional Responsibility as Responsibility Towards Academics?

Many respondents see the university and technical education as competing with other universities globally and nationally. The respondents mention Aalto most frequently, but also Lappeenranta University of Technology, the University of Oulu and the University of Turku as the national competitors. Other Finnish universities offering technical degree education are viewed as taking advantage of the perceived decrease in the role of technology at Tampere: "Nationally there are investments made in technical education in e.g. Lappeenranta, Oulu and Turku. If technology is not really strong and visible in the profile of the new university, the focus will move to these other universities in Finland" (Petition for the Stand of Technology by the Student Union).

The references to Aalto as the main competitor in technical education are interesting, as Aalto has been branded a multidisciplinary university. However, it is still strongly associated with the former Helsinki University of Technology (Aula and Tienari 2011). In the responses, Aalto is also regarded as an example of not choosing a multidisciplinary structure in the merger but keeping separate schools. Some respondents see this as a form of appreciation of the different disciplines: "For example, in Aalto, they did not combine arts and technology by force, but gave both their own value and position as independent" (comments on the first proposal). Some responses use Aalto as a point of comparison from a critical perspective: "The main mistake made in Aalto was not creating a clear ICT focus area. This is a mistake that should not be repeated in Tampere … the ICT-field could become a crown jewel in the new university" (comments on the second proposal).

The proposed structure of the new university is criticised for hiding technology amongst multi-disciplinary faculties, which degrades the internal cooperation of different technical fields (especially different strands of ICT). Some respondents also criticised the naming of the faculties in a way that does not clearly indicate that they provide technical education, particularly in comparison to national and international counterparts, including prestigious universities such as MIT and Delft. It is argued that well-known and functioning models should be adopted rather than inventing completely novel structures, which are not self-evident to students, academics or external stakeholders: "In top-notch [technical] universities, there is an ICT faculty" (comments on the second proposal). Many respondents thus advocate for a recognisable academic discipline and an organisational structure based on it (cf. Becher and Trowler 2001). The respondents argue that the stakeholders want a disciplinary structure, and this is important for the university's prestige, although it seems that the academics are the ones advocating for a traditional disciplinary-based organisation.

The comments indicate that high-ranked universities, such as MIT, epitomise the ideal structure that the new university should emulate. It seems that universities that are not highly ranked globally cannot be trailblazers in creating new structures, faculty names and degree programmes but should follow more traditional and recognisable models and the example of world-class universities (cf. Geschwind 2018). The Board did not use this emulation of role models as a justification for either the merger or structure, although it seems that the staff and students would have found this legitimate. Those who gave feedback identified universities that should have been benchmarked when planning the new structure. However, other universities were only mentioned as models in the comments concerning technical education. As Geschwind (2018, 12) notes, "there are indicators that the technical universities to a higher degree refer to a market related logic, including e.g. position, branding and competitors within the same organizational sub-field." Thus, it may be argued that institutional responsibility towards stakeholders is particularly important for technical education.

It seems that the university's ranking and prestige matter to external stakeholders but even more to the internal stakeholders and academic staff. The academics seem to fear that the university will lose its prestige and become a less attractive workplace for top researchers. In addition, the lower ranking of the university could affect the appreciation the academics themselves receive globally. Many of the respondents represent the technical university as an entity and a stakeholder, although it is problematic to present the organisation as a monolithic entity with a set of well-defined interests. In many cases, it seems that the actual stakeholder whose interests are presented as those of the university is the academic staff of a particular field. Academics associate themselves with the organisation, and if the status of the university is compromised, their academic identities are threatened. Indeed, Välimaa et al. (2014, 45–46) argue that the loss of academic identity may be a consequence of a merger. They note that there may be resistance, as academics see the merger as a "top-down organizational reform rather than an organic, bottom-up development."

Responsibility Towards Region and Nation

The increasing role of the university in the local community is reflected in the growing importance of university social responsibility (Chapleo and Simms 2010). The responsibility to the nation and region regarding technical education mostly relates to the national or local economy rather than to civil society. Many of the comments highlight the role of the technical university in securing competitiveness with industry stakeholders by creating local innovation systems. This viewpoint is especially prominent in relation to ICT:

Tampere is a major national and international centre of the ICT industry, including software applications, games and until recently mobile communications and networks .... Tampere University should be organised to meet this need, should forge strong relationships with local companies and make computer science and related disciplines a key part of its educational profile. The alternative is to risk these companies relocating to other places in Finland that can serve their needs better, and where they can compete for the graduates on offer. (Comments on the first proposal)

This quote refers to the industry, the Tampere region and Finland as stakeholders. It seems that failing the responsibility towards industry ultimately means that the university does not serve its local and national stakeholders, which may threaten national and regional competitiveness.

Technical education is more responsible to the local and national economies than other fields, and any perceived weakening of technical education would thus have a negative effect: "The role of technology is weak in the proposal and if it is carried out, the structure will harm the education and research in technical fields in Tampere and through this the whole local economic life and competitiveness" (comments on the second proposal). Strong technical education (here ICT) is seen as crucial to economic growth and sustainability: "If we look into the future of Finland and industry in the Tampere region, it only grows significantly because of ICT fields ... that is why T3 needs a really strong, visible and prominent ICT faculty!" (comments on the second proposal). Another comment expresses a similar view: "IT industry is one of the cornerstones in industry in the Tampere region, and its societal and economic relevance will not dwindle in the long run (on the contrary). Taking this into account, it seems unbelievable that the proposed faculty structure aims at hiding IT fields" (comment on the second proposal).

In these comments, the Tampere region and Finland are seen as the stakeholders; however, they are quite abstract, and the responsibility towards them is also an abstract concept. Competitiveness cannot be traced back to a particular actor but is closely related to industry. It is also clearly something that the university and technical education can provide to its stakeholders; therefore, any perceived weakening of technical education may threaten the sustainability of the local and national economies.

Intertwined Responsibilities

It was not easy to distinguish the different stakeholders to whom technical education is responsible, as they were often linked to each other in the answers. For example, internationally competitive degree programmes, which are relevant to industry, are also attractive to students. The most reoccurring stakeholders were industry and students. It seems obvious that students would be considered an important stakeholder group (cf. Chapleo and Simms 2010). However, it should be noted that the students gave comments on the proposals, which could heighten the importance of the student perspective.

From what is known about the identity of technical education, companies and industry stakeholders are also considered very important. Of the abovementioned stakeholders, industry is the one mentioned most often in the responses. In addition, the regional and national stakeholders often seem to be linked to industry, which further increases the importance of industry as a stakeholder.

However, the most important stakeholders are the academics and the university, as the brand, ranking, prestige and competitiveness of the institution are relevant to itself and all the other stakeholders. In effect, it seems that the university must be responsible to itself to be responsible to other stakeholders. In the responses, the university is represented as a unified organisational entity, perhaps to enhance the impact of the academic staff in technical fields or to hide the otherwise clear self-interest. Importantly, most of the comments were made by the staff of the merging institutions. Thus, the views of the staff are represented in the answers, even though they seldom name themselves as a stakeholder group. Some of these views are also represented as being those of the external stakeholders, while in reality they serve the interests of the academics.

The importance of different stakeholders is often attributed to their financial role in the university or their "potential impact on the strategic direction of the organisation" (Chapleo and Simms 2010, 8). There are also other stakeholders more directly related to the funding of higher education, including the government, ministry, funding bodies or taxpayers. Even though the government was identified in the theoretical part as one of the most salient stakeholders (cf. Benneworth and Jongbloed 2010), it is mentioned in few responses, and when it is, only in relation to the competitiveness and profiling of universities.

In sum, it can be argued that the respondents do not agree with the Transitionary Board on the benefits of interdisciplinarity. Instead, they argue that an interdisciplinary structure threatens the responsibility of technical education to its main stakeholders (Table 8.2).

It seems that if technical education had continued in a technical university or at least in faculties only providing Master of Science (Technology) education, it could meet its responsibilities and the demands of its stake-

Table 8.2 Summary of the aspects interdisciplinarity is considered to jeopardise from the perspective of technical education stakeholders

Stakeholder	University responsibility	Interdisciplinarity jeopardises

Students	Applicable knowledge
	Skills for working life
	Relevant degree
	Employability
	Attractive study choice for
	  prospective students
		Less technical knowledge, less
		  demanding studies
		Less prestigious degree
		Employability of
		  graduates decreased
		Less attractive choice for
		  applicants

Academics	Attractive workplace for top
	  academics
	Good resources for teaching
	  and research
		Less attractive as a workplace
		Academics' reputation
		  influenced by lower ranking
		Resources must be shared with
		  other disciplines

Institution	High-raked top university
	Technical university
		Not resembling high-ranked top
		  universities
		Loses identity as technical
		  university

Industry	Providing highly skilled
	  workforce
	Cooperation in teaching and
	  research
	Innovations
		Less willing to hire graduates
		Less willing to cooperate in
		  teaching and research
		Technical breakthrough in
		  industry less likely

Region/ nation	Local to global competitiveness National economy	Competitiveness decreased Economic growth curbed

holders and it would have particularly be in the interest of the academic staff in technical fields. The technical university academics and students think the association with softer disciplines will negatively affect the perceptions of the stakeholders of technical education. Mainly, they feel that the faculty structure threatens the responsibility of technical education and the university as an institution.

Strong disciplinary fields and organisational structures based on them are perceived to improve interdisciplinary cooperation: "The current strong degree programs in Tampere enable high-quality cross-disciplinary cooperation. For example, ICT needs to become a cross-cutting theme in the new higher education institution, but in order to have a strong knowledge base, it must be concentrated and have a firm foothold in a particular faculty. Cross-disciplinary research is only possible when there are strong enough knowledge basis" (Petition for the Stand of Technology by the Student Union). Thus, the relevance of technical education is based on a strong disciplinary foundation, and interdisciplinarity is not considered to provide added value to the stakeholders.

It may be concluded that the responsibility of technical education to its stakeholders may be threatened, at least according to the respondents, students and academic staff.

Conclusion: Is Technical Education in Jeopardy?

In this chapter, we analysed reactions to the proposal of interdisciplinary faculty structures aimed at increasing the societal impact of the university. In addition, following the different aspects of university responsibility, we examined how the proposed changes were seen to affect the societal impact of technical education in relation to its stakeholders. We identified the main stakeholders mentioned most often in the comments on the proposals and analysed the respondents' views on the stakeholders' expected reactions to the changes.

Based on different aspects of disciplinarity and the idea of becoming increasingly responsible through interdisciplinary approaches, the notion of a new interdisciplinary university, where different disciplines are placed in productive cooperation within the organisational structure, seemed like an approach to increase the social relevance of all educational fields, including technical education. This is particularly relevant, as technical education has been criticised for being unable to tackle the so-called wicked problems through its disciplinary approaches. However, the respondents do not perceive it in this way and feel that disciplinary-based technical education meets the needs of its stakeholders. It is interesting that they do not refer to the main justification for the interdisciplinary structure, namely, better addressing wicked problems. Even though they do not mention wicked problems in their feedback, they claim that technical education is already socially responsible and meets the needs of its main stakeholders. However, these respondents are staff and students and thus internal stakeholders. They claim to speak for the external stakeholders and justify their views by referring to the needs of external stakeholders and the university's responsibility towards them. It appears the respondents are threatened by the new organisational structure and therefore argue for keeping the traditional organisational status quo or making changes aligned with their strategic interests (e.g., ICT as a core area).

We conclude that an interdisciplinary structure is not thought to increase the responsibility of technical education to its stakeholders. Therefore, the intended increase in societal impact and the university's enhanced capability to contribute to solving wicked problems are questionable. The respondents argue for old structures and disciplinary divisions and claim that the visibility and appreciation of technical education would remain higher in a technical university or in separate technical faculties. The respondents view the traditional disciplinary approach as both organisationally clear and consistent with the needs of stakeholders. They were also critical of the planning process and the top-down way the Transitional Board imposed the interdisciplinary structure without consulting internal or external stakeholders. Moreover, they did not think that any disciplinary structural change should be made from the perspective of stakeholders' needs. These internal actors feel threatened by the new arrangements, arguing for "no change" based on the perceived needs of external stakeholders and important blueprints (e.g., Aalto or MIT).

Despite the theoretically positive views on interdisciplinarity increasing cooperation beyond the borders of the university, the current disciplinary approach is seen as functional and serving the stakeholders to whom the university is responsible. Meanwhile, the interdisciplinary structure is perceived to threaten the existing responsibilities of technical education. The respondents also view technical education as a whole and specific field that is in jeopardy because of the anticipated reactions of the key stakeholders—the stakeholders may not recognise or appreciate technical education if the traditional organisational structure is changed. Here, we have only examined the responses of staff and current students in technical fields, but it would be very interesting to explore some of the external stakeholders' views on the proposed structure.

Time will show whether interdisciplinary faculties increase educational cooperation between different disciplines, how different stakeholders react to these structural changes and whether the responsiveness of technical education to its stakeholders is compromised. It will also be possible to evaluate whether the interdisciplinary structure, even though realised in a compromised way, will increase cooperation between different disciplines and enable knowledge and education better suited to solving wicked problems.

It is not surprising that internal stakeholders, who have their own self-interests, oppose structural changes that jeopardise the disciplinary bases of their academic identities. However, it is interesting that they justify their claims through the needs of external stakeholders. The organisational change threatens the identities of academics, which are often based on the disciplinary structures, university identity and status quo. It seems that university leaders as well as national higher education policies promoting and implementing interdisciplinarity will encounter resistance from academics in most disciplines. When examining the data on this particular structural change in a merger process, academics in technical fields seem to be most reluctant to move from disciplinary structures to interdisciplinary structures.

Universities have the responsibility to meet the needs of their stake-holders, but there are conflicting views on these needs from national, institutional and disciplinary perspectives. Consequently, universities oscillate between disciplinary approaches and institutional interdisciplinarity policies to meet stakeholder needs. This may compromise their ability to be responsible to stakeholders, and there is no shared understanding of which approach would improve university social responsibility.

Acknowledgements We would like to thank Professor Jussi Kivistö from Tampere University for his constructive comments on this chapter.

Appendix 1: List of analysed documents and data

First suggestion of the faculty structure of Tampere University by the Board of the University Foundation (24 Nov 2017)

Updated suggestion of the Faculty structure of Tampere University by the Board of the University Foundation (8 Dec 2017)

The Technical University of Tampere Academic Board's feedback on the faculty structure suggestion (18 Dec 2017)

Statement of the Board of Managers of TUT and UTa

Strategy Statement (2 Feb 2018)

The Student Union's response to suggestions on the faculty structure (1 Dec 2018)

Petition for the Stand of Technology by the Student Union (16 Dec 2017)

Statement by TEK Labour Union for technical fields (online statement)

University regulations of Tampere University (draft)

University regulations of Tampere University (accepted on 10 Feb 2018)

Tampere3 strategy (proposal)

Appendix to the Tampere3 strategy (2 Jan 2018)

Feedback collected within the universities (staff and students) on the first faculty structure proposal in Finnish and in English (24–30 Nov 2017) https://wiki.tamk.fi/pages/viewpage.action?pageId=93684095

Feedback collected within the universities (staff and students) on the second faculty structure proposal in Finnish and in English (11–18 Dec 2017) https://wiki.tamk.fi/pages/viewpage.action?pageId=93684095

Feedback from the Deans of TUT and UTa (26 March 2018) on the faculty structure of Tampere University by the Board of the University Foundation dated on 2 Jan 2018

Board of Faculty of Computing and Electrical Engineering (7 Dec 2017)

Statement of the Student Guild Indecs and Manager

Appendix 2: Faculty proposals and distribution of fields

Faculty	Fields
First proposal 24 Nov 2017	
Communication and Data Sciences	Communications, journalism, languages, software engineering/production, signal processing, information studies, literature, theatre studies
Engineering Sciences and Architecture	Communications system engineering, electrical engineering, automation engineering, mechanical engineering, materials science, civil engineering, architecture
Technical and Natural Sciences	Mathematics, physics, chemistry, computer science, statistics
Biomedicine and Health Technology	Medicine, biomedicine, health sciences, psychology, logopedia
Educational Sciences	Education, pedagogics, early childhood education, vocational education
Business and Leadership	Business, administrative science, knowledge management, industrial management
Social Sciences	Social sciences, philosophy, political science, social work, history
Second proposal 8 Dec 2017	
Communication and Data Sciences	Communications, journalism, data sciences, information studies, software engineering/production, artificial intelligence and machine learning
Technical and Natural Sciences	Mathematics, physics, chemistry, telecommunications technology, signal processing, electrical engineering, automation engineering, mechanical engineering, materials science
Environmental Engineering and Architecture	Civil engineering, architecture, environmental engineering, energy technology
Medicine and Health Technology	Medicine, biomedical technology, biotechnology, health technology
Educational Sciences and Culture	Educational sciences, pedagogics, languages, literature, theatre studies
Business and Leadership	Business, administrative science, knowledge management, industrial management, political science
Social Sciences	Social sciences, philosophy, history, social work, health sciences, psychology, logopedia

Faculty	Fields
Structure decided on 7 June 2018	
Information Technology and Communication Sciences	Electrical engineering, information technology, communications, languages
Management and Business	Business, administrative science, knowledge management, industrial management, political science
Education and Culture	Educational sciences, pedagogics
Medicine and Health Technology	Medicine, biomedical technology, biotechnology, health technology
Built Environment	Architecture, civil engineering
Engineering and Natural Sciences	Physics, materials science, environmental engineering, automation engineering, mechanical engineering, biomedical technology, biotechnology
Social Sciences	Social sciences, philosophy, history, social work, health sciences, psychology, logopedia

References

Aarrevaara, T., & Dobson, I. (2016). Merger Mania? The Finnish Higher Education Experience. In R. Pinheiro (Ed.), *Mergers in Higher Education, Higher Education Dynamics* (Vol. 46). Switzerland: Springer International Publishing.

About the United Nations Sustainable Development Goals. (2015). Retrieved April 5, 2019, from https://www.un.org/sustainabledevelopment/sustainable-development-goals/.

Aula, H.-M., & Tienari, J. (2011). Becoming World-Class? Reputation-Building in a University Merger. *Critical Perspectives on International Business, 7*(1), 7–29.

Becher, T., & Trowler, P. (2001). *Academic Tribes and Territories: Intellectual Enquiry and the Culture of Disciplines* (2nd ed.). Buckingham: The Society for Research into Higher Education and Open University Press.

Benneworth, P., & Jongbloed, B. W. (2010). Who Matters to Universities? A Stakeholder Perspective on Humanities, Arts and Social Sciences Valorization. *Higher Education, 59*(5), 567–588.

Brown, V. A., Deane, P. M., Harris, J. A., & Russel, J. Y. (2010). Towards a Just and Sustainable Future. In V. A. Brown, J. A. Harris, & J. Y. Russel (Eds.), *Tackling Wicked Problems Through the Transdisciplinary Imagination*. London and Washington, DC: Earthscan.

Chapleo, C., & Simms, C. (2010). Stakeholder Analysis in Higher Education: A Case Study of the University of Portsmouth. *Perspectives: Policy and Practice in Higher Education, 14*(1), 12–20.

Chettiparamb, A. (2007). Re-Conceptualizing Public Participation in Planning: A View through Autopoiesis. *Planning Theory, 6*(3), 263–281.

Denis, A. B., & Heap, R. (2012). Social Relevance and Interdisciplinarity in Canadian Engineering Education. In A. Beraud, A. S. Godfroy, & J. Michel (Eds.), *GIEE 2011: Gender and Interdisciplinary Education for Engineers* (pp. 255–266). Sense Publishers.

Edström, K. (2017). *Exploring the Dual Nature of Engineering Education: Opportunities and Challenges in Integrating the Academic and Professional Aspects in the Curriculum.* PhD dissertation, Stockholm.

Esfijani, A., Hussain, F., & Chang, E. (2013). University Social Responsibility Ontology. *Engineering Intelligent Systems, 4*, 271–281.

Ferlie, E., Fitzgerald, L., Mcgivern, G., Dopson, S., & Bennett, C. (2011). Public Policy Networks and "Wicked Problems": A Nascent Solution? *Public Administration, 89*(2), 307–324.

Geschwind, L. (2018). Legitimizing Change in Higher Education: Exploring the Rationales Behind Major Organizational Restructuring. *Higher Education Policy, 22*(3), 381–395.

Gibbons, M., Limoges, C., Nowotny, H., Schwartzman, S., Scott, P., & Trow, M. (1994). *The New Production of Knowledge. The Dynamics of Science and Research in Contemporary Societies.* London: Sage.

Harman, G., & Harman, K. (2003). Institutional Mergers in Higher Education: Lessons from International Experience. *Tertiary Education and Management, 9*, 29–44.

Head, B. W., & Alford, J. (2015). Wicked Problems: Implications for Public Policy and Management. *Administration and Society, 47*(6), 711–739.

Hsieh, H.-F., & Shannon, S. E. (2005). Three Approaches to Qualitative Content Analysis. *Qualitative Health Research, 15*(9), 1277–1288.

Jackson, A. Y., & Mazzei, L. A. (2012). *Thinking with Theory in Qualitative Research: Viewing Data Across Multiple Perspectives.* New York: Routledge.

Kogan, M., & Teichler, U. (2007). *Key Challenges to the Academic Profession.* Kassel: Jenior.

Lönngren, J. (2017). *Wicked Problems in Engineering Education: Preparing Future Engineers to Work for Sustainability.* PhD dissertation, Gothenburg, Sweden.

Lyytinen, A., Kohtamäki, V., Kivistö, J., Pekkola, E., & Hölttä, S. (2017). Scenarios of Quality Assurance of Stakeholder Relationships in Finnish Higher Education Institutions. *Quality in Higher Education, 23*(1), 35–49.

Pinheiro, R., Geschwind, L., & Aarrevaara, T. (Eds.). (2016). *Mergers in Higher Education: The Experience from Northern Europe. Higher Education Dynamics.* Cham/Heidelberg/New York/Dordrecht & London: Springer International Publishing.

Ramaley, J. A. (2014). The Changing Role of Higher Education: Learning to Deal with Wicked Problems. *Journal of Higher Education Outreach and Engagement, 18*(3), 7–22.

Stember, M. (1991). Advancing the Social Sciences Through the Interdisciplinary Enterprise. *Social Science Journal, 28*(1), 1–14.

Tampere University web page/News/Together we are greater. Retrieved January 7, 2019, from https://www.tuni.fi/en/news/together-we-are-greater.

Tetrevova, L., & Sabolova, V. (2010). University Stakeholder Management and University Social Responsibility. *WSEAS Transactions on Advances in Engineering Education, 7*, 224–233.

Times Higher Education University Impact Rankings. (2019). Retrieved April 23, 2019, from https://www.timeshighereducation.com/rankings/impact/2019/overall#!/page/0/length/25/sort_by/rank/sort_order/asc/cols/undefined.

Times Higher Education World University Rankings / THE developing ranking based on Sustainable Development Goals. Retrieved April 5, 2019, from https://www.timeshighereducation.com/news/developing-ranking-based-sustainable-development-goals.

Tress, G., Tress, B., & Fry, G. (2005). Clarifying Integrative Research Concepts in Landscape Ecology. *Landscape Ecology, 20*(4), 479–493.

United Nations Sustainable Development Goals/About. (2015). Retrieved April 5, 2019, from https://www.un.org/sustainabledevelopment/sustainable-development-goals/.

Välimaa, J., Aittola, H., & Ursin, J. (2014). University Mergers in Finland: Mediating Global Competition. *New Directions for Higher Education, 2014*(168), 41–53.

Välimaa, J., Papatsiba, V., & Hoffman, D. M. (2016). Higher Education in Networked Knowledge Societies. In J. Välimaa & D. Hoffmann (Eds.), *Re-Becoming Universities?* (pp. 13–39). Dordrecht: Springer.

Van de Ven, A. (2007). *Engaged Scholarship: A Guide for Organizational and Social Research* (1st ed.). Oxford: Oxford University Press.

Vasilescu, R., Barnab, C., Epurec, M., & Baicud, C. (2010). Developing University Social Responsibility: A Model for the Challenges of the New Civil Society. *Procedia Social and Behavioral Sciences, 2*, 4177–4182.

Vellamo, T., Siekkinen, T., Pekkola, E., & Cai, Y. (forthcoming). Technical Identity in a Merger Process – Between a Rock and a Hard Place. In L. Geshwind, A. Broström, & K. Larsen (Eds.), *Technical Universities: Past, Present and Future.* Springer.

Wan Saiful, W.-J. (2006). Defining Corporate Social Responsibility. *Journal of Public Affairs, 6*, 176–184.

Ylijoki, O.-H., & Ursin, J. (2013). The Construction of Academic Identity in the Changes of Finnish Higher Education. *Studies in Higher Education, 38*(8), 1135–1149.

9

Recruitment and Leadership: Issues and Solutions

Jouni Kekäle and Jenni Varis

Introduction and Key Concepts

In this chapter, we describe development projects dealing with leadership and recruitment at the University of Eastern Finland (UEF). The aim of the projects was to find good practices, broadly discuss recruitment and leadership issues within the institution and to foster development in these human resources (HR) areas so that the university could live up its strategic plans, and, while doing so, become more responsible. The projects were genuinely iterative and interactive: the key ideas (proactive recruitment, HR leadership model for a responsible university) presented in this chapter were invented during these interactive development projects.

The strategic role of HR in universities has expanded, as the expectation of actorhood in HE—turning universities in to social actors with specific goal-orientation, responsibility, social planning, innovation policies and mission statements—has progressed (Krücken and Meyer 2006).

J. Kekäle (✉) • J. Varis
University of Eastern Finland, Joensuu, Finland
e-mail: Jouni.kekale@uef.fi; jenni.varis@uef.fi

A key aspect of HR is recruitment, which is increasingly streamlined with universities' goals (Siekkinen et al. 2016). Finding suitable and committed people is also crucial for fostering innovation (Amabile 1988) and for the outcomes of the university. Shattock (2003) has noted that if there were one single component in creating a successful university, this would be making well-suited academic staff appointments.

The following question related to the development projects is relevant in the chapter: How can HR function to support the accomplishment of institutional strategy (and hence, to foster a responsible university) through leadership development and improving recruitments?

The strategic aim is that the institution can innovate, better outcomes can be reached, and the institution can become more responsible in contributing to the strategic aims chosen.

The strategic aims of the UEF link closely to the ideal of a responsible university as we see it. The University's development projects aimed at fostering strategy and merger through HR measures such as developing leadership and recruitments. It is possible to see that all good and productive research, teaching and interaction with the society are, in a sense, responsible, and can contribute to the betterment of contemporary society. However, the aim of (contributing to) solving pressing global problems appears to be one of the most recent and strongest emphases in providing social relevance and acting in a responsible way in higher education. We will especially start from this latter understanding of responsibility. The approach is also in line with the strategy of the UEF, as we will demonstrate below.

In 2015, the UEF launched an institutional project aiming at developing institutional recruitment and leadership practices. Developing leadership had been a target area throughout the history of the UEF, since the establishment of the institution in 2010. These initiatives were launched as the university leadership group saw that successful recruitment is a fundamental way of implanting strategy and enhancing quality (and improving institutional responsibility). Leadership, on the other hand, is a central phenomenon affecting the institution, in various ways, by decision-making and through everyday interaction, and in implementing institutional strategy. In this chapter, we will concentrate especially on leadership and recruitment in the context of strategic research.[1]

By institutional *leadership*, we are referring both to the university leadership (the people, leaders) officially in charge of the institutional strategy, including departmental and faculty leaders responsible for implementing the strategy and other everyday operations. Leadership (the phenomenon, leadership actions) refers here both to human relations aspects and managerial tasks of these leaders.

Recruitment is a process in which new employees (academic faculty is in our focus) are hired to fulfil certain tasks and roles that would help the institution strengthen its roles in the areas chosen.

By *HR*, we refer here to human resources function and leadership (the phenomenon) dealing with people and issues related to people. This involves both administration and institutional aspects of leading and being in charge.

Innovation means the introduction of something new: a new idea, method, or device. In the context of global problems, innovation refers to novel ideas, methods, and so on that contribute to solutions to these problems.

As noted, in this chapter, we will concentrate on some shared ideas on how the overall strategy might be fostered and supported by HR. In other words, we are interested here in HR aspects such as leadership and recruitment development in supporting the fulfilment of these aims. This chapter is not, however, about criticism of the strategy, strategic thinking, or NPM approaches, but a description of a practical and interactive development project trying to find HR solutions to practical questions about strategy implementation. Hence, we do not tackle aspects like links between strategy and macro-level dynamics, nor the actual or overall implementation of strategies, for example (see Fumasoli et al. 2015).

In what follows, we start by discussing the idea and ideal of a responsible university as we see it, and how the UEF Strategy links with this ideal. We then proceed to a discussion of leadership and describe how it has been developed at the UEF. Then we approach a recruitment development project. We will end our discussion with an overview of lessons learned.

As the projects developed, conclusions were drawn and further discussed with participants. In the end of the chapter, we draw together some key aspects university leadership would need to take into account if having similar strategic aims, and summarize key lessons learned from the development projects in the form of a model.

Responsible University

For our purposes, we define a responsible university here as *an institution that carries out quality research and teaching, responds to the needs of society through basic tasks and aims at solving certain global problems of human-kind while venerating the fundamental freedom of science* (for freedom of science in HE policy context see Kekäle et al. 2017).

In their discussion on Responsible University, Grau et al. (2017a) give their interpretation of the topic: Universities are key players in both knowledge-based economy and investment in education, science and technology. Because of this:

> they have the singular responsibility of helping to provide appropriate and adequate responses to both legitimate needs and interests: i) to contribute to overcoming the global challenges of the world, which are very well summarized by the UN Sustainable Development Goals (SDGs), and ii) to contribute to the social, cultural and economic development and international competitiveness of their societies. (Grau et al. 2017a, 38)

The interpretation may be farfetched, as it assumes that the *singular* responsibility lies in universities. However, currently there appears to be good grounds for attaching universities' strategic aims to attempts to solve global problems on a trans- or multidisciplinary basis (Grau et al. 2017a). The missions and relevant tasks of university institutions have been under discussion for a long time, and the expectations have broadly turned towards solving grand challenges. One reason for this is the cumulative knowledge on negative impacts of climate change and environmental crises (http://www.ipcc.ch/report/sr15/). Kaldeway (2018) notes that "grand challenges" have become a dominant theme in scientific discussions and policymakers' funding schemes in the twenty-first century. Many funding mechanisms tend to connect these targets with resources (see e.g. EU Horizon programmes—https://ec.europa.eu/programmes/horizon2020/en/what-horizon-2020).

If "responsive" university (Tierney 1998) was mainly interested in local engagement, "responsible" university, in the sense of Grau et al. (2017a), adds global challenges to the formula. These two need not be mutually exclusive; realistically, global problems tend to give a university a broader strategic focus and a conceptual umbrella, under which the university directs and conducts strategic research and other operations. Global problems may affect all potential stakeholders, whereas local questions tend to be relevant to only a limited number of operators.

A critical question is: Who is the university responsible for? Answers to such questions may depend on the institution in question, its strengths and profiling. There may be different "local" communities to be served. Some of them may be located far from the university campus. There are reservations: It is unrealistic to expect any definition of responsibility to mean that the whole university is totally committed to a similar understanding of strategic aims, such as bringing solutions to pressing global problems identified. Clark's (1998) unified culture does not easily exist in comprehensive universities (Kekäle 2007). Academic freedom is still the legal basis for legislative framework for universities in Finland, while diverse steering mechanisms fundamentally affect this freedom (Kekäle et al. 2017). Need-driven research and curiosity-driven research are present as well. Building on existing institutional strengths, a certain voluntarism, support structures and strategic funding, and recruitment of suitable scholars who want to work in the strategic area (Amabile 1988) might provide suitable ways to improve an institutional profile, and therefore improve responsibility. This is also in line with the UEF strategy. Proactive recruitment can be used for identifying suitable scholars for strategic areas (Kekäle 2017). It also helps if the whole institution benefits from improving its institutional reputation and increasing possibilities attached to the strategy (Grau et al. 2017b). Academic leaders and researchers are supposed to implement the strategy.

Responsibility and the UEF Strategy

The UEF strategy is connected to solving wicked global problems, as identified from the point of view of expertise and strengths of the strongest research areas at the institution (the strategy can be found at the UEF web pages—https://strategia.uef.fi/?lang=en). Our understanding is that even prioritizing solutions to significant global problems would clearly indicate responsibility.

The interdisciplinary topics and grand challenges in focus at UEF are as follows:

1. ageing, lifestyles, and health;
2. learning in a digitized society;
3. cultural encounters, mobility, and borders, and
4. environmental change and sufficiency of natural resources.

There are researchers from different disciplinary backgrounds working on these broad themes. The idea is that researchers from different disciplinary fields and specialisms at the University can cooperate on these topics. It has become increasingly clear that we cannot solve complex and global problems from within single disciplines (e.g. Lasker and Weiss 2003; Dick et al. 2016). The connection to global challenges brings social relevance and coherence to the University's institutional profile.

In relation to the fourth interdisciplinary topic in the UEF strategy, environmental change, for example, according to NASA (2018), 97 per cent or more of actively publishing climate scientists agree in peer-reviewed scientific papers that the measurable climate-warming trends in the past century are extremely likely to have been caused by human activities (https://climate.nasa.gov/scientific-consensus/). According to our current understanding, climate change may even threaten life on earth, or cause unforeseen problems for humankind (http://www.ipcc.ch/report/sr15/). As Wells (2017, 31) notes as an international observation:

> Perhaps never before in recent history has the role of higher education been so intricately tied to the economic, social and environmental fabric of the modern world. The demands from all stakeholders for quality, robust and diverse systems of higher education to take an active responsibility in addressing the challenges of the world's pressing issues is likewise unprecedented.

Attempting to find solutions to global problems is a responsible action, since these efforts may positively affect many or all humans and stakeholders. However, aiming at something is relatively easy; fostering possibilities in outcomes and getting results are more difficult tasks.

What can an institution (or a group of researchers) do in terms of HR if they aim at becoming increasingly responsible? After all, employees (humans) carry out research and are a major cause of work outcomes; therefore, also HR matters. At the UEF, we have focused on the HR measures in leadership training and recruitment development. We will discuss these next, starting with the leadership phenomenon.

Leadership—A Contingent, Contextual, and Significant Phenomenon

Social concepts, like leadership (Middlehurst 1993), are not value-free; an observer can view them from different angles depending on his or her perspective and values. We can attach different meanings to these phenomena, but we can also study them empirically. Hence, the relevance of leadership, for example, has been discussed, and different schools of thought exist.

O'Reilly et al. (2010) note that proponents of leadership argue that leaders are in any case responsible for making decisions that may help (or might hinder) organizations in their basic tasks in competitive environments (e.g. Hogan et al. 1994). In contrast, those who view organizations as heavily constrained claim that leadership is largely an irrelevant social construction (e.g. Mukunda 2012). However, O'Reilly et al. (2010) note that empirical evidence over the past 20 years shows that leadership matters in organizations. An overall conclusion in relation to leadership studies is that there is no one best method of successful leadership, but leadership depends on disciplinary and departmental cultures and other contextual and social factors (e.g. Kekäle 2001).

We can see that significance of leadership has increased in Finland in past years (Kekäle et al. 2017). We base this claim on recent developments in the Finnish HE system, but also results of interviews of human resource directors and labour union representatives in Finnish universities in 2017.

Jenni Varis carried out the interviews. Her doctoral research (*forthcoming*) has progressed alongside the responsible university project. The 10 semi-structured interviews, five of HR directors and five of labour union representatives, have concentrated on researchers and teachers in universities and have been analysed qualitatively (Galletta 2013). We can recognize different meanings and purposes of leadership from the interviews.

Several interviewees notioned that the significance of leadership has increased, but we can also identify several areas in which leadership is especially relevant. Especially, *problem solving* was seen as a remarkable function for leadership. The main role for supervisors in problem-solving situations was to discuss problems with employees, early and enough. Second, a leader was seen as an *enabler*. The enabling role means that a supervisor would facilitate working conditions or share tasks so that an employee could manage his/her tasks as intended. Some interviewees pointed out that the role of leadership is more important in the beginning of an academic career, during which the role of a *mentor and an advisor* is emphasized more than being a representative of an employer. In this context, the role of supervisor is not always clear for scholars in their early years, even for supervisors themselves.

We can say that the role of supervisor is relatively complex. Academic communities are highly autonomous, albeit within the framework of increasing steering mechanisms (Kekäle et al. 2017), but also the tendency of strategic steering has increased. Several interviewees, both HR directors and labour union representatives, notified the role of strategic leading and decision-making, but at the same time, scholars ought to react to strategic demands in their actions. However, we can determine that constructive discussion is the key point in academic leadership. Several interviewees, especially labour union representatives, pointed out that decision-making has centralized, and leaders have more power nowadays in Finnish universities. Anyhow, leadership of an individual scholar's work is indirect rather than direct. Strategic choices made by a university rather guide than force, but in the long term resisting them may affect a scholar's academic career negatively. The negative influence can appear as a lack of resources or differentiation from a research group or other networks. While recognizing these harmful scenarios, it was pointed out that outside today's strategic focus areas, breakthroughs could still be made, or the areas may rise to a strategic centre later.

Leadership Development at the UEF

The UEF is a comprehensive, multidisciplinary university, established through a merger between the universities of Kuopio and Joensuu, starting from the year 2010. A full merger is a major process, which makes it difficult to concentrate on aspects other than internal organization for some years; hence, these development projects were fully initiated some five years after the establishment of the UEF. Leadership, however, has been a target area for development throughout the merger process.

According to some estimations, most mergers fail (Koi-Akrofi 2016), and, therefore, leadership matters even more, which also stresses the importance of leadership development. The full merger process has been described elsewhere (e.g. Puusa and Kekäle 2013, 2015; Tirronen et al. 2016) and we will not describe this in detail here. Let us note that some 2600 employees work at the UEF, there are 15,000 degree students and 15,000 continuing education students. The UEF is one of the largest universities in Finland and is ranked among the top 300 universities in the world in many fields (see https://www.uef.fi/en/etusivu).

The UEF merger has posed many challenges, as has the overall steering by the ministry. For example, after 2010 Finnish university funding has diminished by several hundred million euros. Hence, the aim in leadership development was to arrange leadership education in the turmoil of the merger, and to provide leaders with opportunities for discussion among colleagues.

If the institution and researchers aim to contribute to solving grand challenges, leadership implies fostering such goals: leadership is about getting things done and hiring the best people for specific tasks. If successful, this can aid in solving global problems and all task-oriented work. Contributing to solving global problems would demand identification of strengths and some concentration of resources, among other things. Currently in Finland, the decision on strategic aims of a university rests on university leadership: the University Board will set the official strategies and priorities for the institution (according to the Universities Act (558/2009), the board is to determine the main objectives of the university operations and finances, the strategy and steering principles). Still, researchers also legitimately steer their own research; their commitment is crucial, but funding and leadership support no doubt affects this.

With respect to leadership training, the UEF arranges three annual discussion and development seminars for all academic leaders, involving departmental heads, deans, directors of administration, as well as rectors. In addition, three levels of general leadership training are provided, as well as frequent 360 degree assessments of leadership.

At least the following topics and support structures and mechanisms have been discussed during the UEF leadership training and seminars:

- Strategy and funding
- Feedback and support
- Recruitment policy
- Interaction and direction
- Social atmosphere
- Terms of employment
- Reward systems
- Correction of problems

All these topics connect to leadership and management. They are aspects that support operations, and culture as an internal logic and value/assumption system behind the operations by which the institution appears to be working.

Leadership development is a contextual issue. The institution has arranged numerous different occasions since the year 2010. The key aims of leadership training have been to overcome and to implement the merger, and to implement and foster the strategy. There have been tens of public discussions on the topics. We cannot go into detail regarding these lengthy discussions here. The information serves as a background. It also forms the basis of the forthcoming model (Fig. 9.1).

As Tierney and Lanford (2016, 26) point out, these leadership aspects can either help or hinder productive work. For example, burdensome evaluations can prevent the implementation of innovative programmes and research agendas, and punitive evaluations may frighten individuals from testing novel ideas. Such support structures can affect the moods and support or hinder productive work, even motivation to innovate.

In what follows, the focus will be on the project of recruitment development which has been carried out more in parallel with the timeframe of the Nordic Responsible University project.

Recruitment Development at the UEF—The Process

Recruitment and strategic aims to address global challenges connect in the following way: Success in recruitments—the motivation, quality, and commitment of the faculty—crucially determines academic work outcomes. They also are crucial for responsibility—as value added in the areas chosen. Human capabilities and extended motivation to research a certain complicated area—as opposed to using one's time and energy for something else—is needed if we are to contribute to solving global problems.

Shattock (2003) has noted that if we would single out one component in creating a prosperous (or responsible) university, it would be success in academic staff appointments. A literature review on HR in higher education shows that, in universities, people are the most important asset and are key to long-term organizational performance (Mugabi et al. 2017, 9). Therefore, if an institution and a department aims at concentrating on certain topics, the crucial issue in recruitment is to find researchers who share these goals and who fit the existing research groups (Kekäle 2017).

UEF launched a project on developing strategic recruitment in the summer of 2015. The authors have worked on the development project throughout its existence. External consultants were first involved. However, this external contribution remained rather obscure, and their efforts concentrated mostly on scaling traditional interviews. The UEF terminated cooperation with external consultants since the cooperation did not provide results.

Throughout the development process, recruitments were widely discussed within the university: in the leadership group, with academic leaders of the university, and during two discussion rounds at the faculties. Since 2015, the university's leadership group discussed the topic and operational goals and proposals several times on the basis of international approaches to recruitment practices. Since 2016, in annual leadership seminars with leaders of the university, as well as the university's internal bodies dealing with research, leaders have frequently participated in discussions on how to develop recruitment. In the discussions, we have concluded that the university's vacancy announcements have not reached the global network of scholars to a sufficient degree, at least when considered against the university's strategy, stressing increasing international recruitment. Recruitment has increasingly become proactive, and a model of this has been formed through discussions in an iterative manner (Kekäle 2017).

As noted, the development work was based on international literature, internal discussions among the UEF leaders, and interviews. In the UEF strategy, the university has identified five top-level international research areas. Jouni Kekäle interviewed the professors in charge of these areas. Each interview lasted for an hour. They dealt with best practices and problems associated with recruitments. The ideas behind the proactive recruitment model (Kekäle 2017) were explicitly discussed and tested in the interviews. The research professors interviewed supported the proactive recruitment model, maintaining that, for many practical reasons, they already used a similar approach in identifying potential candidates.

After that, the rector of the UEF and Jouni Kekäle visited each of the four faculties' leadership groups and discussed recruitment issues, explaining and refining the proactive recruitment model. Responsibility, as a catchword, was not used explicitly, but the focus was all the time on the betterment of work outcomes and the implementation of the strategy by HR. Key professors and leaders responsible for recruitment were present. The participant agreed that the proactive recruitment model generally provides a good approach to improving recruitments. Another discussion round in the UEF faculties' leadership groups took place, this time led by the authors. The proactive model was discussed directly.

The proactive recruitment model (see Kekäle 2017) was identified through this interactive and iterative process. According to the model, a research group continuously, and proactively, strengthens its research profile, and constructs international networks of researchers within the research area. The motivation and orientation of a candidate is crucial: internal motivation and continuous improvement, plus suitability to the research interests and profile of the group. The aim is that benefits will follow. The person-organization fit is difficult to assess sufficiently on the basis of traditional open job announcements and interviews, when the candidate is briefly met for the first time. Instead, a long-term, proactive cooperation and information on key candidates is needed.

In Finland, the traditional approach to recruitments has been to declare vacancies open and then wait for the candidates to appear with not much prior headhunting. This was the official approach set by the ministry of Finance before the University Act of 2010, aiming at equal treatment of Finnish citizens in the recruitment of civil servants. The suitability of candidates was assessed mainly on the basis of documents, perhaps with an added interview. Proactive recruitment gives more room and grounds for the assessment process of person-organization fit, by making this a continuous process of networking before the actual recruitment (Kekäle 2017).

A pitfall in the traditional approach is that according to a global survey, the biggest obstacle to changing jobs is that the candidate does not know what it is like to work at an organization (LinkedIn Survey 2015). Overcoming both these problems requires a proactive approach and a broader network of contacts. Only sufficient experience, prior cooperation, and follow-up time can help to bring in information on the suitability of the person-organization fit. The only rational grounds for a recruitment decision are the candidate's ability, merits, and skill in relation to the task, and his or her capacity to cooperate with the recruiting research group. Assessing these well tends to require rather deep (proactive) knowledge. In such a way, an institution can become more responsible.

Yet another intervention on recruitment development was carried out in early 2018. The UEF invested one million euros towards starting strategic recruitments before a former holder of a position retired. The idea is to "bridge" the transition period so that work in the area can continue and the transition is smooth. Jouni Kekäle and the professors in charge of the recruitments discussed the recruitment process and potential problems they have experienced. As agreed on between the faculties and the rector, the funding was promised for costs related to bridging some 30 strategic posts.

The professors in charge of the recruitments had experienced problems in the following issues: problems in finding suitable candidates; the candidate turning down the offer after long negotiations. However, such problems were experienced only in a few cases. The recruitments were well underway, and in most cases looked promising. Proactive elements and prior headhunting had been added to most of them. The actual recruitment decision was to be made after an open comparison of potential candidates' merits, which is in line with the university instructions. Targeted marketing of certain job announcements will be tested on the basis of feedback, in order to enhance networking.

A Model for Fostering Responsible University

Since the UEF aims at novel solutions and insight in overcoming critical problems in the areas chosen in the strategy, and in doing so enhancing responsibility, the overall ability to innovate—to bring new insights—appears to be a crucial strategic asset. Otherwise, potential solutions will not materialize. By improving recruitments, leadership, and other HR measures, the UEF attempts to foster a responsible university.

After thorough discussion within the organization about the proactive model, leadership and recruitment issues, the authors turned their interest to the question: How is it possible to foster innovations and what aspect should leaders pay attention to when recruiting in a proactive manner if they are to foster novel insights and solutions? The UEF aims at the strategy to find solutions to critical problems in certain areas; since specific solutions are so far missing, innovations are the target. The discussion that followed was theoretical: the intention was to give leaders guidelines in their future work. We did not have empirical evidence on the forthcoming model (Fig. 9.1), but logical reasons and prior empirical research gave grounds for putting it forward.

Committed and motivated people are needed for innovation (Amabile 1988); therefore, recruiting people who can contribute to solutions and add to current knowledge and capacities is a key issue when fostering the strategy via HR measures. Again, the process involved discussions among UEF leaders. One of the faculties and the dean wanted to discuss these issues in detail, so we arranged a two-hour discussion session. The discussions involved the following model for fostering innovations; the leaders present in discussions saw the approach as relevant and agreed with it.

If there is a strategy and a vision, an operational plan is needed. An institution needs to consider its means and measures within the limits of its power and direction rights. In the following, we shall put forward a model, which draws together aspects and which potentially fosters innovations and novel solutions to global problems. By fostering these, leaders might be able to provide good conditions fostering the outcomes in selected areas. In terms of leadership, one can support prerequisites and good conditions, but cannot guarantee breakthroughs. Recruitment is a most crucial issue, as the academic outcomes will depend on academic faculty (Shattock 2003).

Fig. 9.1 HR leadership model for a Responsible University: How leaders can foster innovations

In the model (Fig. 9.1), the surrounding circle of topics represents the leadership areas and themes discussed during the lengthy round of UEF leadership seminars. Many of these topics also connect to Jenni Varis' research findings above. These leadership topics and support structures are relevant (but the fundaments are even more relevant in fostering innovations). At the UEF, these themes and leadership structures are seen as crucial in terms of supporting good work. These are also practical means and ways of supporting the development of a responsible university via university leadership. In the model, they are referred to as support structures. We have discussed these intensively during the leadership training programmes (see section "Leadership—A Contingent, Contextual, and Significant Phenomenon").

As noted, support structures do play a role by supporting responsible action, but they alone cannot provide innovations if the fundaments are lacking. Amabile (1988) notes that as far as qualities of organization that support innovation go, the sufficient freedom, good project management, good resources, and encouragement appear to be crucial ones (Amabile 1988, 147). Nevertheless, if, for example, fundamental intrinsic motivation is missing, reward systems cannot facilitate innovations on their own.

In the strategic questions (How is it possible to foster innovation in the strategic areas, and therefore foster the possibility that the university can contribute to solving critical problems with new insights?), to become more responsible, the fundaments in the middle of Fig. 9.1 appear to be crucial.

The Fundaments: Intrinsic Motivation, Autonomy, and Diversity

Creativity and innovation are crucial if one wishes to solve problems, let alone so far unsolvable and critical global challenges. As noted, from the perspective of university leadership, one can only foster prerequisites for innovation, and, in that sense, fostering the fundaments (Fig. 9.1) would appear to be crucial according to previous research findings.

Tierney and Lanford (2016, 22) note that research literature from different relevant disciplinary fields points to three factors that appear almost invariably to impact innovation in a positive manner. These are *diversity* (of thinking, backgrounds, and people, etc.), *intrinsic motivation*, and *autonomy*.

Recruiting scholars with persistent *intrinsic motivation* in the strategic areas appears to be a fundamental prerequisite for a group's ability to innovate. Based on her several studies, Amabile (1988) found that various personal traits (such as persistence, curiosity, energy, and intellectual honesty), self-motivation (internal motivation where the task itself is to be the greatest motivator), cognitive abilities, and expertise, as well as synergy and support from the group appear to be aspects that best promote creativity and problem-solving capacity. On the other hand, lack of motivation, external motivation, lack of skills and inflexibility inhibit creativity and problem solving. They can inhibit responsibility in our meaning.

As motivation "may be the most important component" in fostering creativity and innovation (Amabile 1988, 133), finding intrinsically motivated and skilled scholars who share the strategic goals of the university appears to be crucial. Proactive recruitment (Kekäle 2017) offers a model for identifying suitable scholars with intrinsic motivation. The idea is to proactively, before the actual recruitment decision, facilitate collaboration among scholars and groups with similar interests in order to learn about their motivation, skills, working pattern, and professional orientation. In this way, the pool of potential candidates becomes broader (Kekäle 2017).

Diversity appears to be a fundamental tenet of innovation; diverse teams tend to produce more creative results than teams with only members from a similar background. For example, Hewlett et al. (2013) found in their broad survey that (inherent and acquired) diversity in organizations unlocks and drives innovation. Phillips (2014) points out that decades of research (by organizational scientists, psychologists, sociologists, economists, etc.) demonstrate that socially diverse groups (diversity of race, ethnicity, gender, and sexual orientation) are more innovative than homogeneous groups. Moreover, groups with people of diverse individual expertise are better than a homogeneous group at solving complex, non-routine problems. Social diversity also seems to work in a similar way. Social innovations are embedded in diversity, and not only internal organizational issues, since they tend to involve universities, business, government, and civil society in quadruple helix partnerships (some diversity in strategy, too, might be useful).

Research has identified that there is a particularly strong relationship between intrinsic motivation and *autonomy*, and, given this, Tierney and Lanford (2016, 24) boldly stress that autonomy is required for innovation in higher education. By challenging conventional wisdom, and often by advancing unpopular theories that undergo refinement, research can lead to important technological and other advances, which positively influence the overall quality of life for millions of people (Tierney and Lanford 2016, 24). These features appear to be essential in fostering innovation, and, therefore, in being or becoming a responsible university in the sense that we are dealing with the topic.

Discussion and Conclusions

Leadership and recruitment can foster responsibility. For our purposes, we defined a responsible university as *an institution that carries out quality research and teaching, responds to the needs of society through basic tasks, and aims at solving certain global problems of humankind while venerating the fundamental freedom of science.* HR, as a shared leadership function, is crucial for accomplishment of this. We have presented a model that sheds light on key issues in leadership and recruitment within the aim of becoming a responsible university. The model which was discussed within the university also describes the overall outcomes and focus of the development projects we have described here.

Having presented a model for fostering a responsible university by the means of leadership, we still feel that there are some useful reservations to be made. Some of them are related to leadership in fostering responsibility and strategy; some others deal with the basic tasks and responsibility in academia.

First, we have already noted that leadership can mainly keep up and provide good conditions for successful work but cannot guarantee innovations or breakthroughs in relation to critical problems. The role of institutional leadership in relation to HR issues is that of a facilitator, but there is a big role to be filled anyway.

Second, the idea of a responsible university also returns to the complexity encompassing different disciplines and leadership of multidisciplinary and cultural projects. The integration, or at least the coexistence, of once deeply divided disciplinary cultures in human studies and natural sciences (Snow 1962) may be needed for the solution of global problems humankind is facing—and a responsible university is trying to solve. This has been a great leadership challenge for years.

Third, a topic related to leadership and innovation is that the cooperation on different platforms, which might be needed with external stakeholders, is far from easy (Tierney 1998). Different time perspectives and expectations can undermine fruitful cooperation. The business world, for example, may wait for short-term business solutions where profit can be calculated, whereas universities deal with long-term complex problems where business logic cannot always be at the forefront. If a fruitful cooperation is to take place, promising developments in line with stakeholder interests should be visible if one wishes to maintain commitment and motivation among participating stakeholders. This also means that different stakeholders can view responsibility in a different manner: business partners may hold different views than academics.

Fourth, a topic related to this is that while leadership is needed, for example, in Finland, the freedom of science is based on constitutional legislation (The Constitution of Finland, 731/1999, 16.3 §). This limits and frames the possibilities of leadership and directional power at the institutional level, and underlines the adage that leadership is persuasion, not domination. Leadership means that others voluntarily follow: most of all this requires mutual interest, good arguments, and negotiations. However, in recruitment situations, there is more room to direct research and to consider if there are mutual interests—by recruiting scholars who are committed to the aims of the institution.

With regard to lessons for other universities and "beyond the Nordics", it appear that the pressure to contribute to the solutions to pressing critical problems is global. Contributing to a focused set of aims in these matters would be responsible indeed. The process we have described here has been highly interactive. It requires mutual trust and interaction. The situation in other universities may be very different and local solutions could therefore differ. The case here can serve as an illustration of one approach in fostering such demanding strategic aims by HR means.

Leadership development is like chasing a moving target. As the world changes, working solutions may need to change as well. The process we have described is ongoing. It has been an iterative learning process in which HR and academics have been cooperating. Such mutual learning appears to be difficult: it requires resilience, trust, and willingness to understand different parties. Still, at least the process at the UEF appeared to bring synergies and benefits that would not otherwise have materialized.

Acknowledgements We wish to thank the participants of the responsible university project and all the leaders and scholars at the UEF who have contributed to the insights presented here. We thank Mikko Kohvakka for commenting on our paper, Romulo Pinheiro for his feedback on the early versions of the chapter, the project participants, and the editors for their comments.

Note

1. Education is also to be considered as a tool in becoming a responsible institution. Universities train future leaders and provide them with meta skills like critical thinking, problem solving, and learning to learn. The alumni, then, will find their way and provide relevance to society. Hence, the potential practical solutions to global problems may indirectly result from higher education, but not necessarily invented within the campus walls.

References

Amabile, T. M. (1988). A Model for Creativity and Innovation in Organizations. *Organizational Behavior, 10,* 123–167.

Clark, B. (1998). *Creating Entrepreneurial Universities: Organizational Pathways of Transformation.* Paris: International Association of University Press.

Dick, M., Rous, A., & Nguyen, V. (2016). Necessary But Challenging: Multiple Disciplinary Approaches to Solving Conservation Problems. *Facet, 3*(1), 67–82. Retrieved from https://www.facetsjournal.com/doi/full/10.1139/facets-2016-0003.

Fumasoli, T., Pinheiro, R., & Stensaker, B. (2015). Handling Uncertainty of Strategic Ambitions—The Use of Organizational Identity as a Risk-Reducing Device. *International Journal of Public Administration, 38*(13–14), 1030–1040. https://doi.org/10.1080/01900692.2014.988868.

Galletta, A. (2013). *Mastering the Semi-Structured Interview and Beyond: From Research Design to Analysis and Publication.* New York: New York University Press. eBook Collection (EBSCOhost).

Grau, F. X., Escrigas, C., Goddard, J., & Ha, B. (2017a). Editors' Introduction. In Grau, et al. (Eds.), *Towards a Socially Responsible Higher Education Institution: Balancing the Global with the Local. GUNI—Global University Network for Innovation.* Higher Education in the World. Towards a Socially Responsible University: Balancing the Global with the Local. Retrieved from http://www.guninetwork.org/report/higher-education-world-6.

Grau, F. X., Goddard, J. H., Hall, B., Hazelkorn, E., & Tandon, R. (2017b). Recommendations for Academia, Academic Leaders and Higher Education and Research Policymakers. In Grau, et al. (Eds.), *Towards a Socially Responsible Higher Education Institution: Balancing the Global with the Local. GUNI—Global University Network for Innovation.* Higher Education in the World. Towards a Socially Responsible University: Balancing the Global with the Local. Retrieved from http://www.guninetwork.org/report/higher-education-world-6.

Hewlett, S. A., Marshall, M., & Sherbin, L. (2013). How Diversity can Drive Innovation. Harward Business Review, December 2013. https://hbr.org/2013/12/how-diversity-candriveinnovation.

Hogan, R., Curphy, G. J., & Hogan, J. (1994). What We Know About Leadership. Effectiveness and Personality. *American Psychologist, 49*(6), 493–504.

Kaldeway, D. (2018). The Grand Challenges Discourse: Transforming Identity Work in Science and Science Policy. Minerva, 56 (2) 161–182. Retrieved from https://link.springer.com/article/10.1007/s11024-017-9332-2.

Kekäle, J. (2001). *Academic Leadership.* New York: Nova Science Publishers.

Kekäle, J. (2007). Developing an Entrepreneurial and Innovative University—The Case of the University of Joensuu. In L. W. Cooke (Ed.), *Frontiers in Higher Education.* New York: Nova Science Publishers.

Kekäle, J. (2017). Proactive Strategic Recruitment in Research Groups. *Tertiary Education and Management, 24*(2), 1–10. https://doi.org/10.1080/1358388 3.2017.1407439.

Kekäle, J. (2018). *Changing Higher Education Policy and the Quest for the Ideal of Socially Responsible University.* A paper presented in CENS Nordic Challenges—Conference in Helsinki, March 9, 2018.

Kekäle, J., & Varis, J. (2018, February 21–22). Responsible University and Institutional Leadership—A Nordic Perspective. Towards the Responsible University—Perspectives from the Nordic Countries KTH, Stockholm.

Kekäle, J., Diogo, S., & Varis, J. (2017). *Changes in the University-Society Relationship and Its Outcomes in Major Higher Education Reforms in Finland.* A paper presented at the Good University Aarhus workshop. Unpublished Manuscript.

Koi-Akrofi (2016) Mergers and Acquisitions Failure Rates and Perspectives on Why They Fail. International Journal of Innovation and Applied Studies 17 (1), 150-158. Retrieved from https://www.researchgate.net/publication/305406845_Mergers_and_Acquisitions_failure_rates_and_perspectives_on_why_they_fail.

Krücken, G., & Meyer, F. (2006). Turning the University Into an Organizational Actor. In G. S. Drori, J. W. Meyer, & H. Hwang (Eds.), *Globalization and Organization: World Society and Organizational Change.* Oxford: Oxford University Press.

Lasker, R., & Weiss, E. (2003). Broadening Participation in Community Problem Solving: A Multidisciplinary Model to Support Collaborative Practice and Research. *Journal of Urban Health: Bulletin of the New York Academy of Medicine, 80*(1), 14–47.

LinkedIn Survey. (2015). Why and How People Change Jobs. Showing Global Average. A Power Point-presentation. https://business.linkedin.com/content/dam/business/talent-solutions/global/en_us/job-switchers/PDF/job-switchers-global-report-english.pdf.

Merriam-Webster. (2019). Innovation. Retrieved from https://www.merriam-webster.com/dictionary/innovation.

Middlehurst, R. (1993). *Leading Academics.* Suffolk: SHRE & Open University Press.

Mugabi, H., Pekkola, E., Kivistö, J., & Stenvall, J. (2017). *Human Resource Management in Higher Education: A Literature Review. A Manuscript.* Tampere, Finland: University of Tampere.

Mukunda, G. (2012, August 22). Leaders Don't Matter (Most of the Time). *Harvard Business Review.* Retrieved from https://hbr.org/2012/08/leaders-dont-matter-most-of-th.html.

O'Reilly, C., Caldwell, D., Chatman, J., Lapiz, J. & Self, W. (2010) How Leadership Matters: The Effects of Leaders' Alignment on Strategy

Implementation. The Leadership Quarterly 21, 104-113. Retrieved from http://faculty.haas.berkeley.edu/CHATMAN/papers/04_HowLeadership Matters.pdf.

Phillips, K. W. (2014, October 1). How Diversity Makes Us Smarter. Being Around People Who Are Different from Us Makes Us More Creative, More Diligent and Harder-Working. *Scientific American*. Retrieved from https://www.scientificamerican.com/article/how-diversitymakes-us-smarter/.

Puusa, A., & Kekäle, J. (2013). Commitment in the Context of a Merger. *TEAM, 19*(3), 205–218.

Puusa, A., & Kekäle, J. (2015). Feelings Over Facts—A University Merger Brings Organisational Identity to the Forefront. *Journal of Higher Education Policy and Management, 37*(4), 432–446. https://doi.org/10.1080/13600 80X.2015.1056602.

Shattock, M. (2003). *Managing Successful Universities*. New York: SHRE & Open University Press.

Siekkinen, T., Pekkola, E., & Kivistö, J. (2016). Recruitments in Finnish Universities: Practicing Strategic or Pathetic HRM? Work and Life in Academia. *Nordic Journal of Studies in Educational Policy, 2016*(2–3). Retrieved from http://nordstep.net/index.php/nstep/article/view/32316.%20.

Snow, C. P. (1962). *The Two Cultures: and a Second Look*. Cambridge: University Press.

Tierney, W. (1998). *The Responsive University. Restructuring for Higher Performance*. London: The John Hopkins University Press.

Tierney and Lanford. (2016). Conceptualizing Innovation in Higher Education. In M. B. Paulsen (Ed.), *Higher Education: Handbook of Theory and Research* (p. 31). Basel: Springer.

Tirronen, J., Aula, H.-M., & Aarrevaara, T. (2016). A Complex and Messy Merger: The Road to University of Eastern Finland. In R. Pinheiro, L. Geshwind, & T. Aarrevaara (Eds.), *Mergers in Higher Education. The Experience from Northern Europe* (pp. 179–193). Basel: Springer.

Webster. (1994). *Unabridged Encyclopedia*. Bexley: Gramercy Books.

Wells. (2017). In Grau, et al. (Eds.), *Towards a Socially Responsible Higher Education Institution: Balancing the Global with the Local. GUNI—Global University Network for Innovation*. Higher Education in the World. Towards a Socially Responsible University: Balancing the Global with the Local. Retrieved from http://www.guninetwork.org/report/higher-educationworld.

Ylijoki, O.-H., & Ursin, J. (2013). The Construction of Academic Identity in the Changes of Finnish Higher Education. *Studies in Higher Education, 38*(8), 1135–1149.

10

Southeast Asian Universities and Responsibility

**Laila Nordstrand Berg, Rómulo Pinheiro,
Puguh Prasetya Utomo, and Pradnika Yunic Nurhayati**

Introduction

This edited book explores the responsible university in the context of the Nordic countries and beyond. This chapter contributes to the 'beyond' aspect by exploring the responsible university in the context of Southeast

L. N. Berg (✉) • R. Pinheiro
Department of Political Science and Management, University of Agder, Kristiansand, Norway
e-mail: laila.nordstrand.berg@hvl.no; romulo.m.pinheiro@uia.no

P. P. Utomo
Department of Political Science and Management, University of Agder, Kristiansand, Norway

Gadjah Mada University, Yogyakarta, Indonesia
e-mail: puguh.prasetya@uia.no

P. Y. Nurhayati
National Cheng Kung University, Tainan, Taiwan
e-mail: pradhikna.yunik@ugm.ac.id

Asia, namely in Indonesia. Indonesia was selected to reflect one of the ways a Norwegian university, University of Agder (UiA), spells out its mission as being a responsible university. Being 'responsible' not only has local or national connotations but also refers to contributing to the development of emerging economies. UiA has for years collaborated with Gadjah Mada University in Indonesia on teaching and research. This collaboration has many elements; professors from UiA give lectures at Gadjah Mada, Gadjah Mada professors teach students visiting from UiA, UiA educates Indonesian PhD students and there is collaboration on research across the universities. The cooperation with Indonesia is also in line with national policy imperatives by Norway's Foreign Minister, when it comes to promoting democracy and institutional capacity building in regions of need. Contrasting Nordic universities (the scope of this volume) with findings from such a different context can offer fruitful perspectives on how to demonstrate responsibility in different settings, thus assessing the so-called Nordic model from the outside.

Knowledge, skills and human resources are crucial for economic growth and innovation and have been at the forefront of policy agendas in the last two decades (World Bank 1998, 2008). In this chapter, we focus on two actors that are central in this development, namely regions and universities. Regions refer to territorial entities below the nation-state. Regions do not exist in a vacuum, and they function within a so-called regional system (Schmitt-Egner 2002) that encompasses a multiplicity of actors, including those involved with the transmission and creation of knowledge, such as universities.[1] Universities are considered important actors that enable socio-economic development and global competitiveness (Lester and Sotarauta 2007). Policy efforts are underway in many parts of the world, for example, across the OECD (Organisation for Economic Co-operation and Development), to enhance the competitive standing of localities and entire regions (OECD 2005), with universities seen as key actors in such endeavours (OECD 2007; Pinheiro and Pillay 2016).

Universities the world over have, either symbolically or in real terms, adapted their roles and functions to meet the demand for being considered responsible actors of society. They have done this by, inter alia, expanding their recruitment practices to broaden participation by under-represented groups, to increase enrolments and cater for students from such groups and by actively participating in the creation of economic assets through interactions with external actors like industry (Čábelková et al. 2017; Stachowiak et al. 2013). The role of universities is no longer limited to providing teaching and research for educational purposes in the classic sense but, to a larger degree, meeting a societal demand for outreach through so-called third-mission activities (Pinheiro et al. 2015b). This comprises common activities between the universities and partners in the regions as a means for developing and applying new knowledge (Benneworth et al. 2017b). The success of universities in contributing to regional development, however, depends primarily on the interconnections between universities (and their diverse academic communities), state actors at various levels and local communities (Mbah 2016; Benneworth et al. 2017a).

As of today, few studies have investigated the contribution of universities to broadening participation and local economic development within the East Asian context and the so-called emerging world economies (Schwartzman et al. 2015). Indonesia possesses large socio-economic asymmetries amongst its various regions or provinces as well as between rural and urban areas. Despite positive economic growth—averaging 6 per cent of the Gross Domestic Product (GDP) annually in the last two decades—social exclusion remains prominent, particularly in poorer, remote regions. Of a population of 265 million, 26 million (nearly 10 per cent) Indonesians currently live below the poverty line. Following the fall of the Suharto autocratic regime in the late 1990s, the modernisation of the domestic economy has been at the forefront of the policy agenda.

Given this backdrop, the chapter addresses two core themes. At the macro, policy level, we investigate how local governments in two regions of Indonesia attempt to improve access to higher education (HE) for under-represented social groups. At the meso level, we shed light on how universities in the selected regions, both through formalised arrangements and via the ad-hoc initiatives of managers and academics, are reorganising internal rules, structures and procedures to meet the needs of various external stakeholders and hence respond to calls for more responsible action. Given the mandate of this book and its focus on the Nordic context, we also provide an analysis of our findings by contrasting them with ongoing developments within the Nordics. The research questions are fourfold:

1. How does government policy, represented by various levels of local government, conceive the role of universities in regional development, including issues pertaining to widening access and participation?
2. What effect, if any, does a socially responsible agenda have in universities' strategies and academic initiatives?
3. To what extent is there an alignment between policy measures and university strategies and initiatives?
4. What lessons can be learnt, in either direction, in light of current developments in the Nordic countries?

In the remainder of the chapter, we first present the key features of the Indonesian HE system, followed by a discussion of the traditional functions of universities and their role in regional development. Methodological issues are then elaborated upon, and the selected case studies are presented. The main part of the chapter presents the empirical findings and discusses the main issues by relating back to the literature. Finally, the chapter concludes by elaborating on the implications of the findings regarding policy and future research inquiries.

Higher Education in Indonesia

The HE system in Indonesia has undergone considerable change in the last few decades, not least due to the country's drastic political transition into a constitutional democracy since 1998. As far as HE policy is concerned, the period 1996–2005 focused on two main aspects: enhancing social mobility and equity. The financial crisis hit the Indonesian economy in 1997–1998, followed by economic, political and social crisis. As is the case elsewhere, the government's ability to expand the supply of public higher education institutions (HEIs) is constrained by the budget and, consequently, the private sector has dominated HE in the last two decades. By 2017, the HEI sector had more than 3100 private and over 120 public HEIs (PDDIKTI 2017). Public HEIs have higher status due to their higher quality (Ministry of Education and Culture 2012, 13), but many students from the poorest segments are unable to meet the admission requirements of public institutions and opt for private universities. Most private HEIs rely on student fees, which are rather expensive for those from disadvantaged backgrounds (Wicaksono and Friawan 2008, 164).

Furthermore, there is a strong regional clustering of HEIs. More than half of all study programmes are located on the highest populated islands, namely Java and Bali. Java and Bali have populations greater than 1000 inhabitants per square kilometre and contribute more than 50 per cent of the total Indonesian revenue and expenditure. Another 30 per cent of all study programmes are located on the islands of Sumatra and Sulawesi (World Bank 2014, 13).

Access and equity remain two central policy issues, despite HE enrolments' exponential rise since the late 1980s, reaching more than 6 million students in 2014 (see Fig. 10.1). Private HE (87 per cent of total enrolments) guarantees access and equity, fulfilling the aims of massification, while public HE acts as the government's engine to steer the country towards excellence and global competitiveness (Asian Development Bank 2012). The gross enrolment rate (GER) in 2014 was 31 per cent, which is low compared to other Southeast Asian countries such as

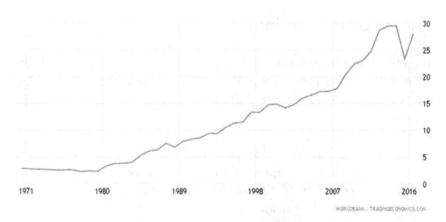

Fig. 10.1 Tertiary enrolments in Indonesia: 1971–2016 (% gross). Source: Economics (2018)

Singapore (70 per cent) and Thailand (53 per cent) (UNESCO-UIS 2014). Turning to equity, Law 12/2012 states that 20 per cent of all HE students should originate from less advantaged groups. In 2016, only 7 per cent of the least well-off households (quintile 1) attended HE, compared to 49 per cent of the most well-off households (quintile 5) (BPS-Statistic BPS 2016, 40). The data also show that in 2016, 31 per cent of students originated from urban areas, compared to 14 per cent from rural areas (Ibid., 113–114).

Universities and Regional Development

The role of HE as an engine for the development of regions is particularly salient in the case of developing and emerging nations within the context of a globalised, knowledge-based economy (Pinheiro et al. 2012b; Schwartzman et al. 2015). Across many national jurisdictions, governments have enacted policy frameworks aimed at establishing universities in peripheral regions or across localities faced with major socio-economic challenges (Pinheiro et al. 2016a). The contribution of universities to local development occurs both in terms of supply and demand. In the supply situation, they provide regions with needed professionals (teachers, doctors, engineers, etc.) and knowledge (technology transfers), with the latter thought to be a critical element in local industrial regeneration (Huggins and Johnston 2009). On the demand side, the presence of universities tends to attract the provision of other economic (e.g. businesses) and social goods (e.g. schools, hospitals), which often have a positive impact on the region's overall outlook and attractiveness (Douglass et al. 2011).

Earlier studies revealed that there are multiple barriers, both structural and cultural, to universities serving as engines of local development. These range from the absence of incentive systems to clashes in norms and values and from gaps in time horizons to a lack of commitment by leaders (Balbachevsky 2008; Pinheiro et al. 2012a). The fiercely competitive environment facing universities worldwide, combined with increasing levels of resource scarcity, makes the regional mission a daunting task (Pinheiro et al. 2015a).

Castells (1993) referred to the traditional functions of universities as pertaining to four main aspects:

- Ideological apparatuses (transmission of norms and values through socialisation)
- The selection and socialisation of (political, economic and cultural) elite groups
- The production and application of knowledge
- The training of a skilled labour force.

In so doing, the author shed light on the contradictory nature of the various societal functions that universities are expected to fulfil. As systems expand and move from elite to mass and then to universal stages, the policy emphasis (system level) tends to shift from elite socialisation towards widening access and knowledge production and transmission (Cantwell et al. 2018).

Trow's seminal work (1970) referred to the 'autonomous' functions that universities tend to voluntarily adopt (e.g. research) from those 'popular functions' they are compelled to address as a result of popular demand or government coercion (e.g. teaching the masses, engagement). Like Castells, Trow pointed to a clash between these two functions. It could be argued that, for the most part, universities (at least in the classic sense) are more committed to teaching and research activities when compared to the so-called third-mission (e.g. regional development), with the latter being relegated to 'nice to have' (Pinheiro et al. 2015a). However, this does not entail the absence of university leaders and academics committed to supporting the economic well-being of their surrounding regions and localities (Benneworth et al. 2017a; Mohrman et al. 2009), but it does suggest that tensions and dilemmas exist.

Gunasekara (2006) made a distinction between the *developmental* and *generative* roles of universities in the context of their importance to the surrounding society/economy. In the latter scenario, the university is the engine or catalyst behind regional development, providing high-level skills and competences as well as knowledge of central relevance to the regional development process. In contrast, in the developmental scenario, universities are but one of many actors comprising the local knowledge and innovation ecosystems, with their role being primarily one of supplying graduates. Studies from North America revealed that despite the presence of adequate local conditions, such as technology transfer offices, policy incentives and industrial outreach projects, 'most research universities have not been particularly successful at technology transfer and have not yet generated significant local economic development' (Feldman and Desrochers 2003, 5). Part of the reason pertains to the fact that universities are necessary but not sufficient conditions for development. The absence of other knowledge actors, such as firms, may result into the outflow of graduates and knowledge, implying low absorptive capacity at the regional level. This is particularly problematic within the context of so-called peripheral or remote regions, thus reinforcing a vicious cycle (Pinheiro et al. 2018b).

Methodology and Cases

Our study adopts a multi-method research design, combining a desktop analysis of major policy initiatives and a case study design with interviews with key actors. Among the desktop material, we analysed the Law 12/2012 on HE (GOL 2012), political initiatives from central and local governments and the profiles and strategic intentions of HEIs. Due to large differences between and within regions in Indonesia, we chose study cases that are as different as possible. Thus, we selected a most different systems design (Przeworski and Teune 1970) and two different case regions. In terms of HEIs, we selected four institutions located in two distinct geographies, namely: the 'central' case, which comes from a vibrant urban area characterised by developed service sectors like tourism, and the geographically 'remote' case located in a less developed region reliant on the primary sector.

Due to the Indonesian system, which comprises a high status and higher standards in public universities and more limited frames for private universities, we selected cases from both groups. In the central case, we chose a public university with comprehensive disciplines and many faculties and a private polytechnic institution focused on applied and practical skills. In the remote case, we selected the opposite: a public polytechnic and a private university. The reason for this selection was to follow our design, which consisted of variation amongst the cases to investigate the role of the university in regional development.

We interviewed three stakeholder groups: (1) politicians from the central and provincial levels, (2) academics from various fields, with managerial positions and at different levels in the universities, and (3) external stakeholders from local industries. Many of these stakeholders had mixed roles between the university and/or at the policy level. A total of 30 interviews were conducted, the majority at the end of 2015, supplemented by a few more in the summer of 2016. A semi-structured interview guide was adjusted to the three groups. The first part consisted of questions centred on equity and access to HE. The second group of questions dealt with regional development and focused on the relevance of education and its impact in the region.

Data Findings

In this section, we highlight the key findings associated with each of the four research questions and respective levels of analysis.

Governmental Policy Within Regions

Due to the widespread decentralisation of Indonesian politics, the authority of national government regarding HE is low and delegated to local governments. The local governments are responsible for addressing the needs of the districts and for developing community colleges according to the needs of the regions, while the role of central government is to monitor quality and accreditation functions. There is a widespread consensus that local governments have the responsibility to enhance access to HE locally. Joint efforts by the universities and local authorities to develop programmes that are specific to local needs are the norm.

> Most of the programmes and curricula follow the national standard. But, the main focus is on the local context. For example, in [local university], they have education orientation relating to [local needs; e.g. fishery, dryland farming]. They follow the national standard, but while teaching they

use the local context as an example. (Local government representative, remote district)

To address the need for HE to foster regional development, governmental organisations, both in the central and remote areas, rely on the expertise of universities, such as experts on infrastructure, medicine and mechanical engineering. These academic experts contribute their knowledge at different stages by surveying, planning and evaluating. Academics also play an important role in shaping policy frameworks both at the local (province) and central levels.

> In almost every ministry, the top management positions are taken by popular people from universities. Many ministers are professors [...] many politicians are professors as well. So, you can imagine that the role of HEIs is very significant at the national level. And this also happens in the regions. (Central government representative)

The participants from the universities in both cases referred to different types of scholarships and affirmative programmes aimed at providing economic support for poor students from remote areas. Some are meant to fully support these students, while others are supplemental, for example, they cover student fees. Scholarships are provided by the central government by regional and local authorities as well as by private actors, such as companies and associations. Both local and central authorities and university staff are concerned that students from remote areas tend not to return to their communities to apply their new knowledge. To counterbalance this trend, the central government provides incentives to educated people with certain skills to move back to remote districts. They are offered better salaries and facilities such as housing and transportation for professionals who are willing to stay in the districts for a period of five to ten years. However, the evidence shows that only a few of these professionals remain in the areas at the end of the period.

University Strategies and Initiatives

The case HEIs applied different strategies and initiatives to act as responsible universities and broaden access for, and participation from, less

advantaged groups. As for strategies to enhance access to HEIs, the interviewees gave examples of initiatives from the universities to change the
recruitment system of new students. By establishing a new entry test, a
higher proportion of students from lower socio-economic groups was
admitted. The strategic initiatives also included accepting lower credits
from students coming from districts where the quality of secondary education was lower. The university strategies also focused on following up
on students from disadvantaged groups. As soon as the students were
admitted, supporting or 'bridging' programmes were offered to help students complete their education and graduate. These could be extra classes
in subjects such as math or chemistry or cultural programmes to help
students from, for example, the jungle adjust to urban life. As for recruitment, the HEIs in remote districts also faced difficulty recruiting lecturers. The strategies of the remote HEIs included recruiting the best
students at their universities as well as students from their islands educated elsewhere.

There seemed to be a common strategy across the cases to involve local
communities in developing the educational content. Research served as a
means to meet the needs of local regions and foster local development.
There were no clear differences between the cases in this respect, and the
differences merely reflected the characteristics of the regions (e.g. regions
focused on eco-tourism, farming in dry land, fishery or the oil industry).
This is expressed by a central university manager:

> As a lecturer, we have three main responsibilities—Tri Dharma. The first is
> teaching, second research, and the third is community service. When we
> create the curriculum, we must involve all stakeholders, including the com-
> munity, so that the curriculum can fit the needs of society. We then apply
> it to our students. It is possible that the research conducted by lecturers will
> be used as material for curriculum and community services. The results will
> be applied to the society. (University manager, central university)

The term 'Tri Dharma' was central in the stories from the participants
and relates to teaching, research and outreach or third-mission activities.
Our study also indicates that many academics were engaged in mixed
roles as university managers, managers in the private sector, public servant roles and as politicians at the local, regional and central levels. In

these roles, they contributed their expertise to develop the regions, but they also received input valuable for the development of the curricula.

Furthermore, teaching and research were closely linked to outreach programmes and so-called third-mission activities. The programmes were designed to meet the specific needs of the various regions, such as improving health, developing tourism, improving fisheries and dry land farming or developing routines to handle natural disasters. All students had to participate in such programmes during their studies, and academics were eager to participate as advisors and in research connected to the programmes. Such programmes were established in both remote and central cases, but where the central academics talked about the programmes in a passionate way, the remote participants were more critical. Perhaps these participants were more critical, as they lived in poorer regions and could see the long-term effects of such programmes. Criticism also came from a civil servant:

> I think that the outreach programmes benefit the universities more than the locals. In [our province], the programmes are designed for the needs of the universities, especially for students to finish the process of education at these universities. (Local government representative, remote district)

Alignment Between Governmental Policy and University Strategies and Initiatives

In general, university stakeholders reported a good alignment with policy measures and cooperation with government at different levels. There was a synergy between the different governmental levels and stakeholders whereby the stakeholders received support and, in return, helped to tackle critical social issues through their local programmes. This synergy was also facilitated through the mixed roles of the academics, who were also engaged in governmental agencies as 'external' stakeholders (e.g. as policy advisors). Another aspect was that most bureaucrats and many of the stakeholders were educated at the HEIs and thus shared common norms and values and had developed cross-sectoral networks. Governmental policies and strategies were not merely developed through top-down processes. Universities were considered think tanks or knowledge repositories for the regions, with the local government seeking to adjust its missions and vision to those of the HEIs. Some visions were driven more by the grassroots than as a result of governmental policy, for example, the growth in the tourist industry. On the problematic side, some participants pointed out that there was a time lag in the development of regional policy because the industry was growing faster than the ability of governmental agencies and the bureaucracy to evolve. As such, there were no major differences between the cases.

Turning back to the HE sector, and regarding the degree of alignment between governmental policies and university initiatives, several dilemmas emerged from the interview data. First, the bulk of academic work was project-based with short-term financing. This made it difficult for the universities in both cases to pursue sustainable strategies, policies and initiatives. Second, the data showed a decoupling of the policy of equity/access for students from all layers of society, which could have been facilitated by the distribution of scholarships. Participants from the remote case were particularly critical of the distribution and the way in which the scholarships were promoted. Information circulation was not widespread and mostly went through channels that benefited civil servants and university bureaucrats, for example, through the internet. The third problem mentioned in both cases was the absence of policies from governments and universities on how to face the expected surplus of students in certain educational fields, such as teaching, nursing and different types of planners. Autonomy by HEIs was also referred to as a bottleneck.

> However, the provincial government does not intervene in the policy in order to improve people's awareness of what will happen in 2030. What should be done by the people and campuses to welcome the 2030 development agenda? The provincial government has no vision at all on these issues. This can lead to huge problems in the future. Further, the government cannot control campuses due to latter's autonomy. (University manager, remote university)

In the next two sections, we discuss the main findings: first, for Indonesia and against the backdrop of the conceptual dimensions presented at the onset in the introduction and second, by reflecting on the data findings from a Nordic perspective.

Discussion

Discussion Part I: Indonesia as a Case

As the country is in a phase of political and social transition from an auto-cratic to a multi-party democracy, Indonesian HE is also shifting from an elite system to a mass system (Trow 1970). Widening participation and local development rank high in the policy agenda, with universities addressing the new policy imperatives and taking the role as 'responsible universities' in the frames of their capabilities, resources and specific local circumstances. Widening participation with a focus on increased access and measures to attract under-represented groups work hand in hand with regional development. Likewise, regions with their public and pri-vate actors actively participate in the development of universities and the entire HE sector by participating in the development of curricula accord-ing to local needs and by 'offering' problems to solve for students and academics in the Tri Dharma regime of third-mission activities.

As studies from other countries have revealed (Pinheiro et al. 2015a), resource scarcity hinders the development of the HE sector. This is also an issue for Indonesia. The majority of HEIs are localised in the central and most populated islands, which is a hindrance for students from remote islands to pursue HE. Critics also point to the fact that few public universities were established in the districts, thus creating problems regarding access to high-quality education and the region's long-term absorptive capacity (Pinheiro 2014). Private universities contribute to massification and access, still supporting inequalities amongst the wealthy and disadvantaged groups, since private HEIs are unable to maintain a high quality of education. As a result, those who can least afford educa-tion tend to pay for low quality, hence supporting the inequality of HE distribution, as found in other countries (Cantwell et al. 2018).

Recruitment to universities is, in theory, based on grades, but in prac-tice, there are several barriers that result in the selection of elite groups, pointing to the elite function within mass HE systems (Cantwell et al. 2018; Palfreyman and Tapper 2008). The first barrier is the quality of secondary education, with grades as the base of student recruitment. There are large variations in the quality of secondary education, and this increases the challenges in relation to access for potential students from these regions. The small number of universities in remote areas is another barrier for poor people who cannot afford to travel to pursue HE. Likewise, differences in quality between public and private HEIs and the urban rural divide play an important role in student choice and university behaviour (recruitment, engagement, etc.). Similar challenges can be observed in other systems that have undergone political and economic transformation and the transition from elite to mass HE systems (Trow 1970). The two cases are Poland, which assisted (late 1990s to mid-2000s) the rise and decline of private universities without adequate quality screening (Pinheiro and Antonowics 2015), and South Korea, which was able to find a proper balance between policy coordination at different levels and the role played by the private sector in promoting access whilst fostering quality and (horizontal) differentiation at the system level (Pinheiro and Pillay 2016).

Another major access barrier pertains to financial aspects, and one way to overcome this is to provide scholarships from public and private actors. However, the distribution of scholarships is not transparent, and information on certain scholarships is not widely distributed. This points to the critical issue of information asymmetries and the notion of HE systems as 'quasi' markets (Dill and Soo 2004; Dinkelman and Martínez 2014). Studies from the US revealed that poor people are often unaware of the support systems available to them (Johnstone and Marcucci 2010). Criticisms from some of the participants that the wealth accumulation of the rich was not distributed to the poorest speak to the wider debate about who benefits from HE and what role governments play in the re-distribution of public goods to promote social mobility (Marginson 2011; Pinheiro and Antonowics 2015). As in other countries (Cantwell et al. 2018), in Indonesia, middle-class students seem to gain the most from the current access and governance policies and university recruitment practices. Financial issues are severe problems faced by both students and universities in the form of short-term and project-based financing. Similar problems were found in earlier studies from Africa whereby international donors funded projects that did not contribute to strengthening core academic activities, ultimately resulting in 'projectisation' (Cloete et al. 2011).

By revisiting the traditional functions of universities and their inherent tensions and contradictions (Castells 1993), local academics critically questioned the ability of their HEIs to act as transmitters of norms and values (socialisation role) in the context of a society and economy in flux and an HE system in transition from elite to mass access (Trow 1970). By taking the role of responsible universities, academics problematised their role in socialising students. They wanted to meet people from diverse cultures with respect. This was challenging, and they questioned whether they had the rights to claim that their values (e.g. knowledge transfers) were better than the more 'primitive' practice of learning by doing. Another related issue pertained to the responsibility of academics to socialise and teach students how to live in fast-growing urban settings, which goes against government policies aimed at attracting professionals and other graduates to the more remote regions from where they originated. As a general notion, the participants reported an alignment between policy measures and the various stakeholders. This can be viewed from the role of universities in the socialisation of students (Castells 1993), as most of the bureaucrats and stakeholders were educated at the same institutions.

Employees from the universities actively participate in society with their expertise and specific skills as planners, politicians, civil servants, managers in the private sector and so forth. Such commitments, combined with teaching and research, are time-consuming and show a high level of engagement. This may, however, be considered a double-edged sword. Such an overlap is positive regarding the sharing of information, coordination and social capital (trust building) but may result in increased dependency on certain individuals as key brokers who might take advantage of this situation to address their own strategic agendas and imperatives (for a similar case in a country in transition, see Hladchenko and Pinheiro 2018). The decades of dictatorship might have undermined the role of HEIs as autonomous institutions. This phase was followed (mid-1990s) by an acute financial crisis, where academic expertise was found to be of high value to the reconstruction of the economy and society nationally and locally. Hence, HEIs played the role of strategic instruments for the accomplishment of policy agendas.

The data support the notion that Indonesian universities act as engines for regional development and thereby take a generative role in society (Gunasekara 2006). Similar findings were demonstrated in earlier studies outside Asia (Castells 1993; Harding et al. 2007; OECD 2007; Pinheiro and Pillay 2016). In less developed areas or outside urban centres, there is an increasing dependence on HEIs as engines or catalysts for development, partly due to the absence of other knowledge and innovation players, such as firms. Recent studies from Norway revealed that similar challenges are at play when it comes to the role of less research-intensive HEIs located in more peripheral geographies (Pinheiro et al. 2018a).

On the teaching front, the case universities supplied programmes that relate to the interplay between breadth and depth. Examples of breadth are educational activities addressing general social needs, represented by the training of teachers, doctors, nurses, midwives, engineers and planners. However, the universities also specialise according to the needs of the regions, for example, fisheries, dryland agriculture, the oil industry and tourism. On the research front, the focus was on projects aimed at supporting the development of different types of industries and efficient government in the regions. These research projects were often developed as part and parcel of outreach programmes and third-mission activities implemented in the context of Tri Dharma, where activities involving researchers, students and local actors were tightly integrated.

Regional development constituted a core activity for the case universities, and this commitment seems to provide reciprocal benefits to both HEIs and the community partners involved—a key principle of engaged scholarship (Brown et al. 2016). This behaviour can be interpreted in the light of socialisation theory (Grusec and Hastings 2014), with respect to both the importance attributed to societal engagement in the context of HE as an institution (Tri Dharma) as well as the role attributed to local norms and values in creating a supportive cultural atmosphere (Breznitz and Feldman 2012). This, in turn, might produce a vicious cycle as universities socialise future professionals to become actively engaged with social issues (Austin 2002), bringing to the fore certain normative preferences (Wildavsky 1987).

Discussion Part II: Assessing the Findings from a Nordic Perspective

In this section, we briefly reflect on how the case findings presented above may be of relevance to understanding the responsible role of universities in a Nordic context, the subject of the current volume. First, it is worth keeping in mind the large differences in populations between Indonesia, with its 265 million inhabitants, and the four Nordic countries, with a combined population of less than 26 million (the largest country being Sweden with close to 10 million and the smallest being Norway with about 5.1 million). Due to size, there are considerable challenges associated with organising and funding the HE sector in Indonesia, as well as challenges related to ethnicity, religion and geographical disparity. Indonesia is also a young democracy facing its own institutional challenges. Second, the Nordic countries currently top the rankings in the UN Human Development Index 2018 (UN 2018), while Indonesia, with its large share of the population living close to the poverty line, is ranked number 116. Still, such a comparison can be fruitful.

The Nordic countries have not always been wealthy, but due to increased focus on HE and access for all layers of the population, universities and other types of HEIs such as more vocationally oriented colleges have been important actors (acting as engines) for the socio-economic development of the societies. This is particularly salient in the cases of Norway, Sweden and Finland, where regional imperatives have long ranked high in the policy agenda, including within HE (Pinheiro 2012b), partly as a result of a geographically dispersed population and significant economic and demographic asymmetries amongst domestic regions. From a policy viewpoint, the regional agenda in Nordic HE (particularly so in the cases of Norway and Finland) has been enhanced by the convergence between regional policy following World War II and HE policy, focusing on widening access and participation and horizontal differentiation along a binary system composed of research-intensive universities and other (more vocationally and locally embedded) HEIs (Kyvik 2009).

The majority of HEIs in the Nordics are public, and education is tuition-free for domestic students at all levels. The sector is funded by the general tax system, which reflects a broader social contract between society and the public sector brokered by the state. In some Nordic countries, as in Norway, both public and private institutions are assigned grants following the same distribution model (Kvaal 2014). This is a significant contrast to how the sector is organised and financed in Indonesia. Just a small share of the universities are public, and the private sector, the bulk of which lacks quality and is concentrated in urban areas where student markets are located, dominates. In Indonesia, only public universities receive public funding and are thus able to provide a better quality of education compared to the private sector.

In Indonesia, both sectors rely on student tuition fees, which are unreachable for potential students from the lower quintiles of disadvantaged groups, thus bringing to the fore a series of equity-related dilemmas, that is, who can access what and where? Although there are different types of financial arrangements targeting public and private actors, this system is not large enough to provide education to the masses. Since the 1950s, the Nordics have offered scholarships and affordable loans to all students as alimonies to remove any potential socio-economic and geographic barriers for accessing HE (Pinheiro and Antonowics 2015). Information on these arrangements is offered by senior high schools and universities and is publicly available. The sharing of information on funding schemes is another hindrance in Indonesia, and the distribution of information of these funding schemes is not well implemented and thereby fails to reach the poorest groups. One consequence, as in many other countries (Cantwell et al. 2018), is that those least likely to afford HE are either the ones gaining access to lower quality HEIs or are completely excluded from the system.

With respect to quality and in contrast to the rigorous oversight by quality assurance agencies and other governmental agencies in the Nordic countries (Pinheiro and Stensaker 2018), as well as proper design and implementation of quality procedures by HEIs (Karlsson et al. 2014), the scale and complexity inherent to the private HE system in Indonesia makes quality assurance and steering by the government a daunting task. This is particularly the case with respect to ensuring the interests of less resourceful students (often located in more remote areas, outside large urban centres) attending private HEIs, since these are ill-served when the state is unable to provide proper quality controls. A 2012 analysis shows that despite the large size of the domestic HE system, including a massive private sector (at that time, 3000 private vs 80 public HEIs), the Indonesian government agency responsible for quality assurance within tertiary education (BAN-PT) employed less than 50 people and had an annual budget of 7 million euro (SEAMEO 2012, 77). In comparison, Norway's quality assurance agency (NOKUT), responsible for supervising about 160 institutions, employed in 2016 a total of 125 employees with a budget of 14 million euro (NOKUT 2016, 39).

The third mission was found to be a core activity of Indonesia HEIs, important both for education and research purposes but also as a practical contribution to the socio-economic and cultural development of the regions. This is in contrast to findings from the Nordics, where third mission is more in line with a 'nice to have' task (Pinheiro et al. 2015b) and the focus is more on the collaboration between academics and public and private sector organisations in the context of knowledge transfers (Benner and Sandström 2000). In the binary Nordic HE system, the more locally embedded HEIs cohere better with the 'responsible university' agenda compared to HEIs centred on the classical Humboldtian model (Nybom 2007). The latter, represented by the 'old' flagship, comprehensive universities, focuses on teaching and research excellence and autonomy as a core value. Interestingly, due to concentration as a result of mergers, more vocationally oriented Nordic HEIs are being integrated in the internal structures of more classic, research-intensive universities where engagement is not seen as a core task (Pinheiro et al. 2016b). Furthermore, as a result of the 'managerial turn' in Nordic HEIs, these have increasingly embraced metrics and excellence as strategic means for managing performance in teaching and research (Pinheiro et al. 2019). This, in turn, seems to have hindered HEIs' motivation to institutionalise third-mission activities as a 'natural part' of their roles and functions (Sima et al. 2017), despite external expectations for doing so.

By viewing the universities in the light of the 'responsible university', the participants emphasised both teaching and research, but what distinguished them from the Nordic context was the emphasis on third-mission activities. This is highlighted as one of the core activities in Indonesia and is an important base for education and research purposes, in addition to the practical contribution to the socio-economic and cultural development of the regions. In the Nordics, and despite an ongoing discourse of HEIs' social responsibility and research impact (also framed within the broader European Union context), the third mission is, as alluded to earlier, more in line with a 'nice to have' task (Pinheiro et al. 2015b). In the Nordics, HEIs as one of many actors are playing a more developmental role (Gunasekara 2006) by supporting local knowledge and innovation ecosystems rather than being the core engine of it (Nilsson 2006).

Conclusion

Based on the data collected, there appears to be a consensus that universities play a responsible role in the context of Indonesian society, both nationally and locally. Respondents from central and local government, academics from private and public universities and stakeholders in both contexts emphasised the role of the university as a central actor in the development of society by playing a generative role (Gunasekara 2006), particularly in more remote geographies. This process takes a multiplicity of forms and is intrinsically connected to the education of students, academics participating on a part-time basis in different areas of society, the provision of technological know-how that poorer regions cannot develop themselves and through outreach programmes, many of which directly involve students as active participants in leveraging the resources of the local community. This could be because there are fewer alternatives in terms of knowledge institutions (e.g. global firms) capable of playing such roles in many of the more remote regions of Indonesia. Still, the regions are not passive recipients of help but also play active roles in engaging with the universities, for example, in relation to curriculum development, which is related to local needs, and by cooperating in third mission and outreach-related activities.

Perhaps unsurprisingly, and mirroring the results from earlier studies (Goddard et al. 2016; OECD 2007; Pinheiro 2012a), we tentatively draw the conclusion that both contextual circumstances and historical trajectories do matter when it comes to the responsible role undertaken by the HE sector. This is particularly the case when assessed against the backdrop of societies undergoing considerable social, political and economic transitions, including, but not limited to, the development of democratic institutions and more equitable educational systems, which are expected to result in a fairer and more inclusive society. In this respect, policy makers and HEIs in Indonesia have much to gain from looking at the so-called Nordic model (Christiansen et al. 2005), given the long historical commitment (as well as track record) to balancing equity (access to critical public goods) with market dimensions (competitiveness), in addition to accountable and efficient government.

In the realm of HE in particular, the Nordic countries provide an important template of how to find an adequate balance between (1) steering at a distance and enhanced institutional autonomy on the one hand and (2) access (widening participation based on tuition-free education) and excellence (teaching quality and world-class research) on the other. In addition, the historical focus attributed to regional decentralisation and horizontal differentiation by policy makers (cf. Pinheiro and Stensaker 2018) offers important lessons to countries like Indonesia that are entering a mass HE expansion phase (Trow 1970). However, the recent policy emphasis put on rationalisation, performance management and concentration (mergers) has brought to the fore a series of new tensions and dilemmas facing all the Nordic HE systems, not least with respect to the interplay/trade-off between global excellence and local relevance on the one hand and horizontal versus vertical differentiation on the other (Pinheiro et al. 2014).

Regarding efforts to broaden participation and regional development, the study has revealed that there is an explicit link between national and local authorities, the 'regulative pillar' (Scott 2008) or 'superstructure' (Clark 1983), universities' policies and strategies ('the middle structure'; Clark 1983) and bottom-up initiatives across the 'academic heartland' (Clark 1998). That said, it is worth stressing that, as is the case with the Nordic countries, local authorities were not found to have any formal mandate on universities, thus constraining the level of coercion they may impose on them to address issues of critical importance to the locality. However, local government was revealed to play a role in terms of influencing curriculum development, research projects and outreach programmes as a result of tight collaborations, which, on aggregate, were found to have a positive effect in instituting a responsible agenda across university policies, structures, activities and normative postures.

Informally, the hybrid nature of the positions played by members of the academic community in society (as experts, policy makers, leaders, etc.) enables them to actively participate in the development of society and to serve as important role models for students and colleagues alike. This is a major departure from established practices across the Nordic countries, where a clearer demarcation of academic roles and responsibilities has traditionally been the norm, helping shape the ethos of the academic profession throughout the region (Vabø and Aamodt 2008). In this regard, one could argue that the Nordic countries have something to learn from the Indonesian experience, where more fluid and hybridised tasks, roles and professional identities facilitate the responsible role of universities in society—what some have termed the rise of the 'third space professional' in contemporary (Western) academia (Watermeyer 2015; Whitchurch 2012).

From a policy prism, the findings suggest that there is a need for a embracing a more systemic or holistic perspective of policy design and implementation that accounts for the complexities associated with HE as a policy sector and the university as a multi-faceted and complex organisation (Pinheiro and Young 2017; Room 2011). More specifically, we urge policy makers and university managers alike to, to the best of their abilities, anticipate the unintended effects caused by the interplay amongst macro-, meso- and micro-level dimensions and to move away from 'one-size-fits-all' solutions that neglect historical trajectories and local circumstances values.

In terms of future studies, we urge social scientists interested in the topic in Southeast Asia, the Nordics and beyond to address critical queries about the accountability of agents with mixed, multiple and overlapping roles, as well as the real autonomy enjoyed by universities and the effects that has in fulfilling their 'responsible' mandates or missions.

There is also a need for further empirical studies on how the abstract notion of the 'socially responsible university' is articulated at different levels of the HE system and amongst different actors both within the university and outside (influential external stakeholders). Finally, future studies could shed empirical light on the roles played by resource allocations (funding streams), competition and professional (managerial vs academic) norms and values in devising and diffusing (institutionalisation) a socially responsible agenda across teaching, research and third-mission activities and the interplay (degree of coupling) amongst them.

Acknowledgement The authors thank the generous funding from the Norwegian Ministry of Foreign Affairs for the institutional cooperation between Gadjah Mada University, Indonesia, and University of Agder, Norway. Also, thank you to the book editors and contributing authors for constructive feedback on earlier versions of the chapter. Any remaining errors are the authors' own.

Note

1. In this chapter, we use the term 'university' to refer to all types of tertiary education institutions. In certain contexts, we refer to the broader term 'higher education institution'.

References

Asian Development Bank. (2012). *Administration and Governance of Higher Education in Asia. Patterns and Implications*. Manila Philiphines.

Austin, A. (2002). Preparing the Next Generation of Faculty: Graduate School as Socialization to the Academic Career. *The Journal of Higher Education, 73*(1), 94–122.

Balbachevsky, E. (2008). Incentives and Obstacles to Academic Entrepreneurship. In S. Schwartzman (Ed.), *University and Development in Latin America: Successful Experiences of Research Centre* (pp. 23–42). Rotterdam: Sense.

Benner, M., & Sandström, U. (2000). Institutionalizing the Triple Helix: Research Funding and Norms in the Academic System. *Research Policy, 29*(2), 291–301.

Benneworth, P., Pinheiro, R., & Karlsen, J. (2017a). Strategic Agency and Institutional Change: Investigating the Role of Universities in Regional Innovation Systems (RISs). *Regional Studies, 51*(2), 235–248. https://doi.org /10.1080/00343404.2016.1215599.

Benneworth, P., Zeeman, N., Pinheiro, R., & Karlsen, J. (2017b). National Higher Education Politicies Challenging Universitites' Regional Engagement Activities. *Ekonomiaz, 92*(2), 146–173.

BPS. (2016). *Potret Pendidikan Indonesia: Statistik Pendidikan 2016 [Portrait of Indonesian Education: 2016 Figures]*. Jakarta: BPS-Statistics Indonesia.

Breznitz, S., & Feldman, M. (2012). The Engaged University. *The Journal of Technology Transfer, 37*(2), 139–157. https://doi.org/10.1007/s10961-010-9183-6.

Brown, K., Shepard, K., Warren, D., Hesson, G., & Fleming, J. (2016). Using Phenomenography to Build an Understanding of How University People Conceptualise Their Community-Engaged Activities. *Higher Education Research & Development, 35*(4), 643–657.

Čábelková, I., Normann, R., & Pinheiro, R. (2017). The Role of Higher Education Institutions in Fostering Industry Clusters in Peripheral Regions: Strategies, Actors and Outcomes. *Higher Education Policy, 30*(4), 481–498. https://doi.org/10.1057/s41307-017-0059-3.

Cantwell, B., Marginson, S., & Smolentseva, A. (Eds.). (2018). *High Participation Systems of Higher Education*. Oxford: Oxford University Press.

Castells, M. (1993). The University System: Engine of Development in the New World Economy. In A. Ransom, S.-W. Khoo, & V. Selvaratnam (Eds.), *Improving Higher Education in Developing Countries* (pp. 65–80). Washington, DC: World Bank.

Christiansen, N. F., Petersen, K., Edling, N., & Haave, P. (2005). *The Nordic Model of Welfare: A Historical Reappraisal*. Copenhagen: Museum Tusculanum Press.

Clark, B. R. (1983). *The Higher Education System: Academic Organization in Cross-National Perspective*. Los Angeles, CA: University of California Press.

Clark, B. R. (1998). *Creating Entrepreneurial Universities: Organizational Pathways of Transformation*. New York: Pergamon.

Cloete, N., Bailey, T., Pillay, P., Bunting, I., & Maassen, P. (2011). *Universities in Africa*. Cape Town: African Minds.

Dill, D. D., & Soo, M. (2004). Transparency and Quality in Higher Education Markets. In P. Teixeira, B. Jongbloed, D. Dill, & A. Amaral (Eds.), *Markets in Higher Education: Rhetoric or Reality?* (pp. 61–85). Boston/London: Kluwer Academic Publishers.

Dinkelman, T., & Martínez, A. C. (2014). Investing in Schooling in Chile: The Role of Information About Financial Aid for Higher Education. *Review of Economics and Statistics, 96*(2), 244–257.

Douglass, J. A., Edelstein, R., & Hoareau, C. (2011). *A Global Talent Magnet: How a San Francisco/Bay Area Higher Education Hub Could Advance California's Comparative Advantage in Attracting International Talent and Further Build US Economic Competitiveness.* San Francisco and Berkeley: CSHE Publications and University of California.

Economics, T. (2018). *Indonesia School Enrolments, Tertiary (% Gross).* Retrieved from https://tradingeconomics.com/indonesia/school-enrollment-tertiary-percent-gross-wb-data.html.

Feldman, M., & Desrochers, P. (2003). Research Universities and Local Economic Development: Lessons from the History of the Johns Hopkins University. *Industry & Innovation, 10*(1), 5–24.

Goddard, J., Hazelkorn, E., & Vallance, P. (2016). *The Civic University: The Policy and Leadership Challenges.* Cheltenham: Edward Elgar Publishing.

GOL. (2012). The Law on Higher Education, Indonesia. *12 CFR.* Jakarta: Ministry of Research, Technology and Higher Education.

Grusec, J. E., & Hastings, P. D. (2014). *Handbook of Socialization: Theory and Research.* London: Guilford Publications.

Gunasekara, C. (2006). The Generative and Developmental Roles of Universities in Regional Innovation Systems. *Science and Public Policy, 33*(2), 137–150. https://doi.org/10.3152/147154306781779118.

Harding, A., Scott, A., Laske, A., & Burtscher, C. (Eds.). (2007). *Bright Satanic Mills: Universities, Regional Development and the Knowledge Economy.* Aldershot: Ashgate.

Hladchenko, M., & Pinheiro, R. (2018). Implementing the Triple Helix Model: Means-Ends Decoupling at the State Level? *Minerva, 57*(1), 1–22. https://doi.org/10.1007/s11024-018-9355-3.

Huggins, R., & Johnston, A. (2009). The Economic and Innovation Contribution of Universities: A Regional Perspective. *Environment and Planning C-Government and Policy, 27*(6), 1088–1106. https://doi.org/10.1068/c08125b.

Johnstone, D. B., & Marcucci, P. N. (2010). *Financing Higher Education Worldwide: Who Pays? Who Should Pay?* Baltimore: Johns Hopkins University Press.

Karlsson, S., Fogelberg, K., Kettis, Å., Lindgren, S., Sandoff, M., & Geschwind, L. (2014). Not Just Another Evaluation: A Comparative Study of Four Educational Quality Projects at Swedish Universities. *Tertiary Education and Management, 20*(3), 239–251.

Kvaal, T. N. (2014). *Finansieringssystem for universitet og høyskoler*. Oslo Norwegian Ministry of Education and Research. Retrieved from https://www.regjeringen.no/contentassets/2af5e2be144c431886f900f9f3432961/finansieringssystemet_universiteter_og_hoyskoler.pdf.

Kyvik, S. (2009). *The Dynamics of Change in Higher Education: Expansion and Contraction in an Organisational Field*. Dordrecht: Springer.

Lester, R., & Sotarauta, M. (Eds.). (2007). *Innovation, Universities and the Competitiveness of Regions*. Tekes: Helsinki.

Marginson, S. (2011). Higher Education and Public Good. *Higher Education Quarterly, 65*(4), 411–433.

Mbah, M. F. (2016). Towards the Idea of the Interconnected University for Sustainable Community Development. *Higher Education Research & Development, 35*(6), 1228–1241.

Ministry of Education and Culture. (2012). *Center for Educational Data and Statistics*. Jakarta: Indonesia.

Mohrman, K., Shi, J., Feinblatt, S., & Chow, K. (2009). *Public Universities and Regional Development*. Sichuan: Sichuan University Press.

Nilsson, J. E. (2006). *The Role of Universities in Regional Innovation Systems: A Nordic Perspective*. Copenhagen: Copenhagen Business School Press.

NOKUT. (2016). *The Year 2016. Oslo: The Norwegian Agency for Quality Assurance in Education*. Retrieved from https://www.nokut.no/siteassets/om-nokut/arsrapporter-og-tildelingsbrev/nokut_year2016_en.pdf.

Nybom, T. (2007). A Rule-governed Community of Scholars: The Humboldt Vision in the History of the European University. In P. Maassen & J. P. Olsen (Eds.), *University Dynamics and European Integration* (Vol. 19, pp. 55–80). Dordrecht: Springer.

OECD. (2005). *Building Competitive Regions: Strategies and Governance*. Paris: Organisation for Economic Co-operation and Development.

OECD. (2007). *Higher Education and Regions: Globally Competitive, Locally Engaged*. Paris: Organisation for Economic Co-operation and Development.

Palfreyman, D., & Tapper, T. (2008). *Structuring Mass Higher Education: The Role of Elite Institutions*. New York: Routledge.

PDDIKTI. (2017). Higher Education Statistics in Indonesia. Jakarta: Ministry of Research, Technology and Higher Education. Retrieved from https://forlap.ristekdikti.go.id/files/infografis.

Pinheiro, R. (2012a). *In the Region, for the Region? A Comparative Study of the Institutionalisation of the Regional Mission of Universities*. Oslo: University of Oslo.

Pinheiro, R. (2012b). Knowledge and the 'Europe of the Regions': The Case of the High North. In M. Kwiek & P. Maassen (Eds.), *National Higher Education*

Reforms in a European Context: Comparative Reflections on Poland and Norway (pp. 179–208). Frankfurt: Peter Lang.

Pinheiro, R. (2014). Regional Policy and Higher Education: The Case of Northern Norway. In T. Aarevaara & E. Berg (Eds.), *Higher Education and Research in Academe—Who Should Pay?* (pp. 53–64). Luleå: Luleå Tekniska Universitet.

Pinheiro, R., & Antonowics, D. (2015). Opening the Gates or Coping with the Flow? Governing Access to Higher Education in Northern and Central Europe. *Higher Education, 70*(3), 299–313.

Pinheiro, R., & Pillay, P. (2016). Higher Education and Economic Development in the OECD: Policy Lessons for Other Countries and Regions. *Journal of Higher Education Policy and Management, 38*(2), 150–166.

Pinheiro, R., & Stensaker, B. (2018). Balancing Efficiency and Equity in a Welfare State Setting: High Participation Higher Education in Norway. In B. Cantwell, S. Marginson, & A. Smolentseva (Eds.), *High Participation Systems of Higher Education* (pp. 386–417). Oxford: Oxford University Press.

Pinheiro, R., & Young, M. (2017). The University as an Adaptive Resilient Organization: A Complex Systems Perspective. In J. Huisman & M. Tight (Eds.), *Theory and Method in Higher Education Research* (pp. 119–136). Bingley: Emerald.

Pinheiro, R., Benneworth, P., & Jones, G. A. (Eds.). (2012a). *Universities and Regional Development: A Critical Assessment of Tensions and Contradictions.* Milton Park and New York: Routledge.

Pinheiro, R., Ouma, G., & Pillay, P. (2012b). The Dynamics of University Transformation: A Case Study in the Eastern Cape Province of South Africa. *Journal of Higher Education in Africa, 10*(1), 95–120.

Pinheiro, R., Geschwind, L., & Aarrevaara, T. (2014). Nested Tensions and Interwoven Dilemmas in Higher Education: The View from the Nordic Countries. *Cambridge Journal of Regions, Economy and Society, 7*(2), 233–250. https://doi.org/10.1093/cjres/rsu002.

Pinheiro, R., Langa, P., & Pausits, A. (2015a). The Institutionalization of Universities' Third Mission: Introduction to the Special Issue. *European Journal of Higher Education, 5*(3), 227–232. https://doi.org/10.1080/21568235.2015.1044551.

Pinheiro, R., Langa, P., & Pausits, A. (2015b). One and Two Equals Three? The Third Mission of Higher Education Institutions. *European Journal of Higher Education, 5*(3), 233–249. https://doi.org/10.1080/21568235.2015.1044552.

Pinheiro, R., Charles, D., & Jones, G. (2016a). Equity, Institutional Diversity and Regional Development: A Cross-Country Comparison. *Higher Education, 72*(3), 307–322. https://doi.org/10.1007/s10734-015-9958-7.

Pinheiro, R., Geschwind, L., & Aarrevaara, T. (Eds.). (2016b). *Mergers in Higher Education: The Experiences from Northern Europe.* Dordrecht: Springer.

Pinheiro, R., Sima, K., Young, M., & Kohoutek, J. (2018a). University Complexity and Regional Development in the Periphery. In R. Pinheiro, M. Young, & K. Sima (Eds.), *Higher Education and Regional Development: Tales from Northern and Central Europe.* Cham: Palgrave.

Pinheiro, R., Young, M., & Sima, K. (2018b). *Higher Education and Regional Development: Tales from Northern and Central Europe.* Cham: Palgrave.

Pinheiro, R., Geschwind, L., Hansen, H. F., & Pulkkinen, K. (Eds.). (2019). *Reforms, Organizational Change and Performance in Higher Education: A Comparative Account from the Nordic Countries.* Cham: Palgrave.

Przeworski, A., & Teune, H. (1970). *The Logic of Comparate Social Inquiry.* New York: John Wiley and Sons.

Room, G. (2011). *Complexity, Institutions and Public Policy: Agile Decision-Making in a Turbulent World.* Cheltenham and Northampton: Edward Elgar Publishing Limited.

Schmitt-Egner, P. (2002). The Concept of 'Region': Theoretical and Methodological Notes on Its Reconstruction. *Journal of European Integration, 24*(3), 179–202.

Schwartzman, S., Pinheiro, R., & Pillay, P. (2015). *Higher Education in the BRICS Countries: Investigating the Pact Between Higher Education and Society.* Drodrecht: Springer Netherlands.

Scott, W. R. (2008). *Institutions and Organizations: Ideas and Interests.* London: Sage Publications.

SEAMEO. (2012). *A Study on Quality Assurance Models in Southeast Asian Countries: Towards a Southeast Asian Quality Assurance Framework.* Bangkok: SEAMEO RIHED. Retrieved from http://www.rihed.seameo.org/wp-content/uploads/2013/FrequentlyRequested/SEAMEO_RIHED_QA_in_SEA_report_2012.pdf.

Sima, K., Benneworth, P., Pinheiro, R., & Beseda, J. (2017). What Are the Cultural Preconditions of Universitities' Regional Engagemnet? Towards a Disciplinary Sensitive Model of the University—Region Interface. *Higher Education Policy, 30*(4), 517–532. https://doi.org/10.1057/s41307-017-0056-6.

Stachowiak, K., Pinheiro, R., Sedini, C., & Vaatovaara, M. (2013). Policies Aimed at Strengthening the Ties Between Universities and Cities. In S. Musterd & Z. Kovács (Eds.), *Place-Making and Policies for Competitive Cities* (pp. 263–292). London: Blackwell.

Trow, M. (1970). Reflections on the Transition from Mass to Universal Higher Education. *Daedalus, 99*(1), 1–42.

UN. (2018). *Human Development Report*. New York: United Nations.

UNESCO-UIS. (2014). *Gross Enrolment Ratio by Level of Education*. Paris: UNESCO. Retrieved from http://data.uis.unesco.org/.

Vabø, A., & Aamodt, P. O. (2008). Nordic Higher Education in Transition. In T. Tapper & D. Palfreyman (Eds.), *Structuring Mass Higher Education. The Role of Elite Institutions* (pp. 57–71). London: Routdlege.

Watermeyer, R. (2015). Lost in the 'Third Space': The Impact of Public Engagement in Higher Education on Academic Identity, Research Practice and Career Progression. *European Journal of Higher Education, 5*(3), 331–347. https://doi.org/10.1080/21568235.2015.1044546.

Whitchurch, C. (2012). *Reconstructing Identities in Higher Education: The Rise of 'Third Space' Professionals*. London: Routledge.

Wicaksono, T. Y., & Friawan, D. (2008). Recent Developments in Higher Education in Indonesia: Issues and Challanges. In S. Armstrong & B. Chapman (Eds.), *Financing Higher Education and Economic Development in East Asia* (pp. 159–187). Canberra: Australian National University.

Wildavsky, A. (1987). Choosing Preferences by Constructing Institutions: A Cultural Theory of Preference Formation. *American Political Science Review, 81*(1), 3–21.

WorldBank. (1998). *World Development Report 1998/99: Knowledge for Development*. Washington, DC: World Bank. Retrieved from http://publications.worldbank.org/index.php?main_page=product_info&cPath=0& products_id=21643.

WorldBank. (2008). *Higher Education and Development: Annual Conference on Developmental Economics—Regional*. Washington, DC: World Bank.

World Bank. (2014). Indonesia's Higher Education System: How Responsive Is It to the Labor Market? Washington, DC: World Bank. Retrieved from http://documents.worldbank.org/curated/en/596601468268792237/Indonesias-higher-education-system-howresponsive-is-it-to-the-labor-market.

Part V

Summary

11

Epilogue

Rómulo Pinheiro, Lars Geschwind, Jouni Kekäle, and Mads P. Sørensen

Introduction

This edited volume explored the 'black box' associated with the meanings, interpretations, tensions and dilemmas related to the notion of the responsible university in the Nordic countries and beyond. In the

R. Pinheiro (✉)
Department of Political Science and Management, University of Agder,
Kristiansand, Norway
e-mail: romulo.m.pinheiro@uia.no

L. Geschwind
KTH Royal Institute of Technology, Stockholm, Sweden
e-mail: larsges@kth.se

J. Kekäle
University of Eastern Finland, Joensuu, Finland
e-mail: Jouni.kekale@uef.fi

M. P. Sørensen
Aarhus University, Aarhus, Denmark
e-mail: mps@ps.au.dk

introduction, we reflected on the multiplicity of, and ambiguity inherent
to, existing perspectives and proposed, rather provocatively, the exploration of the concept of the 'irresponsible university' as an antithesis to the
arguments that have been laid out. From a historical viewpoint, we also
reflected on the extent to which notions of responsibility have, in one
way or another, shaped dynamics within higher education (HE) systems
and institutions in the light of specific imperatives that are contextually
bounded. Furthermore, we touched upon the prevalence of global policy
initiatives, such as the UN's Sustainable Development Goals, that are
intrinsically linked with the grand challenges facing world societies in the
twenty-first century and beyond. We then contextualised how responsibility as a normative idea and hegemonic discourse within national systems and institutions manifests itself in the daily practices and formal
and informal structures of universities at different levels, from the supra
structure of government policy to the middle structure of administration
and further to the academic heartland (Clark 1983). Finally, we concluded the introduction with a brief elaboration of some of the distinct
features of, and recent dynamics within, Nordic HE. Among other
aspects, we pinpointed how the four case systems have evolved during the
last few years towards more stringent financial management, fiercer
national and global competition and the concomitant rise of excellence
and accountability regimes.

In this conclusive reflection, we take stock of the major elements, both
empirical and conceptual, underpinning the case chapters. The chapter is
organised in three distinct sections. First, addressing a largely scientific
audience, the editors attempt to make conceptual sense of the findings
from an organisational theory perspective. Second, we shift our focus to
the wider community of practitioners (policy makers, advisers, university
managers and administrators, etc.) by shedding light on the practical
implications of the volume's core findings for both policy and practice.
Third, we once again address our academic peers by sketching out the
road ahead regarding future studies in the area.

The Responsible University: Analytical Eclecticism Rooted in Organisational Science

The contributions of the volume are diverse and multifaceted and touch upon multiple elements characterising the ways responsible agendas affect the inner dynamics of higher education institutions (HEIs) and the strategic agendas and activities undertaken by multiple internal and external constituencies. By approaching the topic from a holistic and explorative perspective, the editors made a conscious decision to allow authors considerable leeway regarding the conceptual and analytical lenses adopted in the case chapters. This methodological strategy is known in the literature as 'analytical eclecticism', which 'seeks to explicate, translate, and selectively integrate analytic elements—concepts, logics, mechanisms, and interpretations—of theories or narrative that have been developed within separate paradigms but that address related aspects of substantive problems that have both scholarly and practical significance' (Sil and Katzenstein 2010, 10). Eclectic methods move beyond paradigms, seemingly combining elements belonging to different approaches and perspectives to 'develop a causal story that captures the complexity, contingency, and messiness of the environment within which actors must identify and solve problems' (Ibid., 22). In our view, this methodological approach seems rather fitting when investigating the ways in which ambiguous yet prevalent notions of societal responsibility and its various manifestations (impact, excellence, relevance, openness, accountability, etc.) permeate the inner life of universities and the academic, administrative and learning communities composing them (for the use of this method in the field of HE, consult Young et al. 2018).

Thus, to provide some analytical rigour to our analysis and discussion of the key findings, we structure the analysis around seminal concepts and perspectives emanating from the study of organisations and processes of organising. In our view, this strategic posture is justified due to the importance attributed in the extant organisational literature to the role played by formal and informal structures on the one hand and the interplay between environment, organisation and key agents on the other. Hence, we discuss the key findings against the backdrop of five distinct stylised (ideal type) perspectives of the responsible university. Although certain perspectives play a dominant role in the empirical accounts, all of them can be identified throughout each of the individual contributions.

Responsibility as Strategic Choice

This perspective is associated with the *instrumental*, rationalistic view of organisations (Olsen 2007; Christensen et al. 2007) and pertains to the strategic efforts by managers and other rationalisers of the costs and benefits associated with developing and implementing a responsible agenda across the board. More specifically, it focuses on the processes, goals, incentives and outcomes to be achieved and emphasises the role played by so-called strategic agents such as university leaders and administrators to create the conditions for goal achievement and success. Hence, it follows what March and Olsen (2006) described as a 'logic of consequentiality' or outcomes best characterised by the prevalence of self-interested and rationally calculating actors and instrumentalism. Recent government-led policy reforms in the Nordic countries and beyond have attempted to transform universities from relatively decentralised organisations into more coherent and tightly coupled organisational forms (Pinheiro and Stensaker 2014; Pietilä 2018).

In their historical investigation of the transition from a Finnish Keynesian-based welfare state into a Schumpeterian competitive one, Kohvakka, Nevala and Nori (Chap. 2) described how Finnish universities shifted from being principal providers of regional stability to becoming engines for boosting national and international competitiveness. Whilst uncovering the efforts by leaders around HR-related issues and the development of a proactive model for recruitment, Kekäle and Varis (Chap. 9) demonstrated how the recruitment of researchers at the University of Eastern Finland is considered a strategic tool for achieving the university's social mission of addressing global challenges. Vellamo, Pekkola and Siekkinen's (Chap. 8) discussion of the risks posed by interdisciplinarity in a Finnish university merger indicated the importance of multidisciplinary structures as *the* solution for addressing wicked societal problems (e.g., climate change), empirically demonstrating how the quest for acting as a responsible university affects strategy and structure.

In their discussion of the rise of English as the predominant language in Danish academia, Sørensen, Young and Pedersen (Chap. 4) referred to the adoption of bibliometrics and efforts by university management to shape academic behaviour. Similarly, while addressing the question of whether a responsible university really needs a third mission, Karlsen and Larrea (Chap. 7) referred to one variation of the instrumental perspective of organisations associated with power and politics and the concomitant role played by the formation of coalitions and interest articulation (Christensen et al. 2007, 29–30). Barman, MacGrath and Stoehr (Chap. 5) concluded that Massive Open Online Courses (MOOCs) are used strategically to foster broader internal transformation within Swedish universities, with a privileged focus on cost efficiencies and external accountability. In a similar vein, Pulkkinen and Hautamäki (Chap. 6) argued that co-creation is a valuable tool or instrument for achieving universities' social responsibilities by 'applying the corporate social responsibility mode of thinking into a university environment'.

Beyond the Nordics, Benneworth's (Chap. 3) critical take on the topic stressed the government's strategic use of funding allocation models to shape university behaviours, including their response to societal needs. Given the fiercely competitive nature of the UK's and global HE landscapes, as rational actors, universities are expected to prioritise tasks that offer the highest returns in terms of funding and/or prestige. Finally, Berg, Pinheiro, Utomo and Nurhayati (Chap. 10) provided empirical evidence of how the expertise of universities in Indonesia is paramount in addressing local needs. Government and universities have taken steps to promote a socially responsive agenda, for example, in the form of financial incentives for university graduates to return to their localities of origin and by actively involving external stakeholders in devising educational programmes.

Responsibility as Tradition or Moral Duty

This perspective focuses on the normative and cultural–cognitive dimensions underpinning organisational structures and activities. It pertains to the notion of organisations as *institutions*, that is, as a collection of norms, rules and identities that, over time, become deeply embedded in the goals of the organisation and the motivations driving the behaviours of internal actors (Scott 2001). It pertains to the institutionalisation of organisational life, that is, the attitude that specific features that provide a certain organisation with a distinct character or culture are taken for granted (Zucker 1988; Selznick 1996). It basically means that organisations are denoted with a 'life of their own' relatively independent of, and oblivious to, events and strategic imperatives emanating from the outside. It is associated with the 'logic of appropriate behaviour' (March and Olsen 2006), where emerging circumstances (e.g., external events) are matched or addressed by adopting pre-agreed behavioural scripts or routines, often taking an implicit rather than an explicit form. In the realm of HE, these dimensions are intrinsically associated with the historical, path-dependent character of university structures and cherished values and activities (Clark 1992; Krücken 2003). In the context of this volume, this pertains to the internal meanings associated with responsibility as an integral component of academic norms and disciplinary cultures (Becher and Trowler 2001) and their local (university-embedded) variations in both time and space (Clark 1972).

Several of the volume contributors referred to the functional distinction (horizontal differentiation) between the old, research-intensive universities and more recent vocationally oriented institutions such as university colleges (Norway) or polytechnics (Finland). The former are often located in large urban areas and have traditionally catered to the socialisation of future political and professional elites (Castells 2001), even though they also aided the government with providing education to the masses (cf. Tapper and Palfreyman 2010). Not surprisingly, and despite variations from place to place, their general outlook is that of a cosmopolitan academic environment with the nation and the world as their points of normative and strategic reference. This contrasts with the traditional role of more vocationally oriented institutions located in the geographic periphery (cf. Pinheiro et al. 2018), whose structures and activities (at least in theory) tend to cater to the needs and expectations of local stakeholder groups like government and industry.

Kohvakka, Nevala and Nori's (Chap. 2) historical account demonstrated how, during the 1960s and 1970s, universities were expected to support the Finnish government in accomplishing its national mission of state planning, exercised, inter alia, through an emotional bond between the state territory and the citizenry. Fields like the social sciences played a critical role in adopting a state-centric view of regional planning and development with local and global dimensions subsumed into a national frame of reference. This normative posture was contested by the more outward-looking and market-prone technology universities and business schools that favoured institutional autonomy and tight interactions with industry.

Vellamo, Pekkola and Siekkinen's case (Chap. 8) demonstrated the importance of institutionalised domains of organisational life, often manifested in resistance to change. According to the authors, academics voiced their support for old structures, which, in their view, were already interdisciplinary in nature, with the new structures seen as a threat to existing arrangements, including cherished norms and values within specific sub-disciplines. The assertion by internal actors that 'the university has to be responsible to itself in order to be responsible to other stakeholders' is yet another manifestation of the inward orientation associated with the cultural perspective. Sørensen, Young and Pedersen's chapter (4) also reveals interesting elements associated with the role played by institutionalised traditions. During the eighteenth century, the use of Latin in science was associated with tradition, whereas Danish was linked to progress and modernity. Now Danish has become the tradition and English the progressive language for publishing.

Regarding institutionalised practices, Karlsen and Larrea (Chap. 7) pointed to the barriers associated with the linear approach (engagement as a product rather than a process), which is deeply rooted among internal and external actors alike. They also point to the challenge associated with moving from an individual towards a collective (shared) understanding of co-creation. Pulkkinen and Hautamäki (Chap. 6) described co-creation initiatives at Helsinki university that acknowledge the cultural challenges involved with bridging various scientific communities and traditions. Deeply rooted norms and practices, such as peer review, are inadequate in the context of interdisciplinary collaborations where joint development of ideas, open mindedness and constructive dialogue (rather than criticism) are paramount. Barman, McGrath and Stöhr (Chap. 5) claimed that MOOCs are a means for universities to fulfil their societal obligations, as dictated by Swedish law. Through their global reach, MOOCs extend this societal role to the rest of the world, thus acting as a responsible university from a global perspective.

Regarding non-Nordic cases, Benneworth (Chap. 3) argued that the origin of public value failures in Dutch HE is intrinsically linked to policy reforms in the 1990s that had a negative effect (decline or de-institutionalisation) on the traditional democratic decision-making model at universities. Competition and other market-based mechanisms led to the institutionalisation of a 'culture of financialisation'. The prevalence of different versions of responsibility within a single university resulted in the rise of multiple sub-cultures: fiduciary, managerial, meritocratic and so on. Berg, Pinheiro, Utomo and Nurhayati (Chap. 10) highlighted the importance of 'TriDharma' in instituting a culture of moral duty and community service across different types of universities in Indonesia, including those located in large urban areas. Role overlap enabled the emergence of a hybridised culture, with academics acting as 'third space professionals' and connecting the university to the outside world.

Responsibility as Symbolism or Window-Dressing

This perspective is associated with the quest for mostly external, but also internal, legitimacy (Deephouse and Suchman 2008). When faced with external pressures seen as incompatible with organisational goals and/or traditions, internal actors often take proactive steps to protect or buffer core tasks or technologies from environmental influences, minimising the risk of *co-optation* (Selznick 1957). Hence, this perspective focuses on symbolic compliance to external demands and expectations or window-dressing (Greenwood et al. 2011; Oliver 1991), for example, in the form of decoupling between internal activities and external imperatives (Boxenbaum and Jonsson 2008). Such strategic postures have been widely documented in HE (cf. Pinheiro and Young 2017), not least around the third mission (Pinheiro et al. 2015). This process is facilitated by the endogenous loose coupling between units and types of activities (Birnbaum 1988).

Several contributions in this volume point to the symbolic role of strategy in addressing societal challenges. Kekäle and Varis's contribution (Chap. 9) demonstrated how the development of new recruitment models requires the active involvement of academics to secure the necessary input and internal legitimacy. Vellamo et al. (Chap. 8) referred to the fact that the case university's core mission is education rather than the resolution of wicked problems in society, which is an indirect consequence of the latter. In addition, their account suggests that embracing interdisciplinarity is, to a certain extent, associated with the need to secure external support (as well as resources) for the university's goals and structures. Sørensen et al. (Chap. 4) contended that embracing English as the scientific language of choice is in part due to its association with world-class excellence, progress and a global (cosmopolitan) outlook. They also demonstrated that when compared to the insurmountable pressures for (and prestige associated with) scientific publishing, initiatives aimed at increasing societal impact through dissemination or outreach often take the form of 'lip-service'. Karlsen and Larrea (Chap. 7) pointed to a mismatch between the actual (low) level of societal engagement by the University of Agder's academics and the (high) degree of expectation for societal engagement by external stakeholders. Further, they shed light on the fact that the presence of a formal strategy does not necessarily imply tight coupling or implementation. Pulkkinen et al. (Chap. 6) critically questioned whether co-creation has an intrinsic value (e.g., as a learning tool) or whether it is simply a mechanism for demonstrating accountability. Barman et al. (Chap. 5) indicated that the association of Swedish universities with the MOOC consortia, led by prestigious universities like Stanford and Harvard, raises the question of whether this, by itself, is a means of lifting universities' prestige and legitimacy in the eyes of important stakeholders such as students, funders and other HEIs. The authors referred to the idea of MOOCs as a means of communicating to the outside world that the university is modern and progressive. Finally, outside the Nordics, Berg and colleagues (Chap. 10) reported that in the eyes of some external stakeholders, university-led outreach programmes are thought to be more beneficial to the universities themselves (in securing student graduations) than to their surrounding localities.

Responsibility as Environmental Determinism

This perspective is associated with the role attributed to external imperatives in the inner dynamics of organisations. Advocates of such perspectives contend that 'there is no alternative' and that the lack of compliance to externally imposed demands is likely to result in a major loss or punishment in terms of resources, legitimacy or both (Pfeffer and Salancik 2003). In many respects, this represents the opposite of a strategic (instrumentalist) view and thus underplays the agentic role of internal stakeholders at the expense of the technical and institutional environments surrounding the organisations (Hrebiniak and Joyce 1985; Scott 2001). In the realm of HE, this means that universities are pushed to adopt certain features of their environment, such as market-based mechanisms, even if this may not necessarily be aligned with their formal and informal structures or profiles. The carriers of such features include but are not limited to: the state as the main funder and regulator of HE affairs, and influential 'trend-setters', such as supranational organisations like the OECD, the World Bank and/or the EU. The latter have been found to play a critical role in promoting hegemonic ideas or scripts such as 'world-class' and 'best practices' (Ramirez et al. 2016). Such ideas spread and circulate across jurisdictions and sectors of the economy, acting as rationalised myths (Ramirez and Christensen 2013) and are sometimes, but not always, adapted or translated to local circumstances (Sahlin and Wedlin 2008; Beerkens 2010).

In their account of the University of Eastern Finland's strategy, Kekäle and Varis (Chap. 9) referred to the need to respond to a changing regulative and market environment with a strong expectation of innovation and contributions to solving global problems. Similarly, Vellamo et al.

(Chap. 8) reported how, according to the internal stakeholders, the technical needs of industry require the university to keep certain structures (e.g., degree programmes) unchanged. In addition, the same stakeholders state the need to follow well-established and recognised (prestigious) models present elsewhere (MIT, Delft and Aalto). Sørensen et al. (Chap. 4) showed how Danish universities have been obliged to emphasise language as part of their internal policies as a result of changing regulative and competitive environments. They also point to the existing divide in terms of power and hegemony between 'centre' (the Anglophone world) and 'periphery' (national sphere elsewhere), with the former setting the pace for the adoption of new scientific norms and practices. Pulkkinen and Hautamäki definition of co-creation (Chap. 6) alluded to 'a phenomena in a rapidly changing environment' underpinned by a shift in the relationship between science and society and characterised by a change in knowledge regimes. In Chap. 5, Barman and colleagues showed how, as a means of covering rising costs, MOOCs providers are now moving away from tuition-free models towards closed, tuition-based systems. They also demonstrated how the regulative environment in which Swedish universities operate creates barriers to the development of more competitive business models. Beyond the Nordics, in Chap. 10, Berg et al. highlighted the challenges associated with low-quality secondary education (outside the control of universities), which introduces serious challenges to widening access to HE in remote regions. Finally, in the UK context, Benneworth (Chap. 3) showed how the need to respond to external demands (declines in funding and fiercer competition) has led to the modernisation of university structures and the widespread adoption of market-like postures such as managerialism and performance-based models.

Responsibility as Resilience

Resilience pertains to the ability of organisations to withstand or overcome internal and/or external shocks while retaining a sense of identity or stability (Kayes 2015). In other words, it is associated with adaptability within the context of a changing external environment. Resilience and learning are interconnected as organisational actors exploit existing assets and competencies and explore future alternatives (March 1991). In the realm of HE, resilience relates to the ability of universities to maintain a sense of stability and continuity—in terms of structures, activities, norms and values, etc.—amidst changing external circumstances. Several historical accounts have shown that, as organisations, universities have been rather successful at adapting to changing external circumstances while keeping their essence relatively intact (Wittrock 1985; Meyer and Schofer 2007). This perspective thus views universities as complex, self-organising, evolving entities characterised by a multiplicity of forms, goals, values and sub-cultures (Clark 1983; Pinheiro and Young 2017). Among other aspects, it sheds light on universities' abilities to accommodate multiple and sometimes conflicting institutional logics (Berg and Pinheiro 2016), often resulting in new hybrid structures that are thought to foster long-term adaptability to an ever-changing and increasingly complex environment (Billis 2010).

Kohvakka et al.'s historical account of system evolution in Finland in Chap. 2 showed how old and new features coexist (at least for a period) despite the changing policy landscape. In spite of considerable change in the Finnish economy and society, the domestic HE landscape remained relatively stable between the mid-1990s and 2010. In a similar vein, Kekäle and Varis (Chap. 9) associated responsibility with the complexity inherent to different disciplines and cultural orientations, referring to the coexistence/integration of disciplinary cultures as a key element in addressing society's manifold problems. Similarly, in Chap. 8, Vellamo et al. contended that interdisciplinarity (a form of exploration strategy) is an integral aspect of the university's ability to address the needs and expectations of multiple stakeholder groups. Sørensen et al. in Chap. 4 offered evidence of academics, particularly but not exclusively of the younger generations, adapting to new circumstances by shifting their research focus from the local to the global. Further, they stated the importance of keeping Danish journals alive as a prerequisite to 'maintaining a public intellectual space' in the country (p. xx).

In Chap. 7, Karlsen and Larrea highlighted a key feature of resilience systems, the possibility for fostering experimentation and for diversity (heterogeneity), by allowing individualised practices and informal norms to emerge organically (bottom-up) rather than by imposing stricter rules and guidelines from the top down. They also contended that the context specificity and complexity surrounding universities' third mission requires the adoption of multiple definitions and perspectives of engagement rather than a single view or policy. Co-generation rather than linearity is thought to provide a more sustainable (and resilient) alternative for solving societal problems. Pulkinnen and Hautamäki in Chap. 6 highlighted the ability of the entrepreneurial university model to respond innovatively to societal demands without changing the character of universities from public goods into private businesses. Somewhat surprisingly, they found that firms are seeking long-term partnerships to address problems rather than short-term solutions and that co-creation nurtures a 'living lab for experimentation' (p. xx). Barman et al. (Chap. 5) shed light on MOOCs as a disruptive practice in HE. They found that in Sweden, they are being used primarily as mechanisms for driving internal change or adaptation (through innovation) within universities as part of a 'paradigm shift' (p. xx). Benneworth in Chap. 3 warned against the pervasive effects associated with centralised decision-making structures within universities in the quest for reducing ambiguity and complexity, leading to failures and dilemmas. Finally, Berg et al. in Chap. 10 pointed to the Indonesian government's inability to adapt to shifts in student demand across certain fields, compounded by limitations regarding the autonomy enjoyed by universities and individual campuses.

Implications for Policy and Practice

Having grouped the analysis of core findings along five conceptual perspectives, largely addressing a social science research audience, it is now time to reflect on the implications of the volume's empirical insights when it comes to policy and practice. For several decades, universities have been increasingly expected to demonstrate short-term social relevance and to react to external demands for accountability. This trend has manifested in different steering mechanisms; funding is connected tightly to results; and ministries have introduced diverse assessment mechanisms. However, freedom of research and enquiry has remained, in principle at least, unchanged. The discussion of a 'responsible university' is yet another attempt to clarify universities' role in changing societies to provide added value to society. Academic freedom is embedded in the concept, as responsibility includes the notion of volunteerism and free will. If forced, one cannot be held responsible. So, the question remains: how can universities provide added value on a voluntary basis?

One could argue that universities have always provided additional value to society and fulfilled certain moral and strategic expectations. However, societal expectations of HE systems and providers have changed in the Nordics and elsewhere. In the 1960s, the overall expectation by (Western) societies was that the brightest minds should come up with new ideas and solve problems relatively freely; that is, they were given considerable freedom without much external interference and guidance from the government or university managers. The 1970s harkened the introduction of centralised planning to HE steering, reflecting the spirit and beliefs of the era. After the collapse of the Soviet Union, the market economy, management by objectives and a hegemonic neoliberal economic doctrine replaced centralised planning as the basic philosophy of HE policy (Rinne 2004). The rise of the evaluative state has been well documented (Neave 1998, 2012): accountability and value added in return for public funding has been expected. The expectations of short-term evidence have increased as the economic value in a quartile economy is perceived as increasingly important and as the once-high trust in the long-term outcomes from HE has apparently deteriorated, or at least transformed.

If we take Finland as an example, the 2000s saw an intensified discussion in which the business sector and many politicians expected increasing contributions from HE to the economy, most notably regarding employment. Such discussions appeared to contribute to the new university Act of 2009, where universities were given more freedom but were also subjected to a stronger accountability regime. However, as the national HE budget was cut by several hundred million euros in the forthcoming decade, the new, legally established 'independent universities' faced the task of having to adapt to a rather different environment. Similar trends can be detected in other Nordic countries (e.g., budget cuts in Denmark), but pressures on short-term relevance have been present elsewhere. Reorganisation of HE systems in the form of mergers has occurred across the Nordics, centred on fewer but larger and more globally competitive institutions (Pinheiro et al. 2016).

In recent years, triumphs of right-wing populism in global politics have changed the landscape and increased overall unpredictability. The civic university, as a concept, stresses civic involvement, which appears to be lacking, especially in new settings. Universities are increasingly expected to take responsibility for this function (Goddard et al. 2016). The emphasis on public attention and expectations has increasingly turned to global problems, such as climate change, that threaten human-kind and our collective way of living, including eternal economic growth with traditional industry and the production of goods. Universities are again called to contribute to a changing set of expectations. However, there remains a high political responsibility in public engagement and global problems.

This description of external changes is simplified. However, it high-lights some of the general developments. Given the independent nature of academic institutions, the outcomes in which responsibility is prac-tised are bound to vary according to each institution and individual. An institution can identify its own strengths and is expected to communicate the value it can best produce for science, the society and external stake-holders; this also applies to individual scholars. The term 'responsibility' also encapsulates the capacity for one's own (moral) decisions, rational thought and action, which are crucial in HE. Organisations typically aim to have positive impacts in all areas; this approach can be considered responsibility, and it includes orientations towards business (research, instruction and the third task in the case of universities), people (employ-ees and stakeholders), the environment, the community and more.

In this volume, our cases and discussions mainly dealt with responsi-bility in basic tasks for society and stakeholders. As shown, there are vari-ations to the basic approach: Sørensen et al. discussed responsibility for local communities through language policy; Pulkkinen et al. discussed social responsibility in terms of employability; Kekäle and Varis discussed leadership and HR implications to solve problems; Benneworth took a critical stance towards the concept of responsibility and its most crude implications. The basic approach of responsibility in basic tasks demonstrates that the tasks of a university, the relevance the institution produces and the attached funding schemes are much discussed at present.

In recent decades, there has been a growing pressure for accountability when it comes to the basic tasks of universities. However, the best foresee-able contribution to society—demonstrated responsibility—from universities depends on the strengths and capabilities of each institution, faculty, department and individual scholar. Universities' contributions to society may also be slow to materialise, and it is important for society to be patient. It takes a long time to become an expert in a field, and changes in institutional and individual profiles are not easy to carry out. Moreover, academic behaviour is, to a large extent, determined by long-established professional and disciplinary norms as a result of socialisation in a given field. There are also more localised norms and ethos that pertain to the immediate local settings, such as university, department, geographic location, and so on. These norms and traditions are not always aligned with the needs, expectations and values of external stakeholders, often resulting in a 'clash of logics'.

Institutional profiling may help to make various expectations more manageable and thus reduce the burden of expectations that some scholars and institutional leaders may experience. In recent years, we have seen a constant 'add on-process' when it comes to university tasks. Clark (1998, 131) spoke of a crossfire of expectations on a global scale. Enders and Boer (2009) refer to the 'mission overload' facing modern universities as they attempt to address multiple and ever growing external demands. More recently, Fumasoli et al. (2015, 1) noted that 'public organizations face two seemingly contradictory pressures: on the one hand they have to handle more diversified demands from their environments; on the other hand, they are increasingly required to act as strategic organizations and display coherent behavior'. They argued that organisational identity can be designed to reduce the risks of uncertainty about the future and issues related to evaluation and assessment. That said, identities are difficult artefacts for managers to work with, and most universities, as shown in many of our accounts in this volume, have multiple, often competing, identities and sub-cultures. This makes it difficult for managers to align internal characteristics and external dynamics and demands, but the main lesson here seems to be that 'one size does not fit all', and different approaches are required in the light of specific circumstances and local, normative and strategic postures. Whereas one could argue that, in principle, all university staff should take responsibility seriously, in practice this implies flexibility in allowing each individual academic or sub-unit considerable leeway in interpreting how this can be done in real terms.

In deciding what aspects, initiatives and expectations an institution should react to, leadership at all levels is crucial. Institutional leaders have a special responsibility to allocate resources and enable a cultural environment that is conducive to responsible behaviour whilst respecting sub-disciplinary norms, values and traditions. Yet, academics also have a responsibility to carry out teaching and research activities in a scientifically sound way for the benefit of the scientific community and society at large. These are not mutually exclusive dimensions, and there are plenty of examples, including from the Nordic countries, of the important role that academic groups have in addressing issues of social relevancy, such as climate change, whilst simultaneously excelling at their research endeavours. Following Perry and May (2006), it is indeed possible to be both relevant and excellent.

Concluding Thoughts and One Way Forward

This volume set out to provide clarity on the widespread notion of responsibility within HE and its manifold manifestations, largely within the context of Nordic HE systems. The empirical contributions show clear evidence that there are multiple ways to demonstrate responsibility, and this is likely to prevail so long as universities continue to remain relatively independent or autonomous actors. Responsibility, autonomy and accountability are intertwined and must be assessed against the backdrop of a performance management regime that has become an integral part of Nordic HE systems (Pinheiro et al. 2019). Greater institutional autonomy results in increasing oversight ex post (regarding outputs and outcomes). External expectations of accountability and responsibility are not likely to disappear anytime soon. Politicians and other external stakeholders will continue to place their expectations on universities so long as these remain publicly funded, as is the case in Nordic countries. The gradually growing dependency on external forms of income is likely to exacerbate the degree of influence by certain external actors and their particular conceptions of and claims to responsibility.

The cases included in this volume, whilst not exhaustive, are nonetheless representative of the complex realities facing contemporary HE systems in the Nordics and beyond. The examples provided in this volume demonstrate the multiple ways and attempts of taking responsibility into account. Some effects are already being felt in universities' structures, activities and cultures, while others will take much longer to materialise. Responsibility is a process that is constantly evolving (a moving target) and is shaped by temporal and geographic conditions. It is a process laden with normative meanings and positions and, if not handled carefully, may have the unintended consequence of exacerbating the cultural divisions already present within the university as a heterogeneous fiduciary institution whose primary public values are being challenged by the rise of the marketplace and critical voices regarding the role and legitimacy of knowledge and experts in world society.

Future research could, for example, investigate how different stakeholder groups within and outside the university make sense of the rise of responsible agendas in HE. It would also be interesting to shed empirical light on the long-term effects (e.g., as regards institutional profiling, performance, resilience) associated with the implementation of responsible strategies in universities' primary functions and the ways universities and other HEIs adapt to new emerging circumstances.

References

Becher, T., & Trowler, P. (2001). *Academic Tribes and Territories: Intellectual Enquiry and the Culture of Disciplines.* Buckingham: Society for Research into Higher Education & Open University Press.

Beerkens, E. (2010). Global Models for the National Research University: Adoption and Adaptation in Indonesia and Malaysia. *Globalisation, Societies and Education, 8*(3), 369–381.

Berg, L., & Pinheiro, R. (2016). Handling Different Institutional Logics in the Public Sector: Comparing Management in Norwegian Universities and Hospitals. In R. Pinheiro, F. Ramirez, K. Vrabæk, & L. Geschwind (Eds.),

Towards a Comparative Institutionalism: Forms, Dynamics and Logics Across Health Care and Higher Education Fields (pp. 145–168). Bingley: Emerald.

Billis, D. (2010). *Towards a Theory of Hybrid Organizations.* London: Palgrave Macmillan.

Birnbaum, R. (1988). *How Colleges Work: The Cybernetics of Academic Organization and Leadership.* San Francisco: Jossey-Bass.

Boxenbaum, E., & Jonsson, S. (2008). *Isomorphism, Diffusion and Decoupling.* In R. Greenwood, C. Oliver, K. Sahlin, & R. Suddaby (Eds.), *The Sage Handbook of Organisational Institutionalism* (pp. 78–98). London and Thousand Oaks: Sage.

Castells, M. (2001). Universities as Dynamic Systems of Contradictory Functions. In J. Muller, N. Cloete, & S. Badat (Eds.), *Challenges of Globalisation. South African Debates with Manuel Castells* (pp. 206–233). Cape Town: Maskew Miller Longman.

Christensen, T., Lægreid, P., Roness, P. G., & Røvik, K. A. (2007). *Organization Theory and the Public Sector: Instrument, Culture and Myth.* Milton Park: Taylor & Francis.

Clark, B. (1972). The Organisational Saga in Higher Education. *Administrative Science Quarterly, 17*(1), 178–184.

Clark, B. R. (1983). *The Higher Education System: Academic Organization in Cross-national Perspective.* Los Angeles: University of California Press.

Clark, B. (1992). *The Distinctive College.* New Brunswick, NJ: Transaction Publishers.

Clark, B. R. (1998). *Creating Entrepreneurial Universities: Organizational Pathways of Transformation.* New York: Pergamon.

Deephouse, D., & Suchman, M. (2008). Legitimacy in Organisational Institutionalism. In R. Greenwood, C. Oliver, K. Sahlin, & R. Suddaby (Eds.), *The Sage Handbook of Organisational Institutionalism* (pp. 49–77). London and Thousand Oaks: Sage.

Enders, J., & Boer, H. (2009). The Mission Impossible of the European University: Institutional Confusion and Institutional Diversity. In A. Amaral, G. Neave, C. Musselin, & P. Maassen (Eds.), *European Integration and the Governance of Higher Education and Research Higher Education Dynamics* (pp. 159–178). Den Haag: Springer Netherlands.

Fumasoli, T., Pinheiro, R., & Stensaker, B. (2015). Handling Uncertainty of Strategic Ambitions—The Use of Organizational Identity as a Risk-Reducing Device. *International Journal of Public Administration, 38*(13–14), 1030–1040.

Goddard, J., Hazelkorn, E., & Kempton, L. (2016). *The Civic University: The Policy and Leadership Challenges*. Cheltenham: Edward Elgar.

Greenwood, R., Raynard, M., Kodeih, F., Micelotta, E. R., & Lounsbury, M. (2011). Institutional Complexity and Organisational Responses. *The Academy of Management Annals, 5*(1), 317–371. https://doi.org/10.1080/19416520.2011.590299.

Hrebiniak, L., & Joyce, W. (1985). Organisational Adaptation: Strategic Choice and Environmental Determinism. *Administrative Science Quarterly, 30*(3), 336–349.

Kayes, D. C. (2015). *Organisational Resilience: How Learning Sustains Organizations in Crisis, Disaster, and Breakdown*. New York: Oxford University Press.

Krücken, G. (2003). Learning the 'New, New Thing': On the Role of Path Dependency in University Structures. *Higher Education, 46*(3), 315–339. https://doi.org/10.1023/a:1025344413682.

March, J. G. (1991). Exploration and Exploitation in Organisational Learning. *Organization Science, 2*(1), 71–87.

March, J. G., & Olsen, J. P. (2006). Elaborating the "New Institutionalism". In R. A. Rhodes, S. A. Binder, & R. B. A. (Eds.), *The Oxford Handbook of Political Institutions* (pp. 3–22). Oxford: Oxford University Press.

Meyer, J. W., & Schofer, E. (2007). The University in Europe and the World: Twentieth Century Expansion. In G. Krücken, A. Kosmützky, & M. Tork (Eds.), *Towards a Multiversity?: Universities Between Global Trends and National Traditions* (pp. 45–62). Berlin: Transcipt-Verlag.

Neave, G. (1998). The Evaluative State Reconsidered. *European Journal of Education, 33*(3), 265–284.

Neave, G. (2012). *The Evaluative State, Institutional Autonomy and Re-engineering Higher Education in Western Europe: The Prince and His Pleasure*. Dordrecht: Springer.

Oliver, C. (1991). Strategic Responses to Institutional Processes. *Academy of Management Review, 16*(1), 14.

Olsen, J. P. (2007). The Institutional Dynamics of the European University. In P. Maassen & J. P. Olsen (Eds.), *University Dynamics and European Integration* (pp. 25–54). Dordrecht: Springer.

Perry, B., & May, T. (2006). Excellence, Relevance and the University: The "Missing Middle" in Socio-Economic Engagement. *Journal of Higher Education in Africa, 4*(3), 69–92.

Pfeffer, J., & Salancik, G. R. (2003). *The External Control of Organizations: A Resource Dependence Perspective*. Stanford, CA: Stanford Business Books.

Pietilä, M. (2018). *Making Finnish Universities Complete Organisations: Aims and Tensions in Establishing Tenure Track and Research Profiles*. PhD dissertation, Helsinki: University of Helsinki.

Pinheiro, R., & Stensaker, B. (2014). Designing the Entrepreneurial University: The Interpretation of a Global Idea. *Public Organization Review, 14*(4), 497–516. https://doi.org/10.1007/s11115-013-0241-z.

Pinheiro, R., & Young, M. (2017). The University as an Adaptive Resilient Organization: A Complex Systems Perspective. In J. Huisman & M. Tight (Eds.), *Theory and Method in Higher Education Research* (pp. 119–136). Bingley: Emerald.

Pinheiro, R., Langa, P., & Pausits, A. (2015). One and Two Equals Three? The Third Mission of Higher Education Institutions. *European Journal of Higher Education, 5*(3), 233–249. https://doi.org/10.1080/21568235.2 015.1044552.

Pinheiro, R., Geschwind, L., & Aarrevaara, T. (2016). *Mergers in Higher Education. The Experience from Nordic Countries*. Dordrecht: Springer.

Pinheiro, R., Geschwind, L., Hansen, H. F., & Pulkkinen, K. (Eds.). (2019). *Reforms, Organizational Change and Performance in Higher Education: A Comparative Account from the Nordic Countries*. Cham: Palgrave.

Pinheiro, R., Young, M., & Sima, K. (2018). *Higher Education and Regional Development: Tales from Northern and Central Europe*. Cham: Palgrave.

Ramirez, F. O., & Christensen, T. (2013). The Formalization of the University: Rules, Roots, and Routes. *Higher Education, 65*(6), 695–708.

Ramirez, F., Byrkjeflot, H., & Pinheiro, R. (2016). Higher Education and Health Organisational Fields in the Age of "World Class" and "Best Practices". In R. Pinheiro, L. Geschwind, F. Ramirez, & K. Vrangbæk (Eds.), *Towards a Comparative Institutionalism: Forms, Dynamics and Logics Across Health Care and Higher Education Fields* (pp. 35–57). Bingley: Emerald.

Rinne, R. (2004). Searching for the Rainbow: Changing the Course of Finnish Higher Education. In I. Fägerlind & G. Strömqvist (Eds.), *Reforming Higher Education in the Nordic Countries: Studies of Change in Denmark, Finland, Iceland, Norway and Sweden* (pp. 89–135). Paris: UNESCO.

Sahlin, K., & Wedlin, L. (2008). Circulating Ideas: Imitation, Translation and Editing. In R. Greenwood, K. Sahlin-Andersson, & R. Suddaby (Eds.), *The Sage Handbook of Organisational Institutionalism* (pp. 218–242). London: Sage.

Scott, W. R. (2001). *Institutions and Organizations*. Thousand Oaks, CA: Sage Publications.

Selznick, P. (1957). *Leadership in Administration: A Sociological Interpretation.* New York: Harper and Row.

Selznick, P. (1996). Institutionalism "Old" and "New". *Administrative Science Quarterly, 41*(2), 270–277.

Sil, R., & Katzenstein, P. J. (2010). *Beyond Paradigms: Analytic Eclecticism in the Study of World Politics.* New York and Basingstoke: Palgrave Macmillan.

Tapper, T., & Palfreyman, D. (2010). *The Collegial Tradition in the Age of Mass Higher Education.* Dordrecht: Springer.

Wittrock, B. (1985). Dinosaurs or Dolphins? Rise and Resurgence of the Research-Oriented University. In B. Wittrock & A. Elzinga (Eds.), *The University Research System: The Public Policies of the Home of Scientists* (pp. 13–39). Stockholm: Coronet Books.

Young, M., Pinheiro, R., & Šima, K. (2018). Conclusion: University Ambiguities and Analytic Eclecticism. In R. Pinheiro, M. Young, & K. Šima (Eds.), *Higher Education and Regional Development: Tales from Northern and Central Europe* (pp. 191–212). Cham: Springer International Publishing.

Zucker, L. G. (1988). *Institutional Patterns and Organizations: Culture and Environment.* Cambridge, MA: Ballinger Publishing Co.

Permissions

field of academics and their pool of knowledge is as vast as their experience in printing. Their expertise and guidance has proved useful at every step. Their uncompromising quality standards have made this book an exceptional effort. Their encouragement from time to time has been an inspiration for everyone.

The publisher and the editorial board hope that this book will prove to be a valuable piece of knowledge for students, practitioners and scholars across the globe.

Index